# Environmental Degradation and Protection

**Volume I**

# Environmental Degradation and Protection

**Volume I**

*Editors :*


**K.K. SINGH**
**A.K. SINGH**
**ALKA TOMAR**
**VINOD SINGH**



**MD Publications Pvt Ltd**
New Delhi

*Published by*
**MD Publications Pvt Ltd**
"MD House"
11, Darya Ganj
New Delhi-110002
Tel. : +91-11-41562846, 41563325
Fax : +91-11-29235450
E-mail : contact@mdppl.com
Website : www.mdppl.com



ISBN : 978-81-904551-4-5 (Volume 1)
978-81-904551-3-8 (Set of 2 Volumes)

Printed and Published by **MD Publications Pvt Ltd** at Times Press, New Delhi

# CONTENTS

# FOREWORD

Preservation and protection of the environment is not an option any more, it is the only way out. Our existence is at stake. It is we who stand to disappear, and not the biosphere. Nature is too powerful to let us misbehave for long, Like any good mother, she knows when to threaten and when to punish.

Providing sufficient food, shelter and clean environment to the people is becoming exceedingly difficult as the earth's natural endowments are progressively degraded and depleted duc to our excess usage of resources. Depletion of natural resources is a fact of life, but it is its current rate that is alarming. A rate that is directly reflective of rapid population growth, increasing urbanization and indiscriminate industrial development.

Natural calamities such as floods, droughts, tsunamis, earthquakes and volcanic eruptions, seem to be recurring more frequently these days. This is a indicator that all is not well with our only home - the earth. What we are witnessing today are changes that could seriously threaten our collective future.

Every year over 1.5 million hectares of forest disappears. About 12000 million tonnes of fertile soil is washed away. More than 1000 species of animals and 2500 species of plants face extinction. Thousands of human beings are displaced into homelessness by natural and man-made disasters while the several others are not even that fortunate to survive. Millions are affected by the unscientific and indiscriminate use of insecticides and pesticides and are dying of diseases spawned from the abuse of nature.

Our current scenario hence warrants serious alarm and more urgently - action. This book entitled **'Environmental Degradation and Protection'** helps us to do that.

It not only highlights major environmental degradation issues, but also suggests strategies, technologies and techniques for protection, conservation and judicious utilization of natural resources as well as sustainable development. It no doubt is a pertinent addition in the existing literature on Environmental Science.

This reference book covers wide range of topics like the depletion of natural resources, acid rains and its harmful effects, degraded ecosystems, watershed for land and water management, disaster management, indoor pollution, land degradation, nanotechnology, macrophyte decomposition and water quality, ozone layer depletion, equipments and techniques to assess and monitor pollution, landfill leachates, xenophobic exposure in organisms and women & environment.

The compilation is, undoubtedly significant. It presents highly complex fields like Agriculture, Environmental Engineering, Ecology, Biotechnology, Hydrology and Social Sciences in an understandable, reader friendly manner. The technical information contained herein is useful in understanding the science behind degradation of natural resources. The book is sure to help both scientists and environmental activists in working towards assessing degradation of natural resources and monitoring pollution problems and more specifically environment protection. It gives the required lesson that the fundamental principle in developing a rational approach in environmental degradation that management is the principle of relating environmental quality standards to the demands of legitimate beneficial use of the natural resources.

The efforts made by Dr. K.K. Singh, Dr. Vinod Phogat, Dr. A.K. Singh, Mrs. Alka Tomar and Dr. Vinod Singh, in the compilation and meticulous editing of the book are commendable.

**Dr. (Mrs.) Iqbal Malik**
*Founder and Director*
Vatavaran, New Delhi

# PREFACE

Environment is under constant threat from mans' own activities. Population explosion, rapid industrialization, unplanned urbanization and intensive agriculture have caused tremendous damage to our environment. Ignorance towards laws of nature and over-exploitation of natural resources has further aggravated the problem. Development oriented exploitation of non-renewable (coal, ores, petroleum etc.) and renewable (air, water, plants and animals life etc.) natural resources have lead to discharges of waste products, which polluted air, water and land. Sometimes wastes are discharged at a rate beyond the carrying capacity of the environment ultimately degrading the quality of the environment. The degradation has not only led to short-term health and social impacts but also to long-term deterioration of the natural resource base. Faced with such imminent threat, there is a growing realization that rational utilization of environmental endowments of life support system like water, air and soil is a must for sustainable development.

Environmental protection, proper waste utilization and the conservation of natural resources emerged as key of national priorities. However, one must recognize that the situation has not reached the point of no return and by resorting to appropriate environmental management, by integrating the inseparable economic and environmental systems and by creating awareness among the people we can choose ecologically compatible paths of development. The solution for the environmental problems lie in the participation of scholars and practitioners from various disciplines such as biologists, physical scientists, earth scientists and social scientists for requisite and much needed implementation of available technologies in the various streams of environment.

An attempt, therefore, has been made through this book to provide a gist of available waste utilization and environment conservation technologies and tools for improving the quality of life of the people in general and proper strategic environmental protection and management in particular. The contents of the book provide up-to-date, comprehensive and integrated knowledge of ecosystem and the factors concerned with the deterioration of the environment with a view to manage the development programmes in such a way that environmental degradation may not upset the balance of nature. Each chapter of the book is well written by the leading experts and scholars having long standing experience in their respective fields. The treatment of all the topics is in a cogent, lucid style aimed at enabling the reader to grasp the information quickly and easily.

The book is divided into two sections. The first section embodies various fundamental aspects of environmental degradation and depletion of natural resources. The second section deals with various equipments and tools required for assessing and monitoring environmental problems. It is hoped that this comprehensive publication in two volumes would be a reference document to serve the needs of environmentalists, entrepreneurs, researchers, students, consultants and decision makers, as it deals with a wide array of environmental issues and themes.

The editors express their deep sense of appreciation to all the authors for their valuable contribution in the form of chapters. We are also thankful to all the fellow friends whose tireless efforts facilitated us to bring out this publication in time. All the other individuals and organizations who directly or indirectly contributed to this book deserve overwhelming appreciation. We are also thankful to Shri V.K. Gupta, Publisher, M.D. Publications Pvt. Ltd., New Delhi for excellent production of the book.

***Editors***

# LIST OF CONTRIBUTORS

**A.K.Singh,** Asst. Professor, Department of Physics, Dronacharya College of Engineering, Farrukhnagar, Khetanwas, Gurgaon, Haryana.

**Ajay Kumar Naithani,** Department of Geology, Garhwal University, Srinagar Garhwal-246174, Uttaranchal.

**ALEYA Lotfi,** Laboratoire de Biologie Environnementale, Universite de Franche-Comte, 1 Place Leclere, 25030 Besancon Cedex France.

**Alka Tomar,** Dy.Director & Head, Centre for Media Studies (Research House), Community Centre, Saket, New Delhi-110017.

**Amit Krishna De,** Executive Secretary, The Indian Science Congress Association, 14, Dr. Biresh Guha Street, Kolkata-700017, West Bengal.

**B.A.K. Prusty,** Environmental Impact Assessment Division, Salim Ali Centre for Ornithology and Natural History, Anaikatty (PO), Coimbattore-64108, Tamil Nadu.

**Basudeo Prasad,** Scientist & Head, Environmental Monitoring Instruments Division, C.S.I.O., Chandigarh-160030.

**Eline Meulenberg,** ELTI Support VOF Drieskensacker 12-10 6546 M H. Nijmogon, The Netherlands.

**F.A.Lone,** Division of Environmental Sciences, S.K. University of Agricultural Sciences and Technology, Shalimar Campus-191121, Jammu Kashmir.

**G.S. Kanade,** Scientist, National Environmental Engineering Research Institute (NEERI), Nehru Marg, Nagpur-440020, India.

**Girish H.Pandya,** Dy. Director, National Environmental Engineering Research Institute (NEERI), Nehru Marg, Nagpur-440020, India.

**Inderpal Rai,** Assoc. Professor, Department of Home Science, JNV University, Jodhpur, Rajasthan.

**J.C.Sharma,** Department of Soil Science and Water Management, Dr. Y.S.Parmar University of Horticulture and Forestry, Nauni-Solan-173230, Himachal Pradesh.

**Jean-Louis Morel,** Laboratoire Sols et Environment, 2 Avenue Foret de Haye 54505 Vandoeuvre, France.

**Joseph Toscano,** Manager (Quality Control), Bharat Petroleum, Mumbai, Maharashtra.

**K.K.Singh,** Project Directorate (Res.), Agriculture and Soil Survey, Krishi Bhawan, Bikaner, Rajasthan.

**KHATTABI Hicham,** Laboratoire de Biologie Environmentale, universite de Franche-Comte, 1, Place Leclerc, 25030 Besancon Cedex, France.

**M.A.Khan,** Division of Environmental Sciences, S.K. University of Agricultural Sciences and Technology, Shalimar Campus-191121, Jammu & Kashmir.

**Mahadevi Singh,** Teacher, Sophia Sr. Secondary School, Bikaner-334002, Rajasthan.

**N.R. Nadarajan,** Environmental Impact Assessment Division, Salim Ali Centre for Ornithology and Natural History, Anaikatty (PO), Coimbatore-64108, Tamil Nadu.

**P.A.Azeez,** Principal Scientist, Environmental Impact Assessment Division, Salim Ali Centre for Ornithology and Natural History, Anaikatty (PO), Coimbatore-64108, Tamil Nadu.

**Paromita Ghosh,** Scientist B., G.B.Pant Institute of Himalayan Environmental and Development, Garhwal Unit, Srinagar Garhwal-246174 (Uttaranchal).

**R.P.Bajpai,** Director, Central Scientific Instruments Organization, Chandigarh-160030.

**Sanjeev K. Chaudhary,** Department of Soil Science and Water Management, Dr. Y.S.Parmar University of Horticulture and Forestry, Nauni-Solan (HP)-173230, Himachal Pradesh.

**Subodh Kumar Maiti,** Asst. Professor, Centre of Mining Environment, Indian School of Mines, Dhanbad-826004, Jharkhand.

**V.Gayathri,** EIA Division, Salim Ali Centre for Ornithology and Natural History, Anaikatty, Coimbatore-641108, Tamil Nadu.

**V.K. Kandawar,** Scientist Environmental Engineering Research Institute (NEERI), Nehru Marg, Nagpur-440020, India.

**V.M. Shinde,** Scientist, National Environmental Engineering Research Institute (NEERI), Nehru Marg, Nagpur-440020, India.

**Vinod Singh,** Lecturer, Department of Geography, Govt. Dungar College, Bikaner-334001.

**Y.P.Sundriyal,** Department of Geology, Garhwal University, Srinagar, Garhwal-246174, Uttaranchal.

# CHAPTER 1

# DEPLETION OF NATURAL RESOURCES

**Joseph Toscano**

Manager (Quality Control),Bharat Petroleum, Mumbai.

## ABSTRACT

The loss of resources is determined by the behavior and rate of consumption of people. Their behavior is motivated not only by greed - to sell and buy an increasing number of consumer goods, but also by necessity, since it is easier to successfully fit into society and swim with the stream than to drop out or swim against the stream. Their problem is their over consumption and dependence on a great and cheap resource base to fuel their economy and the setup of their society. These problems are grand in scope and it is unfortunately impossible to be an expert on all aspects of the problems and therefore, experts tend to focus too much on their own area and might even be completely ignorant on other areas which is worse. The developed world consume the greater amount of power which indicate that they also have the greater power in the geopolitical sense. Depletion of main natural resources like forests, oil and ozone with typical examples are discussed in this chapter.

**Key word :** Natural resources, depletion

## Introduction

In the 21st century the world must solve two great problems which are:

- Overpopulation in the developing world, and
- Over consumption in the developed world.

And these issues are related to resources. Either too many people consume a few resources each totaling a lot of resources, or a few people, each consume too many resources again totaling a lot of resources. What is important to note is the absolute consumption, not the relative consumption.

It is difficult to differ between the developing world and the developed world, but the canonical values usually used are that:

- The developing world has 80% of the world's population and consumes 20% of its resources.
- The developed world has 20% of the world's population and consumes 80% of its resources.

The ecological systems from which the developing world derives its food, water, and energy can not be sustained with an increasing demand from an increasing population base. If the demand keeps increasing, the systems will eventually collapse. As the systems collapse, the population which is a part of these systems will collapse, die off, or try to escape to places where resources are more abundant.

The resource base from which, the technically more adept developed world derives its food, water, and energy will eventually be depleted in such a way that the production rates will fall due to physical restrictions. This will change the geopolitics and the economic system of the developed world. Eventually, this will lead to a paradigm shift.

The problems mentioned above have similarities and they are not separated as the developed world interacts with the developing world in many ways. The problems in the developing world are water shortages, droughts, floods, famines, forest losses, soil erosion and loss of biodiversity. These all, decrease the carrying capacity of the life support system. The number of people and their behavior determine the rate of loss of this support system. Usually, their behavior is motivated by personal survival instincts, *e.g.*, energy is required to cook and make the available low-quality foods edible, but as most of the trees have been cut down already, dung is collected and burned which in turn, decreases soil fertility and increases erosion. Many of these people already live using a minimum amount of resources. Their problems are determined by their huge numbers which increase rapidly, since most choose to have many children.

The problems in the developed world - and these problems are not so visible - are pollution, damage of ecosystems, loss of bio-diversity, loss of forests, soil erosion and depletion of the mineral and energy resource base on which their society is based.

## Forest Depletion

Three kinds of reserves of natural resources can be identified : continuous resources, such as sunlight and wind, the use of which does not lead to a reduction in their size; renewable resources, such as wood and crops that can be harvested but not faster than their rate of replenishment; and non-renewable resources, such as fossil fuels and minerals. The last are created by very slow geological processes, so slow in human terms that their use diminishes the available stocks. Resources, such as clean water, fertile soils and biodiversity, given the time required for their recovery, can also be considered to be non-renewable. Sooner or later, at the current rate of consumption, the reserves of certain resources will be exhausted. This may be a long way off for a number of fossil fuels and mineral ores, but other resources such as biodiversity and fertile soils are being used up so quickly that there is a danger of crossing the critical thresholds.

This drain on biotic resources is particularly alarming; biodiversity and fertile soils are being rapidly used up.

Research by World Wild Fund (WWF) indicates that the 'health' of the world ecosystem, based on measurements of the loss of forest area and freshwater and marine animal species, has declined by 30% in 25 years (WWF, 1998). Half the natural forest cover worldwide has already disappeared, 13% in the last 30 years. Europe only has 1% of its original forest cover left. And there is no sign of this attack on biodiversity diminishing (Table 1).

**Table 1 :** Some trends in the depletion of natural resources

| | **Decline** | **Expected trend** |
|---|---|---|
| Health of the world ecosystem | -30% in the last 25 years | Continiung decline |
| • Area of natural forest | • -13% in the last 20 years | |
| • Freshwater ecosystem index | • -50% in the last 25 years | More rapid reduction |
| • Marine ecosystem index | • -4% in the last 25 years | |
| Fertile soils | -25% in the last 50 years | Same or greater reduction |
| • Africa | • -30% | |
| • Asia | • -27% | |
| • Latin America | • -18% | |

**Source** : WWR, 1999, Anonymous, 1999

Poverty is an important underlying cause of further deforestation, of which about two-thirds is carried out by small farmers clearing land for cultivation and to obtain wood for fuel. Commercial logging for timber is responsible for most of the rest. The pressure on the remaining forests is increasing as the number of people with a low income and worldwide demand for commercial timbers products grow. The demand for food, and therefore demand for agricultural land, will also rise sharply as the world's population rises and people's diets contain more protein. Almost, all the best agriculture land is already cultivated and so less suitable land is being brought into cultivation, leading to more soil erosion and loss of biodiversity.

Fertile soil is the basis for agriculture production. In the last 50 years, 25% of all fertile soils have been lost and / or degraded, and intensive efforts will be needed to prevent this process speeding up. The poorer countries are worst affected, and major problems are forecast in a number of important food producing areas in third world countries. Soils recover naturally at an extremely slow rate and the costs of restoration are so high that they are, in effect, unaffordable for these countries.

The growth in biofuels is also increasing the pressure on the reserves of suitable agricultural land. The national Institute for Public Health and the Environment (RIVM) in the Netherlands has calculated that, a large-scale conversions to biofuels – stimulated by greenhouse gas policies and the reduced availability of fossil fuels implies that 20- 25% of all suitable agriculture land will be needed for biofuel crops by 2050. It is hardly conceivable that this could happen, given the considerable rise in the demand for land for the production of food.

Long ago, the Earth had a green belt of rain forests around its middle that covered almost 12% of the earth's land surface. Today, the rain forest covers 2% of the earth's land surface and it is declining rapidly. The following will be a description of the rain forest, factors in its destruction, and if there are any answers to slow or halt the process. Today, we have reached a turning point; we can no longer use the excuse of ignorance. People need to try harder to stop rain forest depletion. There are two major areas on earth where rain forests are located. One of these areas is called The Old World Tropics, which includes Africa and Asia. In Africa, the rain forests are primarily located around the Zaire river. The other area in which rain forests are located is called The New World Tropics, which comprises Central and South America. The New World tropics are in lower altitudes as opposed to the Old World tropics, which are at higher altitudes. Rain forests are located around the equator. This location of the rain forests makes them warm and humid all year round. There are never cold winters in the rain forests. During winter in the rain forests, people comfortably are able to wear T-shirts and shorts. The rain forest has a rainy season which usually persists most of the year. The rain forests of the world are home to more than half of the animal species that live on earth. Many of these creatures are some of the most beautiful and odd creatures in the world, such as the large rodent Capybara, the Anteater, and many different colorful exotic birds. There are many beautiful creatures living in our Earth's rain forests. Many people are ignorant to the effects of rain forest depletion on our environment, and this ignorance is a major cause in the beginning of the destruction of the rain forests. European settlers exploited the rain forests for timber and cleared them for agricultural purposes. The name scrub, which was originally applied to the rain forest by European settlers, became a term for land seen as useless until subject to axe, fire, and plough. People did not think of the affects on the environment because the little knowledge that was known about the effects, was not very widespread. Another cause in the destruction of the rain forest is people's values. Many people value species according to their worth to human beings. People often ignore the problems with the environment simply because they do not want to deal with it. Natural checks against over exploitation have been ignored because those who are now consuming the products of the rain forest are not those who experience the immediate effects of its degradation. Many people believe that they will not live long enough to face the consequences of the destruction but they do not realize, how fast the rain forests are depleting. Recently, in Borneo's Sarawak rain forest, 24 cavers and scientists are braving the rain forests elements and creatures to save the region's natural riches. The cavers and scientists are trying to find plant and animal life diverse enough to protect it from mining and to declare it a national park. Whether, the government sets aside the area this year, in five years or never depends on what's discovered out there. This is a case that often occurs in rain forests. Many governments see no reason to protect the rainforest unless there is an important plant or creature that lives in it. With chain saws, bulldozers, and other powerful equipment, we can bring the giant trees of the rain forest, the very symbol of strength and majesty, crashing to the ground from their lofty heights in just a few hours. All of this destruction and havoc is leading our world straight into events that will threaten life on earth itself. Some of the possible results in the future if the depletion does not stop immediately are global warming and increasing ultra violet radiation as the ozone layer of the atmosphere becomes thinner. Already, 80% of rain forest frogs and 40% of rain forest birds are rare, declining or threatened with distinction. The depletion of tropical species affects much of the biodiversity of rain forests. Preservation of the variety of living things and their environment is very necessary in the survival of life. People sometimes become more interested in protecting individual species of animals that may be endangered than preserving the animals' habitats, which are so necessary for survival. Hoping to repair the damage done to the rain forests, unfortunately leads to unpleasant news. Trying to repair the damage would be like trying to put a band aid over a gaping wound. While we cannot rebuild the rain forests, scientists believe it may be possible to establish small islands of artificial rain forests using tree planting of a range of rain forest tree species. The best solution in the present to maintain and preserve our environment is to merely put a stop to chopping, burning and literally torturing Earth's rain forests. If the destruction would stop now, life on Earth would be much more prolonged. If every person in the world knew about the rain forest being destroyed and the future effects, destruction would not be tolerated. Humans cannot understand what they do not know. People who do not know what is going on do not see anything wrong with the destruction of the rain forests. Education about the rain forest needs to be popularized among masses. The rain forest is a very beautiful and mystical place. It is full of wonders and creatures that look as if they are imaginary and were derived from a dream. It has so much meaning to our world that it is hard to imagine why people would destroy it. People may think that they are just rain forests, and if they were destroyed, they would be the only thing destroyed. The earth must really love it's rain forests because if they go, so does the earth. Destroying the rain forests is like taking away the earth's imagination and ability to dream. People have to seek harder in stopping the rain forest's damage. If every person just stopped and stepped out of their busy worlds of business and society, and would take sometime to give a little bit of money or spread the word, they could buy our rain forests peace. Solving the rain forest problem could be one of the biggest steps ahead in history, the time when humans stepped together to correct their wrong.

## National plan for forest depletion

In Vietnam, the ministries of Agriculture and Rural Development and Natural Resources and Environment have proposed a national strategy to combat the degradation of

Vietnam's special-purpose forests. According to statistics from the agricultural ministry, Vietnam special-purpose forests face a serious threat of degradation as a result of poor management. These forests, covering more than 2 million hectares are home to a multitude of unique flora and fauna, all with priority protection status on the endangered species list. However, many of these forests have been seriously neglected, resulting in a failure to meet the special-purpose forest standards. The ineffective management of the country's 27 national parks, 60 nature reserves and 38 scenic areas has been linked to overlapping and unclear responsibilities for agencies. The forests' management boards suffer from a limited capacity and a lack of funding for biodiversity research and preservation.

In the national strategy, the two ministries have proposed measures to improve special-purpose forests over the next five years, including encouraging local communities to participate in reserve planning, enhancing the capacity of forest management boards, promoting education on sustainable use of natural resources and assisting local farmers to replace outdated farming habits with more advanced scientific production methods.

## In Papua New Guinea (PNG)

The independent state of Papua New Guinea was born with a national constitution which already contained an official commitment to sustainable development, one of its five goals being for Papua New Guinea's natural resources and environment to be conserved and used for the collective benefit of us all, and to be replenished for the benefit of future generations. At the time of Independence, in 1975, the national government already developed a Ministry and an Office (later a Department) of Environment and Conservation. A detailed statement of Environment and Conservation

Principles was endorsed by the National Parliament in 1977, and this was followed, in 1978, by three substantial pieces of environmental legislation - the Environmental Planning Act, Environmental Contaminants Act, and Conservation Areas Act. Unfortunately, the state's fine green clothes have not been clearly visible to the mass of the population and have not always been appreciated by the smaller number of 'elites' who knew of their existence. Provincial governments were never given any role in the enforcement of environmental laws and regulations, but the national department lacked the money and the manpower to police the exploitation of the country's natural resources. Nowhere have these shortcomings been more painfully evident than in the forestry sector. In the wake of a 1979 white paper, which recommended an increase in log exports as a means of raising government revenues, a dubious array of foreign logging companies descended on the nation's shores, and most were allowed to operate without regard to the Environmental Planning Act. Even in those few cases where environmental plans were submitted to the Department of Environment and Conservation (DEC), the Department had no capacity to either assess the accuracy of the factual statements, or monitor the operator's compliance with the promises, which were included in these submissions, several of which turned out to be the barely distinguishable products of a single word-processor located in the government's own Forest Research Institute. For the better part of the 1980s, DEC had only one officer assigned to the task of monitoring logging operations in the whole PNG.

In April 1987, the Prime Minister, Paias Wingti, appointed an Australian lawyer, Tos Barnett, to conduct a Commission of Inquiry into what Barnett himself later described as the 'heavy odour of corruption, fraud and scandal arising from the timber industry'. Two years of investigations revealed a scene of 'rampage and pillage' in many lowland areas.

Operations were being commenced illegally; forest working plans, if submitted at all, were being widely ignored; logging tracks were being pushed through at the discretion of the bulldozer driver; hillsides and river banks were being logged; and the immature forest resources were bashed and trampled in the reckless haste to get the logs down to the waiting log ships. The dazed and disillusioned forest owners stood watching in disbelief as foreign operators removed their trees before moving on to the next area, leaving environmentally disastrous logged-over hillsides, temporary gravel/mud roads and rotting log bridges to erode and cave in to clog the water-courses.

And the source of the smell which prompted the Commission's work was found in the many documented instances where in order to gain access to the timber, foreign operators misled and bribed local leaders, set up 'puppet' native landowner companies, bribed provincial government premiers or ministers and gave gifts or bribes to national ministers or members of the national parliament or took such people into some form of partnership with them. Similarly, they also bribed and gave benefits to at least one secretary of the Department of Forests and other officers.

Being a highlander whose own interests were primarily tied to the coffee business, Paias Wingti had nothing to lose from Barnett's revelations (Barnett, 1992). But Wingti had been dislodged from office within a year of Barnett's appointment, and his replacement, Rabbie Namaliu, was rather less enthusiastic, primarily because his deputy and coalition partner, Ted Diro, was the commissioner's most prominent target. Nevertheless, the national government was moved to acknowledge its own loss of control over the logging industry by invoking the assistance of the Tropical Forestry Action Plan, and the World Bank was only too keen to lead the TFAP review team to PNG because the Bank's own image could be nicely greened along the way.

In April 1990, a round-table meeting in Port Moresby approved a five-year National Forestry Action Plan which contained sixteen separate projects with a combined cost of about forty million *kina* (the kina then being roughly equivalent to the US dollar). The greater part of this cost was to be met by grants and concessional loans from the international community - most notably the World Bank itself, the UN Development Programme, and the Australian government's aid budget. These funds were to be split roughly equally between projects designed to rationalise the 'development' of the nation's timber resources and projects designed to achieve the alternative goal of conserving selected areas of special ecological or cultural significance. For this reason, the Plan was later renamed the National Forestry and Conservation Action Programme. During the following year the Forests Minister, Karl Stack, did everything he could, to underline the potential contradiction between these two general goals. At the round-table meeting, he astonished the conservationists, and might even have irritated the World Bank, by announcing the imposition of a two-year moratorium on the granting of new timber permits and an indefinite moratorium on the granting of log export permits; but once his Cabinet colleagues had approved these measures, the Minister found so many good reasons to ignore them that he was able to issue new timber permits at an unprecedented rate. Even after Stack had been replaced, and a new Forestry Act had been passed by Parliament in 1991, a rearguard action by vested interests in the bureaucracy delayed its gazettal until the eve of the national election in June 1992.

Having recovered the premiership in the wake of this election, Paias Wingti awarded the Forests Ministry. Another wealthy white citizen, Tim Neville, who did rather better than his predecessor at showing how wealth acquired outside of the rainforest might provide some immunity from the temptations of this particular office. The flow of new timber permits finally dried up, log shipments were delayed while the Minister personally checked their credentials, and rumours of conspiracies to murder him provided an extra touch of heroism in an Australian television programme devoted to his exploits. Under the terms of the new Act, the old Department of Forests was transformed into a corporate body - the National Forest Authority - and its central offices were carpeted, refurnished, and secured, at great expense, to keep the logging lobbyists at bay. By the end of 1993, the newly recruited Canadian commander of this fortress, Conrad Smith (codename 'Nemesis'), was ready to bombard the public with press releases and full-page newspaper advertisements containing the new National Forestry Development Guidelines:

- all existing timber permit conditions and logging agreements would be subject to review and possible amendment;
- log harvests would be limited to sustainable levels and raw log exports phased out completely by the year 2000;
- logging companies were ordered to submit their plans for meeting this contingency by building factories and plants to process timber; and
- a new revenue system would transfer a larger proportion of their profits to representative landowner organisations for the funding of infrastructural development in the vicinity of logging operations.

Each of these volleys, and most especially the last, drew cries of outrage from the self-appointed spokesmen of the landowner companies, as well as from the Forest Industries Association, and thus received a warm round of applause from the motley band of local NGOs with strong environmental sympathies. But the clapping soon stopped when Smith went on to declare that each logging company with a proven commitment to downstream processing would be granted sole access to an enormous 'timber supply area' in order to meet its long-term need for raw materials. This proposal touched the one raw nerve which could be guaranteed to unify the local advocates and critics of the logging industry, by challenging the hallowed right of all native Melanesians to decide what should or should not happen on their customary land. While the hail of xenophobic arrows which resulted from this blunder where ducked by social workers, Paias Wingti found that he had been deserted by his deputy and coalition partner, Julius Chan, primarily because their government had lurched into a massive fiscal crisis. Having been elected to lead a new governing coalition at the end of August 1994, Chan's first move was to force a substantial devaluation of the national currency, while the public service was placed in a state of suspended animation until the money could be found to pay for anything beyond their salaries. A deadly silence fell upon the castle in the forest, hardly even broken when it was announced that the new Forests Minister would be the one member of parliament whose own constituency accounts for roughly half the logs currently leaving the country.

## Ozone depletion

For four months of every year, Antarctica's McMurdo Research Station lies shrouded in darkness. Then, the first rays of light peep out over the horizon. Each day, the sun lingers in the sky just a little longer and the harsh polar winter slowly gives way to spring. Spring also brings another type of light to the Antarctica, a light that harms instead of that nurtures. In this season of new beginnings, the hole in the ozone layer reforms, allowing lethal ultraviolet radiation to stream through Earth's atmosphere. The hole lasts for only two months, but its timing could not be worse. Just as sunlight awakens activity in dormant plants and animals, it also delivers a dose of harmful ultraviolet radiation.

In this season of new beginnings, the hole in the ozone layer reforms, allowing lethal ultraviolet radiation to stream through Earth's atmosphere to Antarctica, only to pass over more populated areas, including New Zealand and Australia. This biologically damaging, high-energy radiation can cause skin cancer, injure eyes, harm the immune system, and upset the fragile balance of an entire ecosystem. Although, two decades ago, most scientists would have scoffed at the notion that industrial emissions could destroy ozone high up in the atmosphere. Researchers now know that chlorine creates the hole by devouring ozone molecules. Years of study on the ground, in aircraft, and from satellites has conclusively identified the source of the chlorine: human-made chemicals called chlorofluorocarbons (CFCs) that have been used in spray cans, foam packaging, and refrigeration materials.

Ozone is a relatively simple molecule, consisting of three oxygen atoms bound together. Yet, it has dramatically different effects depending upon its location. Near Earth's surface, where ozone comes into direct contact with life forms, it primarily displays a destructive side. Because, it reacts strongly with other molecules, large concentrations of ozone near the ground prove toxic to living things. At higher altitudes, where 90 percent of our planet's ozone resides, it does a remarkable job of absorbing ultraviolet radiation. In the absence of this gaseous shield in the stratosphere, the harmful radiation has a perfect portal through which to strike Earth.

Although, a combination of weather conditions and CFCs chemistry conspire to create the thinnest ozone levels in the sky above the South Pole, CFCs are mainly released at northern latitudes--mostly from Europe, Russia, Japan, and North America--and play a leading role in lowering ozone concentrations around the globe. Worldwide monitoring has shown that stratospheric ozone has declined for at least two decades, with losses of about 10 percent in the winter and spring and 5 percent in the summer and autumn in such diverse locations as Europe, North America, and Australia. Researchers now find depletion over the North Pole as well, and the problem seems to be getting worse each year. According to a United Nations report, the annual dose of harmful ultraviolet radiation striking the northern hemisphere rose by 5 percent during the past decade. During the past 40 years, the world has seen an alarming increase in the incidence of malignant skin cancer; the rate today is tenfold higher than in the 1950s. Although, the entire increase cannot be blamed on ozone loss and increased exposure to ultraviolet radiation, there is evidence of a relationship. Scientists estimate that for each 1 percent decline in ozone levels, humans will suffer as much as 2 to 3 percent increase in the incident of certain skin cancers.

## Exploring earth's atmosphere

Like many lines of scientific inquiry, research leading to the prediction and discovery of global ozone depletion and the damaging effects of CFCs followed a path full of twists and turns. Investigators did not set out to determine whether human activity affects our environment or did they know much about chemical pollutants. Instead, they began with basic questions about the nature of earth's atmosphere - its composition, density, and temperature distribution. The composition of our planet's atmosphere fascinated humans long before chemistry became a formal science. "The storm thundered and lightened, and the air was filled with sulfur," Homer wrote in the Odyssey, referring to the sharp odour, created during thunderstorms, of what later became known as ozone. By the late 1800s, atmospheric scientists had isolated carbon monoxide and inferred the existence of a second combustible gas in the air, which they tentatively identified as methane the simplest hydrocarbon. But in attempting to further analyze the composition of the atmosphere, researchers at the turn of the century faced a major stumbling block: virtually all gases, except for molecular nitrogen and oxygen, exist in such minute concentrations that available equipment could not detect them. Help, however, was on the way. During the 1880s, scientists had begun perfecting a new, highly precise method of identifying a compound by recording a special kind of chemical fingerprint--the particular pattern of wavelengths of light it emits or absorbs. This pattern was called as spectrum by scientists.

In the 1920s, G.M.B. Dobson developed a spectrometer that could measure small concentrations of ozone. By measuring the spectrum of air, the Belgian scientist M.V. Migeotte demonstrated in 1948 that methane is a common constituent of the atmosphere with a concentration of about one part per million by volume. Soon, scientists had the tools to detect other atmospheric gases that occur in concentrations one-tenth to one-hundredth as great as that. By the 1950s, researchers had identified 14 atmospheric chemical constituents. Despite this progress, researchers were still missing a major piece of the atmospheric puzzle. All of the compounds detected possessed an even number of electrons, a characteristic which typically gives chemical stability. Other less common compounds with an odd number of electrons known as free radicals readily undergo chemical reactions and do not survive for long. These compounds play crucial roles in such phenomena as urban smog, the loss of stratospheric ozone, and the global removal of atmospheric impurities. Scientists had not detected free radicals because they reside in the atmosphere at concentrations well below the part-per-million level that state-of-the-art equipment in 1948 could detect. But unrelated research in an entirely different field, analytical chemistry, soon came to the rescue. Analytical chemists had begun developing a cavalcade of new instruments and methods to measure minute quantities of compounds in the laboratory. Such research spurred advances on two fronts: a substantial increase in the precision and accuracy of measurements of atmospheric gases and a striking decrease in the minimum concentration of a compound that must be present to be detected. As a result, the number of atmospheric compounds identified by scientists has increased from 14 in the early 1950s to more than 3,000 today. Detectors today routinely measure compounds at concentrations below one part per trillion, and some can record gases that occur in concentrations one-thousandth as great at that. Even in some of the most remote locations on earth, scientists have detected hundreds of compounds. Curiously, some of the substances that occur in the smallest concentrations rank as some of the biggest players in altering the atmosphere. A case in point; the group of chemicals known as CFCs.

CFCs were invented about 65 years ago during a search for a new, nontoxic substance that could serve as a safe refrigerant. One of these new substances, often known by the DuPont trademark freon, soon replaced ammonia as the standard cooling fluid in home refrigerators. It later became the main coolant in automobile air conditioners. The 1950s and 1960s saw CFCs used in a variety of other applications: as a propellant in aerosol sprays, in manufacturing plastics, and as a cleanser for electronic components. All this activity doubled the worldwide use of CFCs every six to seven years. By the early 1970s, industry used about a million tons every year. Yet, as recently as the late 1960s, scientists remained unaware that CFCs could affect the atmosphere. Their ignorance was not from lack of interest, but from lack of tools. Detecting the minuscule concentrations of these compounds in the atmosphere would require a new generation of sensitive detectors. After developing such a detector, the British scientist James Lovelock, in 1970, became the first to detect CFCs in the air. He reported that one of these compounds, CFC-11, had an atmospheric concentration of about 60 parts per trillion. To put that measurement in perspective, the concentration of methane (natural gas) is 25,000 times greater. Twenty years earlier, merely detecting methane had been considered a major feat. Lovelock found CFC-11 in every air sample that passed over Ireland from the direction of London. That was not surprising, because most major cities, including London, widely used CFCs. However, Lovelock also detected CFC-11 from air samples directly off the North Atlantic, uncontaminated by recent urban pollution.

This unexpected discovery prompted Lovelock to do further studies. Accordingly, he asked the British government for a modest sum of money to place his apparatus on board, a ship traveling from England to Antarctica. His request was rejected; one reviewer commented that even if such a measurement succeeded, he could not imagine a more useless bit of knowledge than finding the atmospheric concentration of CFC-11. But Lovelock persisted. Using his own money, he put his experiment aboard the research vessel Shackleton in 1971. Two years later the British researcher reported that his shipboard apparatus had detected CFC-11 in every one of the more than 50 air samples collected in the North and South Atlantic. Lovelock correctly concluded that the gas was carried by large-scale wind motions. He also stated that CFCs were not hazardous to the environment, a conclusion soon to be proven wrong.

## Ozone Loss: The Chemical Culprits

In 1972, the life of atmospheric scientist F. Sherwood Rowland took a critical turn when he heard a lecture describing Lovelock's work. Like, other researchers at that time, Rowland had no inkling that CFCs could harm the environment, but the injection into the atmosphere of large quantities of previously unknown compounds piqued his interest. What would be the ultimate fate of these compounds? Rowland, joined by Mario Molina, a colleague at the University of California, Irvine, decided to find out the facts.

The scientists showed that CFCs remained undisturbed in the lower atmosphere for decades. Invulnerable to visible sunlight, nearly insoluble in water, and resistant to oxidation, CFCs display an impressive durability in the atmosphere's lower depths. But at altitudes above 18 miles, with 99 percent of all air molecules lying beneath them, CFCs show their vulnerability. At this height, the harsh, high-energy ultraviolet radiation from the sun impinges directly on the CFCs molecules, breaking them apart into chlorine atoms and residual fragments.

If Rowland and Molina had ended their CFCs study with these findings, no one other than atmospheric scientists would ever have heard about it. However, scientific completeness required that the researchers explore not only the fate of the CFCs, but also of the highly reactive atomic and molecular fragments generated by the ultraviolet radiation. In examining these fragments, Rowland and Molina were aided by prior basic research on chemical kinetics--the study of how quickly molecules react with one another and how such reactions take place. Scientists had demonstrated that a simple laboratory experiment will show how rapidly a particular reaction takes place, even if the reaction involves the interaction of a chlorine atom with methane at an altitude of 18 miles and a temperature of $-51^{o}C$. Rowland and Molina did not have to carry out even a single laboratory experiment on the reaction rates of chlorine atoms. They had only to look up the rates already measured by other scientists. Basic research into chemical kinetics had reduced a decade's worth of work to two or three days.

After reviewing the pertinent reactions, the two researchers determined that most of the chlorine atoms combine with ozone, the form of oxygen that protects Earth from ultraviolet radiation. When chlorine and ozone react, they form the free radical chlorine oxide, which in turn becomes part of a chain reaction. As a result of that chain reaction, a single chlorine atom can remove as many as 100,000 molecules of ozone. Unknown to Rowland and Molina, the same chlorine atom chain reaction had been discovered a few months earlier by Richard Stolarski and Ralph Cicerone. In 1974, Rowland and Molina made a disturbing prediction: if industry continued to release a million tons of CFCs into the atmosphere each year, atmospheric ozone would eventually drop by 7 to 12%. To make matter worse, other scientist had demonstrated that an entirely different group of compounds could further reduce ozone levels. Paul Crutzen first showed in 1970 that nitrogen oxides react catalytically with ozone, playing an important role in the natural ozone balance. Soil-borne microorganisms produce nitrogen oxides as a decay product, and Crutzen's work spotlighted how microbe-rich agricultural fertilizers might lead to reduced ozone levels. His research and that of Harold Johnston also focused attention on the effect of nitrogen oxides spewed by high-altitude aircraft. These emissions may also reduce ozone levels in the stratosphere.

Earlier studies, which had investigated whether exhaust emissions from the supersonic transport and other high-speed aircraft could damage the environment, had already begun to document the effects of ozone loss. Compiled because of the perceived threat from these aircraft, the data were brought to bear on the very real threat from CFCs and nitrogen oxides. With less ozone in the atmosphere, more ultraviolet radiation reaches Earth. Scientists estimated that increased exposure would lead to a higher incidence of skin cancer, cataracts, and damage to the immune system and to slowed plant growth. Because some CFCs persist in the atmosphere for more than 100 years, these effects would last throughout the twenty-first century. Concluding that such long-term hazards were unacceptable, Rowland and Molina called for a ban on further release of CFCs. Alerted to this clear and present danger, the United States, Canada, Norway, and Sweden in the late 1970s banned the use of CFCs in aerosol sprays.

## Ozone Hole

As it turned out, the ozone problem was far worse than Rowland and Molina could have imagined. The first warning signs of a bigger crisis did not appear until the late 1970s, but the studies that uncovered these findings had their roots in research dating back nearly a century.

In the 1880s, W.N. Hartley discovered that a broad band of ultraviolet light reaches earth almost unimpeded. This band, known as UV-A, has wavelengths just slightly shorter than ordinary visible light. The ozone layer partly absorbs another ultraviolet band, known as UV-B, before it can reach earth. During the 1920s, G.M.B. Dobson managed to measure the ratio of UV-A to UV-B in incoming sunlight. By doing so, he determined for the first time the total amount of ozone in the atmosphere. Dobson hoped his study would lead to a new method of predicting the weather. Instead, he became interested in the seasonal variations in ozone concentrations. An instrument that he developed, the Dobson spectrometer, has become the standard for monitoring ozone. The rapid development of new scientific tools after World War II--many of them based on wartime instrumentation--led to a hallmark of research in earth science. In 1957-1958, this led to a worldwide scientific effort known as the **International Geophysical Year (IGY).** The year sparked an international outpouring of research on the oceans, the atmosphere, and unexplored land areas of the planet.

Monitoring ozone levels in the south polar region, researchers found them to be consistently about 35 percent higher in late spring than in winter. Annual monitoring showed the same seasonal pattern through the late 1970s. But in 1978 and 1979, the British scientists found something different. In October, the beginning of spring in the southern hemisphere, the researchers detected less ozone than had been detected during the past 20 years. During the next several years, October ozone levels continued to decline. In 1984, when the British first reported their disturbing findings, October ozone levels were about 35% lower than the average for the 1960s. The U.S. satellite Nimbus-7 quickly confirmed the results, and the term Antarctic ozone hole entered popular language.

## Oil depletion

Depletion of resources is an obvious concern from the point of view of the needs of future generations. Is our rate of depletion of the earth's resources unsustainable? Are we compromising the abilities of future generations?

Opinions on this, even among experts, are divided but it is generally accepted about our depletion of oil reserves. Although, the level of proven reserves has risen in recent years, our consumption of oil cannot be regarded as sustainable. The curve is flattening out, and if no more oil were found, with usage increasing at 2% per year, the existing known reserves would be used up in about 40-50 years. That might be enough for the present generations that are the concern of sustainable development, and they are going to be significantly more numerous.

The world's population has more than doubled in the last half of the $20^{th}$ century from 2.6 to 5.9 billion. A further doubling is forecast in the first half of the $21^{st}$ century. Virtually, all of this growth is taking place in the developing world, which can be expected to become progressively more industrialised and therefore make additional demands on global resources. Plastics will play a key role in the conservation of oil reserves. The production of plastics uses a tiny proportion of total consumption of oil and gas, but products made from plastics, including packaging, reduce our use of these resources in the major consuming applications such as energy and transport in several ways. For example, the production of food is energy intensive. By minimizing food loss, plastics packaging prevents energy waste.

## Renewable raw materials

Faced with concerns about resources depletion, the production of plastics from renewable raw materials might be considered as a logical goal. To date, efforts to replace conventional plastics with plant –derived alternatives have embraced three main approaches:

1. Converting plant sugars into plastics.

2. Producing plastics inside micro organisms.
3. Modifying corn and other crops so that plastics are produced within them as they glow.

The energy needed by these processes, either to convert the plant material into plastics, or, if plastic is produced inside the plants, to extract it from them, is in most cases greater than the energy used to make plastics from fossil based resources. For example, a study by Dartmouth College in the USA has shown that 3 times energy is needed to make polyhydroxyalkanoate (PHA) from corn plants than is needed to make polyethylene(PE) in the conventional manner. Overall, the study suggests that a more environmental friendly option would be to develop renewable energies, which would benefit not only the production of plastics - be they biodegradable or not – but many other production processes. Provided there is no energy or other environmental or economic penalty, making plastics from renewable raw materials may open interesting possibilities in some applications. For the time being, polylactide (PLA) seems to be the most promising.

Today the primary energy source is oil. Oil accounts for 40% of all energy use. Therefore, continued access to this resource or an equivalent or an improved replacement is essential to continue the world as we know it.

To solve a problem one must understand the magnitude of the problem. Energy is consumed by humans at a rate of about 13TW (1TW equals one (US) Trillion Watts). A very large fraction (around 40%) comes from oil. Oil is therefore the primary energy source, which should concern us. The world consumes 77 million barrels (one barrel is 42 (US) gallons or 159 litres of petroleum) daily, which makes 26 billion barrels annually. The biggest extractors are Saudi Arabia, Russia, the United States, and Mexico. The biggest exporters are Saudi Arabia, Russia, and Norway. The biggest importers are the United States, Japan, Korea and Germany.

A nuclear power plant produces about 0.5-1.0 GW. It does not run continuosly and is offline some 20-40% of the time. A rough calculation shows that a replacement of the energy of oil by nuclear energy will require the construction of at least 5,000 nuclear power plants. A modern off-shore wind turbine produces about 2MW depending on the wind speed. Hydroplant power depends on the site. Solar power using PV cells depends on the sun facing area of the cells.

A nuclear power plant produces electricity, and one can not use electricity to make plastics, fertilizer, and a whole bunch of other industrial products. Additionally, the world's transport system is based on the internal combustion engine which in terms of output/mass is much more effective than any other engine (steam, stirling, electric, etc.) only gas turbines are more effective, but they are not as robust, and they also depend on fossil fuels. Electricity is an inconvenient source of energy for many purposes. It is only transportable through batteries, by cable, or by converting water into hydrogen. Both conversion methods loose energy in the process, especially the former. Therefore, oil is a source of energy as well as a mineral source which is difficult or impossible to replace. Even if the energy problem is solved, the world will still be facing water shortages, top-soil loss, and loss of biodiversity. One can only hope that possible replacement sources will be used wisely.

## Oil follows the extraction pattern of all other resources

Generally, the easy to reach and rich resources will be found and used first. These resources can be exploited using simple technology and often a hole in the ground in the right place which is not so hard to find, will do the trick. Later more complex technology is required. Oil fields will be smaller, require more effort, and ultimately yield less oil than the first big fields. Later still, advanced technology like 3D or 4D seismic searches, directional drilling, steam injection, and drilling in difficult terrain like off shore or arctic conditions is required. At some point the effort, namely the energy which goes into the process i.e. of manufacturing drilling rigs, actually finding the oil, keeping the crews supplied, and getting the oil to the surface will surpass the energy yield at which point further drilling makes no sense. Presently, the limits are determined by economical arguments i.e. the money-price of oil since the energy yields are still much greater than the energy efforts. If the development of an oil field will cost less than the estimated price of the oil which is pumped up, the field will be developed.

There is some uncertainty attached to the estimation of oil resources. Although, it is reasonably clear how much oil has been extracted from the ground (cummulative production) and what the current rate of extraction is, it is debated how much oil is actually left (resources) and how much of it will be extracted (reserves). It turns out that there are actually two quite opposing views, because people confuse reserves with resources and tend to focus too much on one or the other. Reserves include the amount of oil which can and will be extracted with a given probability. The P90 reserve i.e. the amount of oil which can be extracted, with a 90% probability is usually referred to as proven reserves. A P50 reserve is called proven and probable.

The two different views are:

1. Since the amount of oil is in principle amount, we can never know how big the resources are. What is relevant is whether we can find more oil or not. A rise of oil prices rise will motivate people to develop new

methods to find more oil, to extract more oil from known wells, or to make development of shut-in wells economically possible.

2. Although, the total amount of oil is unknown it is still finite. Once all resources have been turned into reserves no more oil can be discovered. The total amount of reserves can be estimated by noticing that the biggest fields are found and developed first after which increasingly smaller fields are found and brought into production. Eventually, the new fields will be small and hard to find. Plotting the so-called creaming curves i.e. the cumulative discoveries against the cumulative number of wildcats (exploration wells) the asymptotic value will indicate the ultimate amount of reserves.

Governments and oil companies some of which have economic turnovers compared to the GNP of entire countries might not benefit from revealing their true reserves, since many political and economic decisions depend on these numbers. Thus, data are divided into freely available official data and confidential "technical" data which determine the development strategies of the oil companies. The freedom in reporting official data leads to so-called "reserve growth" which is not true growth, since the amount of oil in the ground does not increase, but there is an increase in the reported official number.

## Reserve growth

Reserves are inherently unknown, but they can be estimated within a range and assigned to a probability. A P90 estimate denominate the amount of oil which can be extracted economically with a probability of 90%. Naturally, a P10 estimate will be higher than a P90 estimate, and oil companies are free to report whatever number suits their purposes. Usually, they will not even give the probability but simply give the official reserves.

Economists may then add all these official numbers and arrive at the total world reserve which tend to grow suggesting that more and more oil is discovered/available. This growth is not surprising. Initial estimates will be conservative since a company would develop the field only if they were quite sure that the investment would be returned. As the initial estimate is conservative, later times will demonstrate that the field most likely contains more oil. As the fields are likely to be bigger than what is reported most likely the reserves will "grow" in subsequent reports. Updating of the official number will tend to increase the stock value of the company.

The opposite view is that the initial estimate was wrong and the reserves (amount of oil) has not grown. Instead of marking the increase as newly discovered oil, the addition is backdated and added to the original estimate of the size of the field at the time when it was first discovered. This gives a discovery curve which has been corrected for wrong initial estimates.

Today, about 6Gb are discovered and 26Gb are consumed each year. Since, oil has to be discovered, before it can be extracted the known reserves are being depleted. This is clearly not sustainable. As Jon Thompson, President of Exxon Mobil Exploration Company once stated:

> ... We estimate that world oil and gas production from existing fields is declining at an average rate of about 4 to 6% a year. To meet projected demand in 2015, the industry will have to add about 100 million oil-equivalent barrels a day of new production. That's

> equal to about 80% of today's production level. In other words, by 2015, we will need to find, develop and produce a volume of new oil and gas that is equal to eight out of every 10 barrels being produced today. In addition, the cost associated with providing this additional oil and gas is expected to be considerably more than what industry is now spending. Equally daunting is the fact that many of the most promising prospects are far from major markets -- some in regions that lack even basic infrastructure. Others are in extreme climates, such as the Arctic, that present extraordinary technical challenges.......

Policy makers have previously been concerned with R/P ratios to strategically account for resource depletion.

$$R/P = \frac{\text{Total amount of reserves}}{\text{Current production rate}}$$

This number does not take into account that the reserves may grow, and in particular it does not consider that the extraction rate will change later on. The R/P ratio gives the false impression that the current rate of extraction can continue for a time of R/P until we, one day abruptly run out. In a more realistic scenario, one would expect that the extraction rate would decrease and finally slow to a trickle after which it might not even be feasible using either money-economy or energy-economy to extract the last drop. In that case the resource might in principle last forever, but that is irrelevant to society. What we are interested in is the extraction rate, at present and in the future. The extraction rate determines the amount of oil which will reach the market in the near future. After it has passed through the refineries and the distribution systems, the free market will try to determine the market value. The market value is quite susceptible to the supply rate. So-called swing producers use this to control/increase the prices. Oil importers can counteract/decrease the prices by selling oil from their strategic reserves to the market or by decreasing their demand, perhaps involuntarily.

## Peak extraction rate

Adding the extraction rates for all the wells in an oil field gives the total extraction rate for the field as a function of time. According to the central limit theorem, the total extraction rate of several such fields is distributed as a Gaussian (bell shaped) curve, if they all have the same individual distribution. The integrated area under this curve is the total amount of oil which will ever be extracted. It is evident from the curve that the extraction rate will decrease after half of the oil has been extracted. This point is called the peak year. The peak year is dependent on the estimate of the total reserves. It is not known when the extraction rate will peak. There has been a few local peaks in history, so the peak year will not be known until several years after when it can be confirmed that the extraction rate will never again reach its previous maximum.

The peak year depends on the total amount of oil (unknown), the future extraction rate (unknown) which is correlated to future demand (unknown). Prediction is a highly uncertain business. People have been wrong before and they will be wrong again. However, what is important is not the exact peak year rather it is a range of years. Everybody who subscribes to the Hubbert school calculate a peak year within the next two decades. The most popular year at the moment of writing seems to be around 2007. This is certainly within the life time of most people alive today. It is obvious that oil has to be found before it can be pumped from the ground. A plot of the (backdated) discovery curve shows the extraction curve lagging by about 40 years. The discovery curve peaked in the

1960s. One can get a good estimate of the total reserves by plotting the integrated discovery rate. This graph approaches an asymptotic value as the newly discovered fields are becoming increasingly smaller and more rare. Such a plot is called a creaming curve.

## Oil Depletion—Possible Solutions

### *(a) Replacements*

The world consumes energy at a rate of about 13TW and petroleum accounts for 40%. Predictions estimate a world drop in supply by 3% per annum with less in some regions and more in other regions. Therefore, the world must find a substitute and construct and bring it online quickly enough to alleviate the effects of a diminishing oil supply after the peak year.

Using the above figures about 150,000 MW has to be brought online each year for the next several decades in order to continue to meet demand which will increase, if possible. Compare this number to a large nuclear power plant (1000 MW) or a modern off-shore wind turbine (2 MW). Obviously, the current energy infrastructure is not designed to handle alternative forms of energy and they need to be replaced. Also, the current users like aeroplanes, ships, cars, etc. will have to be replaced as well.

Some replacements under consideration are listed below :

- Hydrogen
- Natural gas
- Tar sands
- Coal
- Coal-bed methane
- Biofuels e.g. ethanol

- Nuclear fission (Upcoming: LWR, FR, IFR, ADS and other closed fuel cycles)
- Controlled fusion
- Hydro power
- Solar power
- Wind power

### *(b) Efficiency*

The population pressure of the developed world is already quite high. It has been estimated that 30-40% of the biosphere is already exploited by the human species leaving the rest for all other species. Gains in efficiency allows a further increase of the number of humans which will increase the other limiting factors. Furthermore, gains in efficiency, *e.g.*, more fuel efficient cars, efficient lighting, etc. is typically eaten up by increased use of the efficient device as long as the rate of use has not reached its natural maximum limit. This is also known as Jevon's Paradox.

The price of oil and gas will not signal shortages until the decline is upon us. For many years after the peak, we will have progressively less energy at progressively higher prices. This contradicts our usual expectation that rising prices will quickly result in greater supply. Higher prices, no matter how high they are, will not create enough new supplies of transportation fuel to prevent sustained contraction of the economy. The resulting paradoxes will create confusion in an economy that depends on economic growth, believes in economic growth, even worships economic growth. The economy will contract, every time fuel prices rise sharply, knocking the price of fuels down as recession reduces demand for them. An unregulated market will neither invest large amounts of fuel in the deployment of alternative fuels in these circumstances, nor will an unregulated market make the "uneconomic" investments needed before the peak to prevent being caught in such cycles. Government must compensate for this deficiency of the market. They must acknowledge the peak of oil and gas production, and introduce appropriate market incentives ahead of the peak.

Those who need most to understand the function of energy in our economy don't understand it, at all. Energy differs from other commodities. Nothing can be done without energy. Nothing can be moved, built, manufactured, planted, fertilized, harvested, or mined, without the liquid transportation fuels that petroleum provides so well, and for which no competitive replacement has ever been found. As a consequently, new energy sources require large investments of energy itself. In particular, the energy investments needed to obtain alternative energy sources and fuels are not only large, but they are much larger than the energy investments needed to obtain fossil energy. These energy investments are so large that some forms of alternative energy will never serve as primary sources of energy. For example, solar electricity from photovoltaic cells will not provide enough energy for the mining, manufacturing, transportation, transportation infrastructure, installation, transmission infrastructure, maintenance, and decommissioning required by the existence of the solar cells. This is not a question of building more solar cells. The ratio of energy returned to energy invested is too small. Solar cells don't work as a primary energy source, although they have other uses. Similarly, ethanol from corn doesn't work as a primary energy source, although it has other uses.

These properties of energy as a commodity invalidate a fundamental assumption made by economists. Rising prices will not result in the smooth substitution of alternative sources of energy. The large energy investments needed by alternative energy sources, and the smaller energy output produced by them, will mean that alternative energy sources will not fully compensate for the decline of oil and gas. Progressively less transportation fuel will be available for use outside of energy production. In spite of our best efforts, the world's economy will contract for many decades.

In addition to their failure to understand energy, and the other factors, there is an ideological explanation for the failure of mainstream economists to acknowledge what is about to happen. Government direction of markets will be needed to mitigate the damage caused by post-peak decline. Any new or restored regulation of markets by governments is offensive to free market dogma. The free market fundamentalists are in the driver's seat. They reflexively deny the reality of problems that require collective action. Perhaps only an economic crash will knock them out of the driver's seat.

## Conclusions

It matters far less to propose detailed solutions than to get people and governments to accept that radical change will happen. The tendency of our society, perhaps of our race, is to deprecate problem statements that don't have proposed solutions attached. Progressive adaption will come from the collective imagination and experience of thousands or millions of people responding to a clear threat. But the threat is not yet seen by those whose engagement is needed. The hardest thing will be to agree that action is needed before change is forced on us. If we wait, we will be trapped with too little of the critical resource needed for adaptation to its own disappearance. Acting before the change, rather than waiting for it to happen, will make the difference between great political difficulty on the one hand, and chaotic disruption and misery on the other hand.

Government, funding institutions, and universities must promote study and understanding of the function of energy in the economy. Government policy workers must allow an understanding of the function of energy to spread their view of the world. Energy conservation, from better insulation to fuel efficiency, must be encouraged and mandated by government as an investment in a more appropriate infrastructure for the difficult times ahead. The prospects for alternative transportation fuels are not promising. Fundamental problems have not begun to be solved; providing the energy to manufacture the alternative fuels and the infrastructure to distribute them. Government must start encouraging radically more efficient transport for freight and passengers--railways, etc. We should stop using natural gas as a fuel for new electricity generators, or for upgrades to existing electricity generators. Although, its lower $CO_2$ emissions are attractive from an environmental perspective, natural gas will soon disappear. We must reduce our reliance on natural gas now, or at least stop increasing our reliance on it, or face much more serious disruption than necessary. We must reconsider coal and nuclear generation of electricity, looking for ways to make them more acceptable environmentally. We must provide at least as much economic incentive for wind and solar compared to oil and gas. None of these measures will prevent a great reduction of consumption, but may prevent serious social disorganization. We need to figure out how to retain social cohesiveness while going through the reduction.

## References

Barnett, T.E. (1992) Legal and Administrative Problems of Forestry in Papua New Guinea. Resources, Development and Politics in the Pacific Islands. Crawford House Press.

De'Ath, C. (1980) The Throwaway People- Social Impact of the Global Timber Project, Madang Boroko Institute of Social and Economic Research : Monograph No. 13.

Filer, C. (1996) The Social Context of Renewable Resource Depletion in Papua New Guniea. Case Studies from Australasia, Melanesia and Southeast Asia. Oxford University Press, Melbourne.

Kortendick, O. (1996) Renewable Resource Depletion Created: http://lucy.ukc.ac.uk/lien/PNG/paper.html

Oil Depletion : One of the world's most Important Problems of the world (2004) http://quasar.physik. unibase.ch/-fisker/401/oil/oil.html.

Rowland, S. F. (2004) The Path from Research to Human Benefit Beyond Discovery. The National Academy of Sciences,Washington, D.C.

# CHAPTER 2

# ACID RAIN AND ITS HARMFUL EFFECTS

**A.K.Singh[1], Alka Tomar[2], K.K.Singh[3] and Vinod Phogat[4]**

[1]Department of Physics, Dronacharya College of Engineering, Farrukh Nagar, Khetanwas, Gurgaon (Haryana).

[2]CMS Environment, Research House, Saket, New Delhi-110017

[3]Project Directorate (Research), Agriculture & Soil Survey, Krishi Bhawan, Bikaner (Raj.) - 334001

[4]Dept. of Soil Science, C.C.S. Haryana Agricultural University, Hisar (Haryana)

## ABSTRACT

Human existence is based on man's natural environment. Man was brought forth and is sustained by what is known as the planetary ecosystem. The planetary ecosystem is a network of complex natural and cultural components, in which micro-organisms, plants, animals, including *Homo sapines*, and their non-living surroundings are interrelated. The Planetary ecosystem unites the multitude of subsidiary ecosystems. Within this system, man alone has a dual role; he is a natural symbiotic component of the ecosystem and he is able to change his environment in a beneficial or in a detrimental way.

**Keywords** : Acid rain, harmful effects, vegetation, wildlife, human health.

## Introduction

One of the changes in the world's ecosystem, brought about by human activity, is the occurrence of acid or acidic precipitation, which in daily speech is referred to as acid rain.

This term includes other forms of precipitation such as snow, hail, dew or fog. Precipitation is by definition acidic if it has a pH below 5.6. Along with the acid-forming agents, a number of accompanying pollutants, such as heavy metals and organic compounds, are transported through the air. Acid deposition is a major environmental concern in most of the industrial world and it may become more widespread if more and more countries start using higher and higher quantities of fossil fuels like petroleum and coal. Burning coal in various industries and thermal plants, and burning of fuels by all sorts of vehicles from two wheelers to heavy vehicles including aeroplanes produces carbon monoxide (CO), carbon dioxide ($CO_2$), sulphur dioxide ($SO_2$) and different forms of nitrogen oxides like NO, $N_2O$, $NO_2$, $N_2O_3$ and $N_2O_5$. Out of these, sulphur dioxide ($SO_2$) and nitric oxide are the predominant forms of gases produced and liberated into the atmosphere. These gases readily dissolve in rain water, mist, snow, and other water sources forming dilute acids like sulphuric acid, sulphurous acid, nitric acid, nitrous acid, etc. The plants are continuously exposed to acid deposition through these contaminated water sources. The gases may also diffuse through the stomata of the leaves of plants and dissolve in the cell sap making it acidic. The extent of acidity produced depends upon the amount of acid producing gases in the atmosphere and the duration of their presence. The acidity so produced may affect the various biochemical mechanisms of different organisms living in the environment (Jaypragasam, 2003).

In addition to, the man-made polluting gases, lighting contributes to some quantity of oxides of nitrogen formed by the reaction of atmospheric nitrogen and oxygen. These oxides of nitrogen may dissolve in rainwater making it slightly acidic with a pH of about 5.6. In a study in Romania, 60-70% of the rain occurred in a region in open field was found to be acid rain of pH less than 5.0 (Trujillo *et al.*, 2001). The annual mean pH of rain water falling over a forest area, in Chongqing

(Southwest China) was 4.7 and was lower in winter than that in summer (Fu Zhu *et al.*, 1996). Sulphate alone contributed over 90% of the total anion content of the rainwater. Serious damage symptoms were observed on several trees around a refinery in May, 1993 in the north of Spanish country and was attributed to an acute emission of $SO_2$ on 2$^{nd}$ May, 1993 (Mesanza *et al.*, 1996). On the east coast of North America, the acidity of precipitation was most common and the pH of precipitation was as low as 3.0 sometimes, which brought down the pH of different surface water sources. Lowering of pH in water sources, like rivers, streams, lakes and ponds would require the input of a large amount of hydrogen ion over relatively a short period of time. The pH of two mountain streams that flew into the Harp lake of central Ontario (Canada) decreased from 6.7 and 6.3 before rain to 5.6 and 4.7 respectively immediately after rain (Beverland *et al.*, 1997). Increased emission of sulphur and nitrogen with the onset of the industrial revolution has been linked to the acidification of surface waters, decline of forest health and corrosion of sensitive buildings and bridges (Newell and Skjelkvale, 1997).

A coloured rain even originating from the Sahara desert occurred on 9-10 April, 2000 at Thessaloniki, Northern Greece. The radioactive nuclides that were determined in a coloured rain dust sample were $^{137}C_S$ of Chernobyl origin, $^{7}Be$ of cosmogenic origin and $^{40}K$ of terrestrial origin. Cesium-137 still remained 14 years after the Chernobyl accident, reaching 26.6 Bq kg$^{-1}$ in the coloured rain dust (Papastefanou, 2001).

Acidification has impoverished a number of fresh water ecosystems, caused fish kills, and hastened the deterioration of buildings and structures. Usually, a receptor is considered susceptive to acid rain if the receptor is sensitive, such as limestone, and if the amount of acidic precipitation is sufficient to causes a deterioration in the health of ecosystem. There is evidence to suggest it may alter other types of ecosystems, affect some agricultural crops, reduce forest productivity and be detrimental to human health. What is new is the realization that it is perhaps, the most pernicious global problem. Subtle but lethal, acid rain is rising up as the most crucial ecological issue, particularly in European countries.

## Acid rain

Rain has traditionally been regarded as the harbinger of growth & productivity and prosperity. Mankind has always acknowledged 'the useful trouble of the rain'. The 110,000 $km^3$ of rain that fall each year have kept much of the earth's life support system alive. Rain is the most important source of fresh water, available to all, free of cost. This source of joy, provides a new lease of life by greening the landscape (Varshney, 1983).

However, the rain has taken on a new and threatening complexity. Describing the alarming phenomenon in its State of Environment Report, the United Nations Environment Programme (UNEP) notes the way in which the rain reacts with the sulphur and nitrogen oxides that pollute the air to produce "acid rain". Now-a-days one hears much about the so-called "acid rain". A few years ago, it became a jargon term among scientists to describe certain changes in atmospheric chemistry and caught the fancy of the layman and the press alike.

The term **'acid rain'** first appeared in a remarkable 1872 book of Robert A. Smith, "Air and Rain : Beginnings of Chemical Climatogy". Smith's observations of atmospheric acidity in industrial Manchester, England, date back 20 years earlier. As early as the $17^{th}$ century, Robert Hooke recognized atmospheric sources of nutrients for the growth of plants. In the meantime, the chemical composition of "bulk deposition" from the air (rain, snow and dustfall) was characterized and documented in Europe, Scandinavia and North America. By the $20^{th}$ century, atmospheric deposition of sulphur and nitrogen was accounted for as a part of the required fertilization for agricultural crops, as well as forest systems. Because of interest in nutrient deposition, large scale deposition, precipitation monitoring began by 1948 in Norway, Denmark and Finland; by 1956, this monitoring was extended and coordinated as the European Air Chemistry Network by the Stockholm International Meterological Institute (Hidy, 1995).

The imaginative leadership of the Swedes Carl Gustaf Rossby and Erik Eriksson invigorated the embryonic science of atmospheric chemistry. Interpretation of the European monitoring data yielded insight about the origins of the acidity in rainfall, particularly in relation to transport of air pollution over great distances exceeding 1000 km. Interest in the European monitoring data stimulated similar studies in the United States, initiated in the 1950s by Christian Junge, and later in the 1960's by the U.S. National Center for Atmospheric Research.

Clean rain is not pure water. Rain water originates from the evaporation and transpiration of water vapour at the surface. Once the pure vapour enters the atmosphere, however, it condenses on solid particles and soon reaches equilibrium with atmospheric gases. One of the gases is $CO_2$ as it dissolves in the water, carbonic acid ($H_2CO_3$) forms. Gases, such as sulphuric dioxide ($SO_2$) and hydrogen sulphide ($H_2S$) which come from natural sources like volcanoes and forest fires can also alter the composition of precipitation. Sulphur dioxide and hydrogen sulphide are oxidized and hydrolysed in the atmosphere to form sulphuric acid. Nitrogen oxides (NOx), originating from forest fires and many other sources are similarly converted into nitric acid ($HNO_3$). Hydrochloric acid (HCl) can also be formed from forest fires. If these acidic gases are present in significant quantities, they depress precipitation below 5.6. The chemistry of natural precipitation, then, depends on the relative amounts of these various substances in the atmosphere. Sulphur, nitrogen and chlorine also enter the atmosphere as the result of human activities. In reaction with water they form strong acids, which lower the pH of precipitation below 5.6. Anthropogenic nitrogen oxides (NO, $NO_2$ and $NO_3$) may also contribute significantly to the acidity of precipitation. They come from the oxidation of organic nitrogen in fossil fuels.

Scientists in Europe and North America have called attention to marked increases in the acidity of precipitation over recent decades. Rain water normally has a pH of about 5.6 owing to the presence of $H_2CO_3$ formed from the $CO_2$ in the atmosphere. But in or nearby areas with large-scale combustion of fossil fuel or with smelting of sulphide ores, the pH of precipitation may be as low as 4.0. In extreme cases of dense fog, the pH may drop to nearly 2.0, which is a potential hazard of much concern to environmentalists (De Young, 1982).

Acid precipitation, popularly called acid rain, is apparently due to the oxidation of nitrogen and sulphur containing gases that dissolve in the water vapour of the atmosphere to form nitric acids. Reactions such as the following are thought to occur :

$$\underset{\text{Nitric oxide}}{2NO} + O_2 \rightarrow \underset{\text{Nitrogen dioxide}}{2NO_2} \xrightarrow{H_2O} \underset{\text{Nitrous acid}}{2HNO_2} + \underset{\text{Nitric acid}}{HNO_3}$$

$$\underset{\text{Sulphur dioxide}}{2SO_2} + O_2 \rightarrow \underset{\text{Sulphur trioxide}}{2SO_3} \xrightarrow{2H_2O} \underset{\text{Sulphuric acid}}{2H_2SO_4}$$

Figure 1 shows how these nitrogen and sulphur oxides can move into the atmosphere, be converted to inorganic acids, and return to the land in rain and snow. Such cycling may be responsible for lowering the pH of precipitation in the northeastern part of the United States and in eastern Canada.

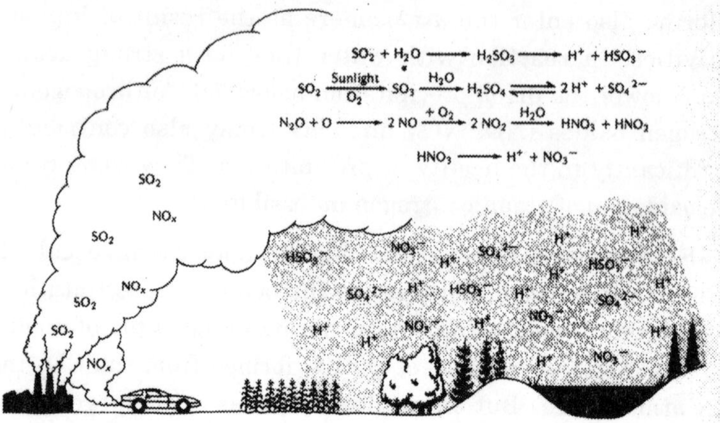


**Fig.1 :** Formation of Nitrogen and Sulphur Oxides from combustion of fuel. These help acidify rainwater, which falls on soil as "acid rain".

## Origin and definition of acidity

Acid rain is an umbrella term, which is used to cover a number of different pollution processes. It is used to describe all precipitation - rain, snow, fog, dew and dry acidic deposition - which are more acidic than normal. It refers to any precipitation which has a pH value less than 5.6, the pH of uncontaminated rain water. The pH of acid rain can be compared with that of common acid and alkaline substances. Acid precipitation generally ranks between about 5.6 and 3.5, and in some cases even lower. Because acid rain includes other forms of precipitation as snow, sleet, hail, dew, forest and dry fall, it may be appropriate to refer the phenomenon as acid deposition and acid precipitation or "atmospheric deposition" collectively. The real acid deposition, often turn up days later and hundreds of kilometers from the source of emission.

Acidity present in the atmosphere derives from the major acid forming gases - carbon dioxide ($CO_2$), sulphur dioxide ($SO_2$), and nitrogen oxides (nitric oxide NO, and nitrogen dioxide $NO_2$). Small contributions derive from hydrogen chloride (HCl) and organic acids sometimes found in the air. In the atmosphere, chemical reactions take place either in the gas phase or in cloud water to oxidize $SO_2$ to sulphuric acid ($H_2SO_4$). Similarly, the nitrogen oxides are oxidized ultimately to form nitric acid ($HNO_3$). All the acid forming gases in the air have both natural sources and anthropogenic sources. Most of the $CO_2$ is a product of the natural carbon cycle involving, for example, plant respiration and forest fires. $SO_2$ can be produced as an intermediate oxidation product of biogenically emitted compounds such as hydrogen sulphide ($H_2S$) and dimethyl sulphide [$(CH_3)_2S$]. Nitrogen oxides are produced naturally from soil nitrification processes and respiration, as well as from lightening discharge. HCl derives naturally from volcanic emissions. Organic acids also may be traced back as potential oxidation products of hydrocarbon vapour emission from vegetation, or the aerosolization of organic slicks on the oceans. Other acidic species in the atmosphere include acid-forming ammonium salts, e.g., $NH_4HSO_4$, $NH_4NO_3$, and $NH_4Cl$.

Naturally occurring atmospheric acidity is substantially enhanced by air pollution, especially from $SO_2$, NO, $NO_2(NO_x)$, and HCl emissions, from the combustion of fossil fuels. There are also human-derived sources of $CO_2$, $NH_3$, and organic acids.

Acids from the atmosphere reach the earth's surface from precipitation (rain, snow, dew, drizzle etc.) or by direct contact with the surface (dry processes). In the latter cases, atmospheric gases can be absorbed in soils, surface waters and vegetation on contact. Nitric acid and hydrochloric acid, mainly in vapour form near or at the ground, may be absorbed directly on surfaces. Acids suspended as tiny particles (aerosols) in the condensed phase, e.g., sulphuric acid are deposited by fall out (sedimentation), impaction, or Brownian motion on underlying surfaces.

Acidity in the atmosphere depends on the mix of trace constituents suspended in the air that will form both anions and cations when dissolved in water. In addition to the principal anions involved, $HCO_3^-$, $CO_3^{2-}$, $SO_4^{2-}$, $Cl^-$, and $NO_3^-$, the cations derived from soil dust, $K^+$, $Ca^{2+}$, $Mg^{2+}$, and $Na^+$, are important adjuncts to $H^+$. Thus, the acid content of deposition can not be determined from measurement of anionic species alone; it is the balance of cations and anions that determine acidity.

Low pH in precipitation, or dry deposition of acid-forming species, does not necessarily create environmental problems. The underlying aquatic and terrestrial ecosystems need to be considered "susceptible" to acidification. Vulnerability of surface waters depends on watershed soil and rock conditions, as well as watershed vegetation interactions. If the alkalinity or acid neutralizing capacity (ANC) of the watershed surface water is low, then the capability to neutralize acid deposition is low. Examples of acidified water conditions are relatively limited and focus on regions of "thin" soils, silicaceous or granitic watershed and lakes or streams, the residue in granite bowls, and where waters have an ANC near zero (or negative). Such areas are found, for example, in historically glaciated regions of Scandinavia and Northeastern North America. Similarly, terrestrial ecosystems in regions of thin-depth, low alkalinity soils (podzols) are believed to be most susceptible to acid deposition effects. These have sometimes been identified with stands of conifers in part of Europe and North America, such as fir, spruce, and pine.

Of course, acid deposition is often loosely linked with other environmental insults, including the effects of airborne sulphur and nitrogen oxides on humans, material corrosion, and visibility impairment. Though, the linkages of air chemistry, nitrogen oxides are connected with environmental stress from elevated atmospheric ozone ($O_3$) levels near the ground.

## Air chemistry

In recent years, air quality and in particular rainwater composition have become matter of increasing concern all over the world. Because high acidity in deposition has been attributed mainly to $SO_4^{2-}$ and $NO_3$ anions, the chemistry of acid rain has focused largely on their atmospheric behaviour. For both species, the chemistry is quite complex and is blended with the broader aspects of meteorological processes that disperse pollution, as well as create cloud and precipitation (Zilio-Grandi and Szpyrkowicz, 2000).

Although, natural sources of sulphur and nitrogen compounds are important to global-scale air chemistry, these sources are overwhelmed by anthropogenic sources in major industrialized regions of the world, including parts of Europe, the Commonwealth of Independent States (former Soviet Union), North America and Asia (particularly China, Japan and Korea). The phenomena of acid rain is largely confined to regions of 1000-2000 km surrounding and downwind of the industrialized regions. Acid rain is identified with these large regions and largely results from the accumulation of pollution in air that travels over sources that overwhelm the ability of the atmosphere to disperse and rid itself of the pollution.

The 1000-km scale of the phenomenon relates to the

residence time of material in the air. This time scale is a measure of the effective lengths of time a chemical constituent will survive in the atmosphere under the influence of chemical transformation, dispersion, and dry and wet deposition loss at the ground. Residence times are largely determined by chemical reactivity and solubility in water. Some highly reactive chemical species are lost to transformations in seconds, whereas others remain in the air for years. The residence time for sulphur and nitrogen oxides generally ranges between 3 and 5 days; nitrogen oxides are more reactive and are estimated to be somewhat shorter. The "regional scale" of phenomena like acid rain is derived from these time durations, assuming air motion at about 10 km $hr^{-1}$

The principal atmospheric reaction of $SO_2$ is its oxidation to sulphur trioxide ($SO_3$) followed by rapid reaction with water to form $H_2SO_4$. The oxidation of $SO_2$ occurs through homogenous gas-phase reactions with the hydroxyl radical (OH), which is produced photochemically from $NO_x$ reactions with organic species in the presence of sunlight. $SO_2$ also is oxidized in condensed water by reactions with dissolved hydrogen peroxide ($H_2O_2$), and to a lesser extent with $O_3$ or $O_2$. The last reactions are catalyzed by the presence of manganous ion and ferric ion. $H_2O_2$ comes from gas-phase photochemical reactions linked with OH formation. Sulphate in the atmosphere is in the condensed phase; reactions of $H_2SO_4$ with ammonia ($NH_3$) from biogenic sources from complex mixtures of $H_2SO_4$, ammonium sulphate, and ammonium bisulphate, with a variety of other material including soil dust, metal oxides and salts, and carbonaceous species.

Nitrogen oxide chemistry in the atmosphere is more complicated than that of sulphur oxides. $NO_x$ undergoes a series of photochemically stimulated gas-phase reactions with organic species (hydrocarbons and oxygenates) that produce a series of gaseous species, including $NO_3$, $N_2O_5$, $N_2O_4$, HONO, $HONO_2$, and organic nitrate (e.g. peroxyacetyl nitrate of PAN). In urban areas like Los Angeles, this chemistry causes the well-known photochemical smog. Evidence suggests that nitric acid vapour is readily dissolved in condensed water or moist aerosol particles, rather than produced by aqueous reactions. Nitric acid also reacts with $NH_3$ to form ammonium nitrate. Some of the other nitrogen oxide species are quite reactive in air and dissolve in water to form nitrate ion.

Acids can be collected in cloud or precipitation elements (on hydrometers) by vapour absorption, chemical oxidation and water vapour nucleation or by aerodynamic processes involving collision with aerosol particles. If acid material is scavenged inside clouds, the resulting removal is sometimes called rainout. If scavenging occurs in hydrometers falling below clouds, the process is called washout.

Dry deposition of gaseous species depends on their reactivity with the underlying surface as well as fluid dynamic and molecular diffusion processes transferring the gas to the surface. Deposition of acid on particles depends on the stickness or wetness of the surface and the particle, as well as the fluid dynamic process of particle capture. Wet deposition takes place from rain and snowfall, as well as collection of fog (cloud) particles, rime (ice particles), and dew formation on surfaces.

In general, concentrations of pollutants in the atmosphere tend to decrease exponentially with distance from a source to low levels within 100 km. However, if many sources are aligned roughly along the direction of prevailing winds, cumulative concentrations can remain elevated for substantial distances. The so-called long-range transport of air pollutants relates to this cumulative effect, as well as the atmosphere's ability at times to transport large volumes of air for long distances with relatively little mixing of (or dilution by) clean air. A tracing of polluted air by various direct and indirect means suggests that a "zone of influence" of large sulphur and nitrogen oxide sources can be inferred for hundreds of kilometers downstream. This long-range cumulative effect creates the potential for relatively high levels of acid deposition over the distances exceeding 1000 km, affecting pristine areas far from industrial-urbanized environments. Thus, the phenomenon of acid rain is generally not identified with localized air pollution problems in and around large sources or at urban areas but with larger scale regional effects.

Examples of widespread sulphate deposition have been observed in eastern North America. Superposition of $SO_2$ emission densities shows the coincidence between pH in precipitation water and regionally high emission densities. Similarly, there is a correspondence between high emission densities and $SO_4^{2-}$ deposition. Emission-deposition patterns reflecting local effects and long-range transport of pollutants are also observed in Europe, Scandinavia, and Japan. Patterns are also similar for NOx emissions and nitrate; NOx emission distributions in eastern North America and elsewhere tend to coincide with $SO_2$ distributions. The international character of long-range pollutant transport is illustrated in southeastern Canada where it, derives not only from local emissions, but also from transboundary transport northeastward from industrial areas of the United States. Similarly, Scandinavia is exposed to acid deposition from both local sources and long-distance sources in the United Kingdom and industrial Northern and Central Europe. Japan receives acid deposition exposure not only from its own industrial sources, but also from China and Korea westward across the Sea of Japan.

## Indian scenario

In the urban areas of India, motor vehicles contribute more than 50% of the total emission of oxides of nitrogen (NOx). Analysis of four-hourly nitric oxide data generated by the National Environmental Engineering Research Institute (NEERI), Nagpur for 10 urban centers in India indicated the occurrence of $NO_2$ peaks, during peak traffic hours. Delhi the capital city of India is termed as the fourth most polluted city in the world. In some parts of Delhi, suspended particulate matter (SPM) was found to be double the permissible limit of 200μg $m^{-3}$ or even more. The highest level of sulphur dioxide ($SO_2$) recorded in the year 1993 in Delhi was 38 μg$m^{-3}$ and that of nitrogen oxides was 53 μg $m^{-3}$. The concentrations of $SO_2$ and NOx were reported to be 29 and 69 ppb respectively, in Lucknow city. An abnormally high concentration of 3450 μg $m^{-3}$ in case of SPM was observed there. Kolkata city recorded a $SO_2$ concentration of 140 μg $m^{-3}$ against the standard 80 μg $m^{-3}$. Atmospheric concentration of $SO_2$ in the industrial area around the coal mines of Bihar was 96 μg $m^{-3}$. Use of outdated technology in the production of vehicles/machinery and other consumer/industrial products along with the ignorance of a vast majority of people due to poverty and illiteracy has led to tolerance of the pollution and consequent degradation of the environment (Jayapragasam, 2003).

## The effects of acid precipitation

There have been widespread debates on the extent to which acid deposition helps or harms the terrestrial and aquatic systems. Acid rain contains nutrients, such as nitrogen, potash and trace elements, often in a form readily available for plant use. The sulphur contained in the deposition is beneficial to those soils which are sulphur deficient. But too much of nutrients, however, are as bad as not enough. Elevated nitrogen content may predispose trees to winter damage. Nitrogen supplied to high elevational trees through cloud water may result in increased susceptibility to damage from early frost or desiccation.

The effects of acid precipitation are determined by physical factors, such as stream flow, evaporation, stream size, soil and bed-rock type and depth. The damage to nature caused by acid rain is "already unacceptably high", but the future effect is "potentially enormous". It has been shown "beyond my reasonable doubt that forests and fresh water are seriously and detrimentally affected". As industrialization proceeds to developing countries, acid rain is spreading to tropical forests.

The effects of acid precipitation depend on the sensitivity of the receptors. The following sub-paragraphs deal with the actual and possible effects of acid precipitation on soils, terrestrial vegetation, aquatic ecosystems and other receptors.

### *(a) Effect on soil*

Low pH in precipitation, or dry deposition of acid-forming species, does not necessarily create environmental problems. Acid rain is assumed to be responsible for increased acidity in some lakes of the Adirondacks and in other regions of the northeast United States. Since most fish will not tolerate pH levels below about 4.5, the resulting increased acidity of lake water is though to have essentially eliminated most fish in some of the Adirondack lakes.

Effects of acid rain are more pronounced on the acidity of water than on soil acidity. Soils generally are sufficiently buffered to accommodate acid rain with little or no increase in soil acidity on an annual basis. But continued inputs of acid rain at pHs of 4.0-4.5 would have significant effects on the pH of soils, especially those that are weakly buffered. This is also serious for soils that are already quite acidic, since increased acidity could well make them even less fertile.

Acid precipitation in the soil has three possible fates : (i) the acid will be neutralized by reaction with free bases such as $CaCO_3$ and $Na_2CO_3$ in drier regions and in (young) alkaline soils; (ii) acidic ions will enter into exchange reactions which will to a large degree control the pH of the soil and release other ions, in soils which have an appreciable cation exchange capacity (CEC), (iii) after incomplete reaction with soil minerals the acid water may pass into the ground water in soils that are already quite acidic and/or have low cation exchange capacity (CEC).

On entering the soil, solutions undergo many reactions. When deposition dominated by sulphur enters a system previously unaffected by acid deposition, the $SO_4^{2-}$ concentration of the soil solution begins to increase. Some soils have substantial capacity to adsorb $SO_4^{2-}$ on the particle surfaces, and in such cases, this adsorption acts as a buffer, delaying the elevation of solution $SO_4^{2-}$ concentrations. The $SO_4^{2-}$ uptake and cycling capacities of the biotic component of the ecosystem also acts as buffers, slowing the increase in solution $SO_4^{2-}$ concentration. Usually, the soil system will reach an equilibrium at which elevated $SO_4^{2-}$ concentrations in solution become sufficiently high that the outgoing flux of $SO_4^{2-}$ sulphur in the drainage water is approximately equal to the incoming sulphur in acid deposition. Because soils vary greatly in adsorption capacities, the time required before substantially elevated $SO_4^{2-}$, concentrations are observed in the drainage waters may vary from a few weeks to many decades.

As $SO_4^{2-}$ concentrations in soil solutions and water leaving the system increase, charge balance considerations dictate that these anions be accompanied by an equivalent amount of cations. In soils that are even moderately well supplied with bases (i.e. perhaps 15% or more of the negatively charged exchange sites are occupied by the cations $Ca^{2+}$, $Mg^{2+}$, $K^+$, or $Na^+$), these base cations will comprise most of the increase in solution cation concentration. The remainder will be largely $H^+$ or aluminium species, particularly $Al^{3+}$, that comes into solution as a result of exchange reactions or the dissolution of soil minerals, although, in some systems iron or manganese species may be significant. The increase in the rate of removal of basic cations will tend to acidify the system. Because the total supply of these cations in the soil is usually quite large relative to the annual input of H+ in acid deposition, acidification of soils and waters by this cation export mechanism is likely to be a slow process involving decades or even centuries in deep soils or soils containing significant amounts of minerals that release basic cations upon weathering.

Other substances besides acids are deposited from the atmosphere. Some of these like N, P, K, Na, N, Mg and S are nutrients for natural ecosystems but others are not beneficial and may become toxic to plants and soil organisms if in high enough concentrations. Toxic metals include Pb, Zn, Cu, Cd, Ni and Hg. Metals entering the soil from the atmosphere are likely to become exchangeable ions on the clay or organic exchange sites to be complexed by organic compounds, or to remain or become insoluble. In any of these cases, there is a strong tendency for the soil to hold the metals. Thus, only a small portion of the metal compounds entering or accumulated moves through the soil. It turns out that the more fertile highly buffered soils are also the most effective filters for metals. Such metal contamination of soil by aerial deposition has reached localized damaging levels only near urban or industrial sources.

A main component of man-made acid deposition is sulphuric acid ($H_2SO_4$). The availability of phosphorus nutrient is very much affected under acidic conditions of the soil and it gets fixed in the soil as unavailable form. The canopy of pine and fig trees was thinner due to exposure to acid rain and the soil P was less in such forests. A reduction of 75% of the acidity deposition in relation to 1988 is required in order to protect 95% of the forest resources from the effects of soil acidification in Sweden. The sulphate and nitrate ions in rainwater cause additional mobilization of basic cations from the soil into the drainage water. Heavy metal solubility, availability and their loss through leaching and runoff increases in acid soils. Acid rain and dry deposition of $SO_2$ were correlated with accelerated leaching of magnesium and calcium ions and increased the concentrations of aluminium and hydrogen ions in soil.

### (b) Effects on terrestrial vegetation

Forests are highly complex ecosystems and trees have very long life cycles. Forests react to environmental changes and other stresses slowly with subtle and often hard to identify changes. Assessing possible effects of acidic deposition has required the development of an improved knowledge of natural changes in forest systems, as well as knowledge of the impacts of a wide range of stress factors including short-term weather cycles, long-term climate shifts, insects, pathogens, fire, wildlife and human management practices, as well as air pollution.

Forest damage has become a major topic of public and scientific discussion in recent years. Species exhibiting most serious damage due to acid rain are conifers such as fir, pine and spruce. However, deciduous trees like beech are also affected adversely. One of the most damaged area in Germany is the famous "Black Forest", which is largely covered with conifers. Red spruce is declining in Eastern North America and sugar maples of Quebec in Canada are also showing signs of decline (Vogelmann, 1982). In the yearly inventories of damage, reported by Federal Ministry of Food, Agriculture and Forestry, the portion of damage to German forest has risen from 8% in 1982 to 52% in 1985. Forest damages in other parts of Europe have been reported. Instances of severe decline in certain regions of Poland and (formerly) Czechoslovakia appear to be a result of exposure to very high $SO_2$ concentrations associated with nearby industrial emissions. A survey of forest damage in UK has indicated a worsening forest condition. Damage and decline of cedars in Japan have been recognized since the 1960s.

Forest damages may vary from minor foliar injury to large scale destruction and death of forest stands. In 'Crown die back' injury, leaves or needles at the tree top turns yellow, then brown and ultimately drop off. The tree growth may be decreased in association with annual concentration as small as 25-30 μg of sulphur dioxide.

Acid rain has a variety of effects on terrestrial vegetation including agricultural crops (Lee and Weber, 1979; Hileman, 1981; Maiti, 1982; Chevone *et al.*, 1986). Through acid rain nutrients from foliage may be leached, causing lesions on leaves (chlorosis and necrosis) and erosion of external surface of young plant parts. It may also affect photosynthesis and growth of young tissues. Acid precipitation may exert a subtle effect on the reproductive potential of plants. Due to acid rain plant development power is diminished; gross deformation occurs, vitality is snapped and chances for survival are lessened. The direct effects of acid-rain on vegetation are :

(*i*) Damage to protective surface structures;

(*ii*) Distrubance of gas exchange and metabolic and growth processes;

(*iii*) Poisoning of plant cells, resulting in necrotic lesions;

(*iv*) Alternation of leaf and root oxidation processes, affecting associated microbes;

(*v*) Synergistic interaction with other environmental stresses.

Pollutants and acidic deposition have been identified as one of the causes of altitude decline of Norway spruce (*Pices abies*). This new type of disease occurred in all types of parent rocks, on all soil types in widely varying climatic conditions in tree stands with varying nutritional status and in situations where pollution and atmospheric deposition differ considerably (Rehfusess, 1991). Studies carried out in China in a forest covered predominantly with Masson pine (*Rinus massoniana*) showed steady decline beginning 1980s. Adverse signs of the pines included tip necrosis of needles, thin crown, reduced needle length, premature abscission, branch dieback and reduced radial growth. Atmospheric sulphur dioxide and fluoride content were greater in these forests. Between 1973 and 1988 the number of lichen species in an area of Netherlands increased from 56 to 68. Evidence of growth reduction and tree death in Siberian forests due to acid deposition was noticed from the year 1978 when there was increasing industrialization. There was lack of early wood formation and late wood cell thickening was absent. Number of cells per growth ring was decreased. Trunk ring width in *Pinus brectia* was less and resin canals were either damaged or not present due to acid deposition in Turkey.

The plants try to neutralize the acidity in rain water. The external acid neutralizing capacity (EANC) of the plants may be determined by measuring the change in pH induced by soaking fresh leaves in an acidic solution of pH 4.0 for two hours. The buffering capacity index (BCI) is determined by measuring the amounts of acid necessary to produce a change of 5 μeq$H^+$ in the leaf homogenate. EANC and BCI are used to evaluate the plant's sensitivity/tolerance to acid deposition.

The effect of simulated acid rain was studied in several plant species by a number of plant scientists. *Picea abies* needles exposed to dilute sulphuric acid at concentrations found in natural rain exhibited yellowish white to brown necrotic spots. This damage was worse in trees more than 60 years old than that in younger trees. Wet acid deposition decreased the height and stem diameter growth of white oak (*Quercus alba*) and loblolly pine (*Pinus aeda*) under high as well as low fertility soils of Canada.

Germination of the seeds of five tree species viz., *Cinnamonium camphora, Ligustrum lucidum, Castanopsis fissa, Melia azadarachta* and *Koelreuteria bipinnata* was inhibited in acid rainwater of pH 2.0. It also damaged the foliage, increased the cell permeability and acidified the leaf sap of the seedlings. Increased cell permeability makes the membrane leaky and subsequently leads to loss of ions and other nutrients.

Many reports are available on the effect of air pollution and the consequent acid on the aerial shoots. Very little information is available on the underground plant parts like the roots. Presence of acid producing gases in the air had no effect on skeletal root morphology of Norway spruce. However, the growth of fine roots was markedly reduced particularly in the 0-10 cm soil layer where viability of the root was also considerably reduced. Root length decreased by 14% as the pH of nutrient solution decreased from 5.5 to 2.5 while tissue aluminium increased from 0.24 to 0.7 mg $g^{-1}$ in the leaves of forest tree seedlings. The root conductivity was 83% greater in pH 2.5 than in 5.5 pH. Calcium and magnesium concentrations in newly formed lateral branches of shoots were significantly lower in pH 2.5 treatment relative to 5.5 pH.

Stimulated acid rain retarded the development of mycorrhizae on *Pinus thumbergii* and therefore the leaf phosphate content decreased. Sulphur dioxide can bleach the pigments of the leaf at high concentrations. But very rarely atmosphere concentration increases to such an extent. The epoxidation state of the xanthophylls cycle was changed upon $SO_2$ exposure due to a higher concentration of zeaxanthin and a lower violixanthin content. Acid rain of pH less than 3.0 decreased the leaf pigment content.

Exposure to the acid rain also has an influence on the various biotic and abiotic stresses of the plants. Red spruce seedlings exposed to acid mist were more frost hardy as assayed by electrolyte leakage and the area of necrotic spot. Acidity of stimulated acid rain increased the incidence and severity of anthracnose leaf symptoms. Acid rain causes a change in the incidence and severity of different pests and diseases. The situation is more complex and varying since some organisms are able to show increased infestation while some others show decreased infestation under acid rain.

Acid mist increased the foliar iron and potassium concentrations and increased the leaching of calcium, magnesium, manganese and zinc from the foliage of red spruce (*Picea rubens*). The decrease in leaf calcium due to acid smog was 25% in current year needles and 18% in one-year-old needles of red spruce seedlings. Foliar calcium, magnesium and copper were reduced in pH 4.2 and 3.8 treatment in white oak and loblolly pine trees due to acid rain.

Acid mist of pH 2.3 markedly decreased soluble carbohydrates (42%), starch (64%) and hemicellulose (83%) content of the leaf and stem in *Phaseolus vulgaris*. Root starch was drastically reduced in pine trees due to $SO_2$ exposure. The carbohydrate content of the leaf and stem of green pepper was adversely affected.

Exposure to oxidative stress like ozone ($O_3$), $NO_X$ and/or $SO_2$ may result in the formation of various highly reactive compounds in plant tissues, including peroxide and super oxide radicals. As a consequence, many functions in the plants are altered. The ability of plants under these adverse conditions depends on the prevention of the free radical production and the increase of free radical scavenging. Acid rain induced lipid peroxidation and increased levels of hydrogen peroxide in the leaves of *Phaseolus vulgaris*.

### *(c) Effects on aquatic ecosystems*

Perhaps the single most publicized environmental assault from acid rain is the acidification of surface waters. Experience has indicated that the potential for acidification is most likely in areas where the watershed is poorly suited to neutralize acid deposition, and where the waters have low acid neutralizing capacity (ANC). ANC in clear natural waters is defined in terms of aqueous bicarbonate and carbonate ion concentration :

$$[ANC] = [HCO_3^-] + 2[CO_3^{2-}] + [OH^-] + [H^+]$$

Among lakes surveyed by the National Surface Water Survey (NSWS), USA, 4% of some 28,000 lakes were acidic (ANC≤0) and just over half had ANC≤200 $\mu eq\ L^{-1}$. Five per cent had closed-system pH≤5.5. Most acidic lakes were found in the Northeast, Florida, and the upper Midwest; <1% of the lakes in the west Minnesota, and the Southern Blue Ridge subregion were acidic. Total aqueous monomeric Al increased with decreasing pH; concentrations exceeded 50 $\mu gL^{-1}$ in 3.0% of the NSWS lakes.

Atmospheric deposition is the dominant source of $SO_4^{2-}$ in most NSWS surface waters. Among acidic NSWS lakes, 75% are inorganic dominated with $SO_4^{2-}$ as the dominant anion, 22% are organic dominated, and 3% are watershed-sulphur dominated. Among acidic, inorganic dominated NSWS lakes and streams, acidic deposition is believed to be the main source of current acidity.

The early estimates of the extent and severity of lake acidification in Scandinavia and North America relied heavily on limited historical observations based on chemical measurements of highly variable quality. The details of alleged widespread acidification of natural waters in Sweden and Norway, involving thousands of lakes, have not been verified because their survey and historical data have not been made available. Similar assertions of acidification of lakes in Ontario and Quebec, and in the northeastern United States, particularly the Adirondack mountains, are clouded with ambiguity relating to inadequate historical records of water quality and incomplete accounting for naturally acidic waters (Goldstein *et al*., 1984), as well as confounding causes of acidification related to land use and forest and management practices.

Acid precipitation may reach aquatic ecosystems directly or indirectly through runoff from terrestrial ecosystems. Deposited along with the acids are many other toxins and nutrients. All these pollutants may affect organisms and aquatic ecosystems in relatively short time scales, particularly ecosystems with a small number of species, also called oligotrophic ecosystems. Acidification of lakes and streams to pH 5 or less appears to reduce decomposition because of the elimination of some species of bacteria, which may be replaced by other species of bacteria or fungi.

Acidification affects communities of planktonic and benthic algae in lakes and streams. The number of species of phytoplankton in acidic lakes decreases as pH declines (Almer *et al*., 1974, 1978). Diatoms collected from a series of acidophillic species increased between 1949 and the mid

1970's (Leivested, 1976). In Dutch moorland pools, diatom species diversity declined from 1920 to 1978 in acidified pools.

Aquatic macrophytes also show changes related to acidification. In Swedish lakes, macrophytic communities once dominated by Lobella species were later dominated by Sphagnum species (Grahm *et al.*, 1974; Grahm, 1978) or *Juncua bulbosus* (Nilssen, 1980). A similar dominance of *Sphagnum* was evident in an acidic lake in New York (Hendrey and Vertucci, 1980).

In Ontario and Sweden, zooplankton biomass was lower in acidic than in similar non-acidic lakes (Roff and Kwiatkowski, 1977). The number of zooplankton species present in a lake decreased as pH decreased in Sweden (Almer *et al.*, 1974, 1978), Norway (Hendrey and Wright, 1976; Raddum *et al.*, 1980) and Ontario (Sprules, 1975a, 1975b).

Mollusks are highly sensitive to acidification, as would be expected due to the high calcium carbonate requirements of this group for shell formation. Snails were found in Norwegian lakes with pH at or below 5.2, and were rare or reduced at pH 5.2 and 6.6 (Okland, 1969; Raddum, 1980). The snail *Ancylus* species was not found below pH 5.7 in the river Duddon, England (Sutcliffe and Carrick, 1973). Mollusks are not found in Ontario lakes with pH at or below 5 (Scheider *et al.*, 1975; Roff and Kwaiatkowski, 1977).

The crustaceans *Gammarus lacustris* and *Lepidurus areticus* are widespread in Norway and are important fish food organisms where they occur. They are not found in lakes with pH less than 6.0 (Leivested *et al.*, 1976; Okland, 1980). In Sweden the crayfish (*Astacus astacus*) is common in lakes with pH less than 6.0. Some groups of aquatic insects are reduced at low pH while others flourish. Many species of Ephemeroptera and Plecoptera disappear as pH declines.

Raddum *et al.* (1980) found that Coleoptera, Hemiptera and Megaloptera were more abundant in lakes with pH below 4.8.

The primary impact of acidification appears to be on species composition and diversity. Unfortunately, few taxonomic groups have been studied sufficiently to predict species changes with the onset of acidification. Fish populations have been studied that are indigenous to acid sensitive lakes. Fish are affected individually and at the population and community levels; some species are more sensitive than others. In lakes and streams experiencing acidification, fish appear to respond primarily to Al, pH and Ca. Populations in low - Ca waters (an indicator of sensitivity to acid deposition) generally are less productive than those in hard waters. Calcium has a protective effect for fish exposed to acidic conditions typified by low pH and high Al concentrations. Toxicities of fish to Al and pH depend on life stage and concentration in their environment. For example, the primary adverse effect on eggs seems to be related to pH, but toxicity to fish is primarily due to ionic Al.

Actual damage to fish populations from acidification is difficult to quantify. Estimates depend on judgments from evidence that (a) populations of species were once naturally reproducing in a water body, (b) acidity in the water body has increased, and (c) decline or absence of the population or community cannot be explained by other casual factors. Perhaps the best analysis of fish loss based on these three criteria was done in the 1980s for the Adirondack region. These studies suggested that 200-400 lakes may have lost fish populations. By area, this would amount to about 1.5-3.0% of the Adirondack lakes.

Glass and Loucks (1980), observed the decline of the frog (*Rana temporaria*) and the toad (*Bufo bufo*) from a Swedish lake where the pH had declined to 4.0-4.5 and from which all fish had disappeared. Exposure to acid decreased sodium influx in isolated frog skin, and thereby reduced active sodium transport. However, there was no significant change in osmotic permeability of intact frog (*Rana pipens*) exposed to low pH.

Effect of acid precipitation on fish include mortality, reproductive failure, reduced growth rate, skeletal deformities and increased uptake of heavy metals. The earliest recorded impact was on Atlantic Salamon in few southern Norway rivers (Jensen and Snekvik, 1972). Death of fish at low pH has been attributed to the failure of ion regulation or asphyxiation, or to elevated metal concentration associated with low pH. Exposure to low pH water causes edema between outer lamellar cells and remaining tissue, erosion of lamellar and swelling of filaments (McKenna Duerr, 1976). Primary mode of acid toxicity in fish is gill damage, which impairs respiratory, excretory and liver functions. Liver impairment reduces tolerance of fish to other toxicants. Dyne (1981), believed that the death of fish embryos is the result of corrosion of epidermal cells by acid, which interferes with respiration and osmoregulation.

The low pH interferes with respiration through several mechanisms. Elevated hydrogen ion concentration may cause excessive secretion of mucus from the gills, thereby reducing the rate of oxygen diffusion across the gill surface (Dively *et al.*, 1977). At extremely low pH, an increased influx of hydrogen ions reduces blood which in turn, reduces the oxygen carrying capacity of haemoglobin (Spry *et al.*, 1981). Packer (1979) reported reduced oxygen consumption in Brook Trout exposed to acutely lethal pH. The reduced consumption was caused by decreased oxygen transfer and reduced blood oxygen capacity.

The most likely explanation of the physiological effect of

hydrogen ion on fish is that at moderately low pH (4-5) failure of ion regulation is the primary response. At very low pH (<3.5), respiratory failure occurs.

Acidification of surface waters is accompanied by increases in concentration of some metals. Aluminium concentration appears to be very important in determining the effect of acidification on fish (Schofield, 1982). Cronan and Schofield (1979), Baker and Schofield (1980) and Schofield and Trojnar (1980) showed that mortality of Brook Trout in New York was caused by aluminium and pH in combination, rather than by either factor singly.

### *(d) Effects on wildlife*

Several direct and indirect effects of arid rain on the productivity and survival of wildlife population have been reported (Mayer *et al.*, 1984). Acid rain can directly affect the eggs and tadpoles of frogs and salamanders that breed in small forest ponds. Increases in acidity of these waters may impair hatching success or survival of young animals. It has been postulated that acid rain can indirectly affect wildlife by allowing metals bound in soil and sediments to be released into the aquatic systems where toxic amounts may be ingested by wildlife. Other indirect effects of acid rain on wildlife are loss or alteration of plants' food and habitat resources, because abundance and diversity of plants is directly related to that of wildlife, any affect on the former will also affect the latter. For example, lichens are extremely sensitive to pollution and acid rain; the decline of a particular lichen often used as a nesting material by the northern perula (*Perula americana*) may be partly responsible for this species increased rarity.

### *(e) Effect on human health*

Acid deposition is an important concern because of its potential to induce adverse environmental effects. Traditionally, effects on human systems are usually considered at highest priority because of the national and international laws and covenants protecting public health and welfare.

The direct effects of sulphur and nitrogen oxides on human health and welfare have been studied for many years (Hidy, 1995). Knowledge of respiratory stress from high concentrations of $SO_2$, airborne particulate matter, and to a lesser degree $NO_2$ formed the basis of the U.S. National Ambient Air Quality Standards (NAAQS) in 1970. Welfare (economic or aesthetic) effects associated with crop and forest damage and metal or stone corrosion and damage from high concentrations of $SO_2$ and $NO_2$, as well as visibility impairment from sulphate containing haze, also were noted to support the NAQS. The annual emissions of $SO_2$ have decreased in the United States by about 30% since 1970.

Acid rain is known to be highly corrosive in action and results in skin diseases and even severe deaths. The best example of such effects have been reported by Kitagava (1985). Some 600 cases of severe lung diseases that occurred over a period of 8 years were studied. All the victims substomatal chamber resulted in very small wall angles. These small wall angles may not be adequate enough for water penetration of stomata (Schonherr and Bukovac, 1972). All evidences suggest that the main route of substances should be through the cuticle and not through stomata (Evans, 1988).

The acid deposition on the leaf surface reduce the rate of photosynthesis. In addition, the nitrate content of acid deposition combines with the potassium content of leaf's nutrient system which then is leached or chemically washed from the leaf. If this vital potassium is not supplied by the roots, the entire tree may suffer from nutrient stress. Alteration in leaf surface chemistry may increase vulnerability of the leaf to disease agents and toxic materials.

There is a possibility that the forests of the world may be destroyed completely if pollution persists. In contract with natural degradation in which the ecosystem rebuilds itself, trees affected by acid rain will take centuries or even millennia to achieve the predisturbance level of productivity, structure and function. Degrading forests not only results in ecological lived relatively close to a titanium dioxide pigment factory that emitted 100-300 tonnes of sulphuric acid aerosols per month. In one area with the highest incidence of the disease, measurements have indicated that acid concentrations averaged 160 $\mu gm^3$. Average concentration of acid rain and the incidence of lung disease declined with increasing distance from the plant. The incidence of lung disease dropped sharply, furthermore when the plant installed controls to remove sulphuric acid from its emissions. Plants sensitive to these gases show necrosis of leaves or needles at exposures in excess of ~100 parts per million (ppm) $SO_2$, $NO_2$ as well as sulphuric acid droplets for short periods.

The question of the effects of acidity on the human system has proven to be controversial. Studies of the effects of airborne sulphate in the 1970s suggested adverse respiratory response, but these were later disputed. More recently, the influence of strong acidity in aerosols has been considered. Experiments to date have not verified any respiratory effect of airborne acidity, except at concentrations for higher than found in the atmosphere. The occurrence of adverse health effects from either airborne $SO_4^{2-}$ or acidity remains unresolved.

Possible indirect effects of acid deposition on drinking water supplies have been reported. These appear to derive from accelerated dissolution of heavy metals like lead from old pipes and cistern walls, but are not widespread as a hazard for most modern water supply systems. Of all the human system concerns, the impairment of visibility by various airborne sulphate appears to be the best documented. The aesthetic effect is considered by some to merit marginal consideration. Nevertheless, the issue of visibility continues to be raised in conjunction with the environmental effects of acid deposition.

### *(f) Other effects*

In addition to these ecological effects, acid rain and accompanying pollutants cause corrosion and deterioration of structures and materials such as limestone, marble roofing, slate, mortar and metals. The rate of atmospheric corrosion depends on the interaction of different climatic parameters such as humidity, temperature and pollutant concentrations. The corrosive effect has been demonstrated in several laboratory investigations. Acid rain influences corrosion rates by providing to the surface corrosion stimulations in the form of $H^+$ and $SO_4^{2-}$ ions, or by washing away dry pollutants, principally sulphates, deposited during the preceding dry period. Whereas the first process promotes corrosion, the latter decreases corrosion. Increasing amount of $SO_2$, and $SO_4^{2-}$ in the atmosphere, especially in the troposphere, changes scattered solar radiation which in turn can lead to a temperature decrease.

Acid rain accelerates corrosion in most construction materials in buildings, bridges, dams, industrial equipments, water supply networks, underground storage tanks, hydroelectric turbines and power and telecommunication cables. It also assaults historic buildings and cultural treasures by accelerating corrosion. For example, substantial damages to the Parthenon in Athens and Trojans column in Rome are largely due to the acid fall out.

Monuments, statues, building, temples where marble (i.e. rock mainly composed of $CaCO_3$) is used are very vulnerable to acid rain. The sulphuric acid in acid rain reacts with $CaCO_3$ to convert it into gypsum ($CaSO_4.2H_2O$) with nearly two fold increase in volume. Consequently, a pressure develops on the surface leading to peeling, pitting and corrosion. Further, rain washes away the loose aggregates of gypsum formed on the surface leading to severe loss of surface details. The phenomenon is popularly known as stone leprosy. Our national monument Taj Mahal has developed stone leprosy due to impingement of acid fumes emitted by Mathura refinery.

## Remedies against the detrimental effects of acid rain

### *1. Liming*

The damage to lakes and other water bodies can be eliminated by adding lime. Many chemicals such as caustic soda, soda, sodium carbonate, slacked lime and limestone are most popular for raising pH of those water. But while liming, eliminates some of the symptoms of acidification, it is expensive and not practical for many lakes and running water. Most of all, it is not real cure - it does not attack the causes of the problem. It nevertheless is good interim measure, and can concurrently be used to counterbalance the increasing acidification of crop land. Although, liming can restore many species and improve water quality in lakes and streams, it must be repeated periodically (every 3-6 years) to remain effective.

### *2. Emission control*

The obvious and only lasting solution to the acid rain problem is a reduction of sulphur and nitrogen oxide emissions. The use of fuels that are low in sulphur is not really practical because the world supply in these fuels is believed to be limited. Various techniques are also available for scrubbing fuel gases before they are released into the atmosphere. Methods are also available to reduce sulphur emissions from non-ferrous smelters. Oxides of nitrogen can also be reduced through reduction or better control of combustion temperature. Reduction in the emission of acidic gases is necessary and should be part of all new projects. Investment in controlling pollutants at the source is most effective and often the least expensive.

The Stockholm conference in 1982 on acidification of the environment was an important step in the right direction. In March, 1983, the long range trans-boundary air pollution convention accepted an obligation to reduce their 1980 base emission levels by 1993 at the latest.

Alternatively, there are other potential sources of energy instead of fossil fuel, there are many ways of improving energy conservation measures.

### *3. Amelioration of the impact of acid rain*

Recovery from the impact of acid rain may be brought about in two ways : by amelioration of the impact of the pollution, or by its elimination at the source. The first solution that comes to mind usually is to ameliorate the impact of the pollution where the harm is done. One of the consequences of acid rain is acidification of waters and soils. By liming, that is, adding calcium carbonate, one can increase the pH of water and the cation exchange capacity of soils. Liming decreases acidity, but it does not provide for the return of the leached nutrients nor does it remove all absorbed toxic metals. In some acidified lakes restocking of fish by tolerant species has been applied. Certain species can survive at a pH lower than 5.0.

None of the measures to counteract the impacts of acid rain seem to be satisfactory remedies on a large scale. To preserve genetic material which is being lost, it is thus, imperative to take to fight the cause of acid rain and its accompanying pollutants.

### 4. *Elimination of Acid Rain at the source*

The only effective means of reducing the acid precipitation problems is by greatly reducing emissions of the precursors of the acids in acid rain (and accompanying pollutants). This can be done by energy conservation, substitution for polluting fossil fuels by cleaner fuels or other alternatives, or application of abatement techniques to reduce the $SO_2$ and $NO_X$ content before, during, or after combustion. Currently, available $SO_2$-control technology consists of : the use of cleaner burning fossils like low sulphur coal, oil or gas, physical coal cleaning and flue gas desulphurisation of FGD. Emerging control technologies include : fluidised bed combustion or FBC, coal gasification, coal liquefaction, and new burning techniques for the reduction of $NO_X$.

#### (*i*) Energy Conservation

Fuel consumption may be reduced through more efficient use of fuels. In some countries 50% or more of all fuel consumption meets space heating requirements. Improved thermal insulation or district heating schemes could lead to a considerable economization of energy, as could changes in the industry. However, what can be achieved by energy conservation is a slower growth of fuel consumption even perhaps a slight reduction of energy use, but no reduction of any importance.

### (*ii*) Substitution

The use of cleaner burning fuels is the most straightforward control option. Oil and gas are both cleaner burning fuels than coal. The use of low sulphur coal is not always feasible either, since demand exceeds supply and low sulphur coal mines are often remote from power plants or ore smelters, resulting in prohibitive transportation costs.

The use of nuclear energy instead of power generated by fossil fuel combustion certainly reduces sulphur and nitrogen emissions but its use causes other kinds of pollution and risks. The use of hydroelectric power and solar energy have limitations relating to supply and technology, respectively.

### (*iii*) Abatement techniques to reduce sulphur content before fuel combustion

In countries using coal for power generation, coal cleaning is a standard practice, usually at the mine. This technique is of greater importance in the USA than in Europe because of the higher sulphur levels of American coal. The process that is usually applied is relatively simple and involves washing the coal with large quantities of water and drying it in a stream of hot combustion gases.

There are several other precombustion techniques. Desulphurization of liquid fuels is a process for the desulphurization of gas, residual fuel oils, and of other oils. The desulphurization of gas oil, a widely employed process in Europe, involves hydrogenation of the gas oil components after atmospheric distillation in the presence of a catalyst. With most crude oils this process is capable of desulphurisation to 90%. The energy consumption is about

3.5% of the fuel to be desulphurised. In another technique, the residual fuel is treated with hydrogen at high temperature and high pressure in the presence of a catalyst. These techniques can reduce the sulphur level from 30-80% with an energy consumption from 5-8%.

### 5. Abatement techniques reducing the emission during combustion

An emerging technology that shows significant potential for a clean burning process is fluidised bed combustion, or FBC. A fluidised bed boiler consists of a reaction chamber in which the fuel containing sulphur is burned in the presence of finely fragmented limestone or other material capable of absorbing sulphur dioxide at combustion temperatures. During combustion the fuel and crushed limestone are kept in a state of turbulent motion by a stream of gas from below. As a result the entire surface area of the fuel particles is exposed and there is a higher rate of combustion. In addition to this increase in thermal efficiency, the fuel is stripped of sulphur during the process.

While the combustion temperature is high enough for efficient combustion, it is low enough to ensure a decrease in nitrous oxide emissions. At the moment a 30 Megawatt FBC-plant is operating at Rivesville, West Virginia, U.S.A. Preliminary data from this plant inidcate that a 85-89% $SO_2$ reduction is feasible. The technology is potentially energy efficient.

### 6. Abatement techniques reducing emissions after combustion

Flue gas desulphurization, or FGD-control systems remove $SO_2$ from combustion gases after burning through absorption in an alkaline solution. This technology employs "stack gas scrubbers". FGD-systems can be classified into two general types : non-regenerable or throwaway systems and regenerable or recovery systems.

The most popular non-regenerable FGD systems are direct lime scrubbing and direct limestone scrubbing. These are wet chemical techniques, in which the gas is washed with an aqueous solution containing lime or limestone which removes sulphur dioxide, sulphate and dry ash, thereby producing a waste product in the form of a slurry or sludge. One of the major problems with these techniques is the disposal of the water, although wallboard could be produced from the waste at high costs. The limestone scrubbing process produces half a ton of sludge for every ton of coal burned. At present, FGD waste is disposed of in the USA by means of ponding, landfill and surface mine disposal. The environment can be at peril because of this kind of disposal in the event of ground water contamination, surface water contamination, fugitive emissions and lack of waste stability or consolidation. The problems of creating an insoluble end-product can be avoided by double alkali scrubbing, a second generation technology. Double alkali systems use scrubbing solutions of soluble alkali salts like sodium for $SO_2$ removal. The spent scrubbing liquid is then reacted with lime outside the scrubber system, thereby forming a slurry which is less difficult to dispose of than the lime and limestone-scrubbing waste.

## Measures against acid rain

The remedy lies in reducing the release of pollutant gases. Hence,

1. Power stations utilizing coal must turn to use low sulphur coal or fuel with less pollution potential.
2. Wherever necessary, arrangements should be made for $SO_2$ or $NO_X$ absorption. Desulphurization

technology is available, but costly. Cost effective desulphurization technology must be evolved. For the time being, less effective, but less costly methods like treatment of flue gases with slurry of $CaCO_3$ etc. may be tried.

3. Mobile sources of pollution, such as automobiles, must be fitted with catalytic converter to clean the exhaust so that $NO_X$ are rendered harmless and CO is converted into $CO_2$.
4. Emission control standard should be strictly adhered to.

## Conclusions

In general, detrimental affects are caused by acidic precipitation and its accompanying pollutants, which is caused by certain emissions of pollutants and their transformation during transportation. The present state of our knowledge about the chemical changes in the soil brought about by the acid and polluted precipitation is far from complete. The effects on human health, certain species in terrestrial or aquatic ecosystems, forests, agricultural crops, and buildings are not sufficiently known. On the other hand, undisputable causal relationships exist between acid and polluted rain, and the acidification of lakes with subsequent fish-kills or reduction of fish stocks.

Acidification need not be caused by acid precipitation resulting from primary pollutants emitted at great distances. It can also be a consequence of local emissions. A good deal of the sulphur dioxide emitted into the air is absorbed directly upon the moist surfaces of plants, soils etc., where it may be oxidised to sulphuric acid. Precipitation may become acidified by fall through forest canopies or by stem flow. Also about 2-5% of the sulphuric acid comes out of the smoke stacks. This disposal of wastes by local industries is bound to have the same deleterious effects, acidification, metal contamination, mobilization or leaching. Metal contamination might also be caused by liming in great quantities. There are further complications in the problem of source identification. Acidification of soils can be due to the use of certain fertilizers or to a certain style of forest management.

In summary, acidification is a cumulative phenomenon. It is very likely to be caused by different sources. Hence, one can not say that a certain source is the source of the acidification but one can only say it is a cause of acidification and its consequences.

## References

Beverland, I.J., Growther, J.M. and Srinivas, M.S.N. (1979) Water, Air and Soil Pollution, 96 : 73-91.

Chevone, B.J., Herzfeld, D.E., Krupa, S.V. and Chappelka, A.H. (1986) JAPCA, 36 : 7 : 813-815.

De Young, H.G. (1982) Acid rain regulators shift into low year. High Technology, 2 : 82-86.

Evans, L.S. (1988) Effect of Acidic Deposition on Vegetation : State of Science. *In : Perspectives in Environmental Botany*, Vol. 2 (Eds. D.N.Rao *et al.*) Today and Tomorrow, New Delhi, pp. 73-119.

Fu Zhu, Z. Fu, Yang, Z.I., Hong Rui, Z., Ogura, N. and Ushikubo, A. (1996) Water, Air and Soil Pollution, 90(3/4) : 407-415.

Goldstein, R.A. *et al.* (1984) Integrated Lake Watershed Acidification Study (ILWAS) : A Mechanistic Ecosystem Analysis. Philos. Trans. Roy. Soc. (London) Sci., B(305) : 409-425.

Hidy, G. (1995) Acid rain, Chapter 1, *In : Encyclopedia of Environmental Biology*, (Ed. William A. Nierenberg), pp. 1-17, Academic Press Inc., Vol. A-E, San Diego.

Hileman, B. (1981) Environ. Sci. Technol., 15(10) : 141-142.

Huckabee, J.W. *et al.* (1989) An assessment of the ecological effects of acid deposition, Arch. Environ. Contam. Toxicol., 18 : 3-27.

Irving, P.M. (ed.) (1991) Acidic deposition : State of Science and Technology. Washington, D.C. : National Acid Precipitation Assessment Program.

Jayapragasam, M. (2003) Acid rain effects on forest environment, Chapter 18, *In : Current Environmental Issues*, (Eds. B.B.S.Kapoor, Ahmed Ali, K.K.Singh and Chandrakanta), Madhu Publications, Bikaner (Raj.), pp. 215-226.

Johnson, D.W. and Lindberg, S.E. (eds.) (1992) *Atmospheric Depositions of Forest Nutrient Cycling*. New York : Singer-Verlag.

Lee, D.O. and Weber, D.E. (1979) The effects of simulated acid on seedling emergence and growth of eleven woody species. Forest Sci., 25 : 393.

Maiti, T.C. (1982) Science Reporter, 360-361.

Mauer, O. and Pulatova, E. (1991) In '*Plant Roots and Their Environment*'. Elsevier Science Publishers, pp. 240-247.

Mesanza, J.M., Casado, H. and Encinas, D. (1996) Journal of Environmental Science and Health, Part A : Environmental Science and Engineering, 31(5) : 1025-1033.

Newell, A.D. and Skjetkvale, L.B. (1997) Water, Air and Soil Pollution, 93 : 27-57.

NRC (1983) Acid Deposition : Atmospheric Processes in Eastern North America. A National Research Council Report (Washington, D.C. : National Academy of Sciences Press).

Papastefanous, C., Manolopoulou, M., Stoulos, S., Ioamnidou, A. and Gerasopoulos, E. (2001) Coloured rain dust from Sahara desert is still radioactive. J. Environmental Radioactivity, 55(1) : 109-112.

Rehfuess, K.E.J. (1991) Environmental Science and Health Part A : Environmental Science and Engineering, 26(3) : 415-445.

Schofield, C.L. (1982) Acid Rain/Fisheries (Ed. R.Johnsn), American Fisheries Society, Bethesda, M .D., pp. 57.

Seinfeld, J. (1986) *The Atmospheric Chemistry and Physics of Air Pollution*. New York, Wiley Interscience.

Trujillo, K.E., Kadooka, C., Tanmoto, V., Bergfeld, S., Shishido, G. and Kuwakami, G. (2001) Plant Disease, 85(4) : 357-361.

Vogelmann, H.W. (1982) Catastrophe on Camel's Hump. Natural History.

Zilio-Grandi, Francesco and Szpyrkowicz, Lidia (2000) The Survey of Acid Rain in the Venice Region (Italy). Pollution Research, 19(1) : 1-29.

CHAPTER 3

# LAND DEGRADATION PROBLEMS IN HIMALAYAS-MEASURES/SUGGESTIONS FOR MANAGEMENT

**J. C. Sharma and Sanjeev K. Chaudhary**

Department of Soil Science and WM, Dr Y. S. Parmar University of Horticulture and Forestry, Nauni-Solan (HP)-173 230.

## ABSTRACT

Scientific management of land resources in the fragile Himalayan region is necessary for food and environmental security. Increased anthropogenic pressure and related developmental activities are exerting undue strain on natural resources in the region, thus accelerating their degradation and causing many land and environment related problems. Presently, more than 50% of the total area in the region is degraded, the severity being more in the states of Mizoram, Himachal Pradesh, Uttaranchal, Nagaland and Tripura as 89, 75, 72, 60 and 60% of the total area, respectively is degraded. Water erosion and physical deterioration are the principal forms of land degradation and the major causes are unprecedented increase in human and livestock populations, deforestation and degradation of forests, shifting cultivation, overgrazing, incidence of landslides/landslips, indiscriminate mining/quarrying, flash floods, exploitation of lands for construction of roads, dams, industrial and tourism activities etc. Runoff (more than 50 % of rainfall) and soil loss are maximum in the Shiwalik hills (80 t $ha^{-1}$ $yr^{-1}$ in North-West) and shifting cultivation region (40 t $ha^{-1}$ $yr^{-1}$) in the North-East. Landslide/landslips and flash floods in region are common occurrences during the monsoon period. Appropriate combinations of various biological and engineering measures involving low cost, locally available material and socially acceptable methods are essential for protecting the lands from degradation and reducing the problems of erosion and runoff, flash floods, sedimentation of reservoirs, landslides/slips. Stable agriculture needs to be popularized to contain the practice of shifting cultivation in North-Eastern Himalayan region. Adoption of land capability classification scheme modified according to the Himalayan conditions needs to be demonstrated and validated on a larger scale. Soil and water conservation on watershed basis needs to be given utmost importance and priority for improving the status of resources and agricultural productivity. Various forms of land degradation and their causes have been discussed in this article and suitable measures suggested which are problem specific.

**Key Words :** Land degradation, Himalayas

## Introduction

Mountain regions occupy about one fifth of the earth's surface and are home to one-tenth of the global population. They provide goods and services to about half of the mankind. Seeing the importance of mountain ecosystems to the well being of high and low land communities, the mountains have already been put on global agenda with the adoption of chapter 13 of Agenda 21 by the United Nations Conference on Environment and Development (UNCED) held at Rio de Janerio in 1992. The Mountain Agenda read as Managing Fragile Ecosystems-Sustainable Mountain Development states: "Mountain environments are essential to the survival of global ecosystem. Many of them are experiencing degradation in terms of accelerated soil erosion, flash floods, landslides and rapid loss of habitat and biological diversity. Hence, there is an urgent need to suggest effective control measures to check land degradation, conserve and manage the mountain resources and also promote sustainable mountain development for livelihood and environmental security". The United Nations general assembly at its $53^{rd}$ session further adopted resolution 53/24 and proclaimed year 2002 as International Year of Mountains. Many activities were organized during the year throughout the world, including Himalayan region to renew our commitments and resolve to work in mountain areas with a focus on sustainable development.

The Indian Himalayas, spread through 14 states in Western and Eastern regions, cover about 16% of the geographical area and 4% of the total population of the country. The Western region includes states of Jammu & Kashmir, Himachal Pradesh, Uttaranchal and Shiwaliks of Punjab and Haryana and occupies 62% of the total Himalayan range. The Eastern region includes Arunachal Pradesh, Manipur, Meghalaya, Mizoram, Nagaland, Sikkim, Tripura and parts of Assam and West Bengal. It stands entirely different not only from South Western region but also from rest of the country. The differences lie not only in dress, language, food habits and festivals but also in socio-economic status, land tenure and farming systems. The major area of Himalayan region is under forests constituting 59% of the total reporting area (Anonymous, 1998). The area under cultivation is small (12%) with per capita availability of 0.17 ha of land. The permanent pastures and grazing lands occupy about 5.5% of the area. A sizeable area of about 23% is under other categories comprising primarily of culturable and unculturable wastelands.

The Himalayas are viewed as towers of water, the largest repositories of biological diversity, preferred destinations for recreation and tourism and providers of a wide range of crucial goods and services. The increasing anthropogenic pressure on the Himalayan resources to meet ever increasing demands for material supplies is, however, leading to their widespread degradation. Today, about half of the area (49%) in Himalayan region is degraded, the severity being more in Mizoram, Himachal Pradesh, Uttaranchal, Nagaland and Tripura (Table 1). The signs of degradation are already evident in terms of declining productivity, loss of biodiversity,

**Table 1 :** Soil degradation in Himalayan region

(Area '000 ha)

| State | Water erosion | Wind erosion | Physical deterioration | Complex problem | Total degraded area | Total geographical area |
|---|---|---|---|---|---|---|
| Jammu & Kashmir | 5460 | 1360 | 200 | -- | 7020 (31)* | 22224 |
| Himachal Pradesh | 2875 | -- | 1303 | -- | 4178 (75) | 5567 |
| Uttaranchal | 1554 | -- | 2280 | -- | 3834 (72) | 5348 |
| Sikkim | 235 | -- | -- | -- | 235 (33) | 710 |
| Arunachal Pradesh | 4327 | -- | 176 | -- | 4503 (54) | 8374 |
| Mijoram | 1187 | -- | -- | 694 | 1881 (89) | 2108 |
| Manipur | 133 | -- | 111 | 708 | 952 (42) | 2233 |
| Nagaland | 390 | -- | -- | 605 | 995 (60) | 1658 |
| Tripura | 425 | -- | 203 | -- | 628 (60) | 1049 |
| Maghalaya | 1168 | -- | 146 | 34 | 1208 (53) | 2243 |
| Total | 17754 | 1360 | 4279 | 2141 | 25434 (49) | 51514 |

*Figures in parentheses denote percentages.

**Source** : NBSSLUP (2004).

increased sedimentation of rivers and reservoirs, drying up of water resources, recurring droughts and flash floods and deteriorating environment. Continued degradation of the fragile Himalayan region is adversely affecting the socio-economic and environmental stability not only in high lands, but in lowlands as well. Different problems of land degradation which the region is facing presently and the measures/suggestions for their improvement have been discussed in this chapter.

## Problems of land degradation

According to UN/FAO, land degradation generally signifies the temporary or permanent decline in the productive capacity of the land. Land degradation is a human induced or natural process which negatively affects the land to function effectively within an ecosystem, by accepting, storing and recycling water, energy and nutrients. Blaikie and Brookfield (1987) suggested that land is degraded when it suffers a loss of intrinsic qualities or a decline in its capabilities.

The problem of land degradation did not appear overnight. It started as soon as the first man cut the first tree to practice arable farming. The major land degradation problems in hills from which the lands are suffering are broadly categorized as under:

(*i*) Soil erosion

(*ii*) Excessive runoff losses

(*iii*) Shallow soil depth

(*iv*) Adverse soil physical conditions

(*v*) Low soil fertility

## Causes of land degradation

Causes of land degradation vary from region to region depending upon the land use systems, population, economy and investment for the conservation. Broadly, they can be classified as abiotic (non-anthropogenic) and biotic (anthropogenic). The former includes geology, geomorphology, rainfall erosivity, floods and all other phenomena over which man has little control. The unstable and weak geology of the Himalayas coupled with monsoonic type of climate prevalent in the region are some of the natural processes abetting land degradation. Superimposed on these, is the impact of anthropogenic factors, both direct and indirect, accelerating the processes of resources degradation. A broad listing of the anthropogenic and non-anthropogenic causes of accelerated land degradation is as given below:

- Rapid increase in human and livestock populations
- Extension of cultivation to marginal and steep sloping lands
- Overgrazing of pastures and forest floors
- Unconsolidated and fragmented land holdings
- Shifting cultivation
- Defective terracing
- Various developmental activities
- Deforestation and diversion of forest lands for other purposes
- Forest fires
- Landslides/landslips
- Mining/quarrying
- Avalanches and cloudbursts

## Soil and water conservation programmes in India

Systematic soil and water conservation programmes in India were initiated as early as in early 20$^{th}$ century by the British Government by launching a scheme to control gullies in then United Province. These have become essential part of five yearly planning in India after independence. The first programme incorporated in India was River Valley Project (RVP), Damodar Valley Corporation by setting up a Department of Soil and Water Conservation at Hazaribagh in Bihar (now in Jharkhand). Soil and water conservation programmes got further momentum in sixth five year plan (1980-85) by setting up a National Land Resource Conservation and Development Commission and National

Land Use and Wasteland Development Board. During this plan, a national policy was adopted to use watershed as a unit of land-water resources development and conservation. Subsequently, watershed management programme was identified as a thrust area of development and it is being continued vigorously in $10^{th}$ plan also.

## Soil and water conservation measures

Soil conservation is not merely an erosion control programme. It means drainage if the land is too wet and irrigation if it is too dry; it means addition of fertilizers and organic matter to soil that is improvised of these constituents. It includes both curative as well as preventive approaches to land use and further improvement of the land productivity.

Soil and water conservation measures are inseparable. Water conservation is a pre-requisite for soil conservation. The major objective of any soil and water conservation programme is to keep the rainfall where it falls as nearly as possible so that it may be absorbed by the soil and to collect excess rainwater from the land slowly and under control so that soil erosion is reduced to a minimum. This can be achieved by keeping the land under cover for a comparatively longer period of time, thereby increasing its percolation capacity and permitting water to be stored in the soil. A local survey on the basis of climate, soil properties, water table, slope *etc.* is often helpful to determine the type of conservation practices and treatment measures to be adopted. Broadly, the soil and water conservation measures are grouped into two categories:

### *(a) Biological conservation measures*

Methods used for controlling soil erosion through crops or vegetation and agronomic practices are known as biological measures. Biological practices provide suitable cover to the land and build up fertility of the soil. Some of the biological practices that can be easily adopted in hilly areas without any extra expenditure result not only in higher production, but also promote effective soil and water conservation, are as below:

- Crop rotation
- Contour farming
- Mulching
- Strip cropping
- Growing of grasses and forest trees

### *(b) Mechanical measures*

The mechanical measures also called engineering measures involve the construction of mechanical structures or land surface modifications primarily designed to slow down the surface flow, impound water for a longer time period, to enable most of it to percolate and allow surplus runoff to flow at non-erosive velocity. These practices when carried out systematically over a longer period of time bring about permanent improvement in the land qualities. According to Rama Rao (1962), the important principles to be kept in mind while planning mechanical measures are:

(*i*) To increase the time of concentration for allowing more runoff water to be absorbed and held by the soil

(*ii*) To break longer slopes into several short ones for reducing the flow velocity below critical limits

(*iii*) To prevent excessive soil and water losses

Mechanical measures, though costly, constitute important component of soil and water conservation programme in hilly areas, providing much needed barrier across the direction of flow of erosive runoff. Important mechanical soil conservation measures are as follows:

- Bunding and terracing
- Contour trenching
- Bench terracing
- Stone terracing
- Check dams
- Retaining wall and slip control works *etc.*

Mechanical and agronomic practices are not the alternatives. They are, instead complementary though each serves a separate purpose (Darby, 1986). The biological measures are adopted when the land slopes are gentle (less than 2% in general) and erosion problems are not severe. However, when land slope exceeds 2%, engineering measures become necessary. Biological measures can be adopted to control soil erosion upto land capability class II. Beyond it, these must be supplemented with mechanical soil conservation measures.

## Problem specific soil and water conservation measures

### *(a) Soil erosion*

The major cause of land degradation in Himalayas is severe soil erosion due to water and heavy runoff losses. Based on the first approximation map of soil erosion rates in India (Singh *et al.,* 1997), the North-Western hills of Jammu & Kashmir, Himachal Pradesh and Uttar Pradesh (now in Uttranchal) and hills of North-Eastern states suffered due to severe soil erosion of more than 20 t $ha^{-1}$ $yr^{-1}$. However, the rates were quite high for Shiwalik hills (>80 t $ha^{-1}$ $yr^{-1}$) and shifting cultivation regions in the North-East (> 40 t $ha^{-1}$

$yr^{-1}$). This acute problem of soil erosion in Shiwaliks and high Himalayas is being manifested in large scale terrain deformation brought about by severe gully erosion and landslides/slips, silting up of rivers, lakes and reservoirs with considerable damage to the ecosystem. In the recent analysis of annual soil erosion rates in India, it was estimated that 5334 million tonnes (16.35 t $ha^{-1}$ $yr^{-1}$) of soil is detached annually due to agriculture and other related activities leading to the removal of green cover from the soil surface. Of this, about 29% is carried away by the rivers into the sea, while nearly 10% is being deposited in surface reservoirs, resulting in the loss of 2% of the storage capacity annually.

Besides biotic factors, others which predominantly influence the extent of soil erosion include climatic factors like intensity, duration and frequency of rainfall and topographical factors such as nature, degree, and length of slope and the vegetative cover which the land wears. Thus, a flat land has less possibility of erosion, but on sloppy or hilly areas, the chances of moving water increase thereby enhancing its erosive power. In addition, the nature and properties of the soil particularly texture, structure, amount of organic matter and amount and kind of salts present in it largely affect the susceptibility to erosion.

### *(b) Runoff*

Runoff is the volume of surplus rainwater discharged by drain, draining the catchment area. It can be surface runoff or ground water runoff or seepage. However, it is the surface runoff which is of paramount importance in hills. It has been estimated that in the Shiwalik region of North-Western states (spread in three million hectares), out of an average annual rainfall of 100 cm, about 50% not only ends in runoff but also causes the problems of floods, sedimentation and damage to agricultural lands and civic amenities. Shiwalik hills which have steep slopes and light textured soils have substantial runoff potential. One of the viable alternatives for sustainable crop production in such region is therefore, runoff farming *i.e.* harvesting surplus rainwater by constructing ground tanks, ponds, check dams etc., and using it for providing supplemental/life saving irrigation as and when needed. This practice of runoff management may give a new direction to resources management and for mutual benefit of the people as well as hilly ecosystems.

## Control measures

### *(a) Crop management*

Different crops vary in their capacity to control erosion. Those with erect growth and non-tillering habit allow more runoff and erosion. On the contrary, others which develop quick canopy or have profuse tillering habit, reduce runoff and soil loss. Thus, erosion resistant crops with good yield potential should be the obvious choice. Fast canopy developing leguminous crops can also be used as cover cum green manure crops not only to control erosion but also to increase soil fertility.

### *(b) Strip cropping*

Combination of erosion permitting and erosion resisting crops grown in alternate strips across the slope is known as strip cropping. The alternate strips consist of close growing erosion resisting crops and erosion permitting crops like row crops. Thus, it is appropriate to make combinations of the two to achieve desired objective. Other cropping systems such as inter-cropping, mixed cropping and crop rotation can be judiciously utilized not only for stabilizing the crop production but also for effective soil and water conservation, thus providing efficient moisture utilization both in high and low rainfall areas.

### *(c) Grassland management*

Management of grasslands plays an important role in minimizing the soil and runoff loss in hilly areas. In shallow, sloppy lands having poor fertility for crop production, grasses should be grown. Grasses intercept raindrops to the maximum through their close canopy and obstruct easy flow of water on slopes. These also collect soil particles from the running water due to sieving action, thus soil loss is reduced to a tremendous extent. Studies on soil conserving values of different grasses have shown that grasses differ in their capacities to reduce soil and runoff losses owing to differences in growth habits (Table 2). Grasses with dense growth reduce runoff and soil loss better than those of more open and luxuriant growth habit.

**Table 2 :** Soil conserving values of different grasses (Work done by Damodar Valley Corporation at Hazaribagh, 1955-60)

| **Grasses** | **Soil loss (kg ha$^{-1}$)** | **Runoff (%)** |
|---|---|---|
| *Cynodon plectostachys* | 57 | 35 |
| *Cenchrus ciliaris* | 136 | 33 |
| *Panicum antidotale* | 409 | 36 |
| *Urochloa stoloniferous* | 79 | 32 |
| *Pennisetum ploystschyon* | 68 | 27 |

Overgrazing causes tremendous biotic pressure on pastures and forest floor. In North-Western Himalayan region of India grazing exceeds yield levels by a factor ranging from two to four. Overgrazing has many adverse impacts such as gully formation on cattle tracks, inhibition of growth and declining productivity. Studies on the management of grasslands conducted at Deochanda farm at Hazaribagh, from 1955-60, demonstrated that overgrazing not only reduced grass cover but also deteriorated the top soil by compaction and soil particle detachment through animal hoofs (Table 3). For effective management of grasslands, affected areas should be closed for grazing, as well as cutting of wood and grasses.

**Table 3 :** Effect of grass land management on runoff and soil loss (Work done by Damodar Valley Corporation at Hazaribagh, 1955-60)

| Management | Runoff (%) | Soil loss (kg $ha^{-1}$) |
|---|---|---|
| Over-grazed | 27 | 2384 |
| Properly grazed | 19 | 795 |
| Not grazed | 11 | 397 |

### *(d) Grassed waterways and diversions*

Grassed waterway is a natural or artificially constructed channel discharging concentrated runoff from slopes, a terrace system or from any other land surface safely. It is an important soil conservation practice since it discharges water safely and thereby protects the land against rills and gullies. Grassed waterways become essential where suitable natural drainage is not available to drain off excess water from agricultural fields. The design of diversion to direct runoff away from acute gully heads, villages, low lying areas *etc.*, is done on the same principles as the grassed waterways and a diversion has comparatively lesser grade as it is laid across the slope while the grassed waterway is laid along the slope.

### *(e) Afforestation*

Forests are one of the most important natural means of conserving soil and moisture particularly in hilly areas and have profound effect on soil physico-chemical and biological properties. The forest canopy intercepts rain drops and abates their beating action thus minimizing the runoff, detachment and transportation of soil particles. Forest litter acts as sponge in holding back a considerable amount of flowing water. Also, water gets enough time for infiltration. Thus, forests check runoff and soil loss from the floor which prevents the reservoirs from rapidly silting up. This helps in maintaining the lifespan of costly dams. According to Rama Rao (1962), successful planning of forests for the purpose of soil and water conservation depends on:

- Amount of organic matter added annually
- Rate of decomposition of organic matter
- Ever-greenness or deciduousness of forests
- Rate of transpiration
- Socio economic requirements

### *(f) Orchard management*

On gentle slopes of hills, it is possible to take care of both production and protection aspects of the land by planting suitable fruit species and following judicious management practices. Studies by Ghosh and Ram Babu (1977) at Dehradun have shown that by allowing natural weeds to grow in the inter-bed areas of strawberry and pineapple plots and in the interplant areas of pomegranate during the rainy season, soil and runoff loss on gentle slopes could be reduced considerably without imparting much adverse effects on the growth of the plants, particularly at early stages of development (Table 4).

**Table 4 :** Effect of orchard management practices on runoff and soil loss (at 11% slope)

| Treatment | Rainfall causing runoff (mm) | | Runoff as % of rainfall | | Soil loss ($t\ ha^{-1}$) | |
|---|---|---|---|---|---|---|
| | 1974 | 1975 | 1974 | 1975 | 1974 | 1975 |
| Strawberry with weed | 1079.4 | 1154.4 | 27.8 | 7.39 | 8.89 | 1.09 |
| Strawberry clean | " | " | 29.4 | 25.83 | 26.00 | 20.14 |
| Pineapple with weed | " | " | 8.8 | 2.39 | 3.29 | 0.09 |
| Pineapple clean | " | " | 11.0 | 9.97 | 11.51 | 5.32 |
| Pomegranate with weed | " | " | 12.4 | 2.08 | 2.62 | 0.16 |
| Pomegranate clean | " | " | 31.1 | 35.92 | 18.69 | 14.08 |
| Grass (*Cymbopogan citrulus*) | " | " | 20.3 | 1.64 | 4.51 | 0.10 |
| Cultivated fallow | " | " | 24.8 | 7.60 | 33.42 | 3.50 |

### *(g) Mulching–effect on soil and runoff losses*

Mulching is not only effective in moisture conservation during the drought spells but also checks soil and runoff loss during rains. Studies at Dehradun (Khybri *et al.* 1980; Table 5) and mid hills of Himachal Pradesh (Sharma, 2005; Table 6) demonstrated the usefulness of mulches which alongwith tillage reduced the runoff and soil loss considerably.

**Table 5 :** Runoff and soil loss under maize crop with mulch (1978-80)

| Treatment | Runoff as % of rainfall | Soil loss ($t\ ha^{-1}$) | Maize yield ($t\ ha^{-1}$) |
|---|---|---|---|
| Normal ploughing | 49.4 | 36.5 | 2.93 |
| Normal ploughing +mulch @ 4 $t\ ha^{-1}$ | 22.3 | 6.2 | 2.75 |

**Table 6 :** Runoff and soil losses under pea and tomato crops in mid hill region of Himachal Pradesh (flat land)

| | **Pea*** | | | **Tomato**** | | |
|---|---|---|---|---|---|---|
| **Treatment** | **Runoff (cm $ha^{-1}$)** | **Soil loss (t $ha^{-1}$)** | **Green pod yield (t $ha^{-1}$)** | **Runoff (cm $ha^{-1}$)** | **Soil loss (t $ha^{-1}$)** | **Fruit yield (t $ha^{-1}$)** |
| Conventional tillage | 1.31 | 1.78 | 7.67 | 13.9 | 7.31 | 16.56 |
| Conventional tillage + straw mulch @ 8 t $ha^{-1}$ | 0.32 | 0.43 | 8.48 | 8.18 | 1.64 | 22.33 |

*Average of three (1996-97, 97-98 & 98-99); ** two (1997 & 98) years

## Gully erosion

Milder forms of soil erosion like splash, sheet and rill erosion go on unnoticed year after year until gully formation starts and large areas of valuable land are converted into gullies and subsequently waste land. Once a gully is formed, it acts like a wild fire and goes on engulfing more and more areas of the table land till the entire area is destroyed and becomes a network of gullies of various sizes and shapes in various stages of development. It is a common feature to note gully type of erosion in hills. The gullies are an indication of neglect and poor management of the land resources. Apart from the fact, that the gullied land has been completely destroyed, it is a menace to the adjoining table lands. The sloping nature of lands having coarse textured soils and weak structure, intense rains during monsoon, improper land use by way of overgrazing and biotic interferences with the natural vegetation cover and faulty agricultural practices are the chief causes of gully erosion. Erosion by gullies has dual effect of destruction of the land on one hand and complementary difficulties relating to silt disposal on the other.

### Control measures

Closure of gullied land to biotic interferences, such as grazing, illicit felling of sparse shrubs and tree vegetation should constitute the first step in control measures. In fact, the best land use for gullies is to put them under permanent vegetation and exploit them as forest or grasslands. An integrated approach of watershed management is perhaps the best answer to the management of such areas. However, owing to increasing population pressure on cultivated lands, it is not possible to retire all gullied/ravinous lands for forest and grasslands. The main demand is to reclaim the gullies to make the affected area at least arable even if it does not make these suitable for growing high value cash crops.

## Stream bank erosion

It is mostly caused by fast flowing water in rivers, streams and flash floods by cutting the agricultural land on either bank. Vegetation over the long stretches of stream banks is also uprooted. This problem is further aggravated in Shiwalik hills by meandering torrents (*choes*) causing extensive damage to land and property.

### Control measures

Effective control of stream bank erosion requires that the mechanical measures must be appropriately supplemented by agronomic measures which can be classified into two groups' *i.e.* direct and indirect protection. Direct protection includes works done directly on the bank itself for buffer or consolidation effect. While indirect measures are not laid directly on the stream banks, but are used in the upper areas of the catchment.

Direct protection includes following works:

- Enclosure to increased human and animal interferences of over exploitation,
- Creation of vegetal cover, covering by brush wood, construction of retaining walls etc.
- Stabilization and protection of stream banks, islands, slopes and degraded areas by planting with fast growing species such as *Salix*, *Eucalyptus, Populus, Alnus nitida*, *A. nepalensis, Betula alnoides, Ulmus wallichiana, Grewia nudiflora etc*. This will not only reduce the action of stream currents but also provide valuable material for various other purposes.

Indirect protection consists of following works:

- Deflection of flood water and deposition of sediment by constructing revetments, spurs and retards
- Channelisation of runoff and taming of the stream to prevent gully and ravine formation
- Gully plugging
- Construction of vegetative and masonry check dams
- Bench terracing
- Contour trenching

## Road-side erosion

The construction of roads in high altitude areas without concurrent arrangements for slope stabilization results in landslides/slips. Quite often, it involves clear felling of existing protective vegetation and blasting of otherwise stable hills. With the emphasis on connecting every village with a road under the scheme 'Pradhan Mantri Sadak Pariyojana' and upgradation and widening of existing roads to ease the heavy traffic load, massive road construction activities are going on in the fragile hills. However, the roads in hills offer certain peculiarities. These are characterized by winding alignment, blind curves, vertical rock cutting overlooking valleys or fast streams *etc.* Inadequate and faulty drainage, combined with certain peculiar geological and soil formations met within areas are the main causes of erosion along the hill. Local peculiarities of weather like high intensity rainfall also play a significant role in this direction. All this makes it imperative that roads in hills be properly constructed and maintained. But the unscientific construction of roads has contributed to deforestation and degradation of mountain gradients and caused extensive landslides. According to Sharma (1987), the sediment load from road cutting in the Himalayas is as high as 8000 $m^3$ $km^{-1}$. Gupta (1974) has ably enumerated the causes of roadside erosion and some of them are as follows:

- Culverts emptying at improper points
- Outfall points being not protected against under cutting
- Drainage outlets being too small, few for high intensity storms and not properly located
- Blocking of drains by landslides
- Unstable geological formations such as sedimentary and metamorphosed rocks especially loose sand stones, shales, schist *etc.*
- Avalanche/glaciers
- Defective alignment
- Destruction of protective vegetation both on the upper and lower hill slopes

## Control measures

### *(a) Preventive measures*

To draw full benefits from the investments on road construction and keep the risk of road side erosion minimum, following preventive measures be followed:

- Construction activities should be properly executed and not staggered over longer period.
- Design wide and gently sloping roads with greater use of retaining walls and cribbing structures.
- Excess of dug out material should be disposed off in a controlled way.
- Use drop inlet structures in areas where excess soil is thrown.
- All gullies and streams which cross the road should be trained from top to bottom by means of stone and vegetative check dams to provide for the disposal of runoff water at safe velocity without causing any undercutting.

### *(b) Curative measures*

The curative measures have to be directed towards the safe disposal of excess water and stabilization of vulnerable portions both on upper and lower sides of the roads. Some of the most useful and practical measures are as under:

- Cross drains should be provided at regular intervals all along the roads to disperse the excess water from the road surface.
- Excess water caught by such drains be spread along the slope through chutes, drop outlets *etc*.
- A catch drain should be provided along the hill side of the road to carry water coming from the slope. The discharge should be made to escape through a culvert or a bridge down the hill through a paved waterway.
- All areas liable to erosion on the hill side of the road should be closed to grazing so that they get vegetated and stabilized.

- Construction of retaining walls and side drains should be attended to wherever there are chances for the soil to slip down.
- The side drains should be pitched with stones with wide and shallow sections to facilitate speedy disposal of water.
- Where slopes are steeper than the natural angle of repose, these should be eased near to their natural angle of repose as possible.
- Dug out earth thrown down the hill should be stabilized concurrently through the construction of engineering structures and by vegetative means. A low retaining wall should be constructed at the lower most point where loose earth rests to check its movement.
- Slopes on hillside of the road and surface of loose earth on the down hill should be covered with wattling with a view to provide physical protection to the exposed soil against flowing water and action of gravity.

## Dams, industrial activity and tourism

Owing to large potential of Himalayan region for hydro-electric power generation and heavy demand from the plains, lot many projects are in operation to generate cheaper energy. The construction of big dams and barrages across Himalayan river systems for the purpose, has severely threatened the environment and ecosystem sustainability in upstream areas and caused siltation of reservoirs of dams in downstream areas.

The scenic beauty and salubrious environment in Himalayas attract large number of tourists from the plains which is putting undue strain on the fragile mountain ecosystems and limited facilities. The development of tourism and industries demands construction of buildings, roads, restaurants and recreation spots which exert unbearable pressure on scarce land resources. Such developmental activities lead to deforestation, defacing and destabilization of land and slope.

### Suggestions

Strict measures to regulate industrial growth and tourist inflow have to be enforced through proper legislation to reduce pressure on natural resources. Safe disposal of dug out material and afforestation of affected catchments should form an integral part of the project plan to protect the Himalayan environment.

## Landslides

Landslide/landslip is a downward and outward movement of slope forming material composed of soil mass, natural rock, artificial fills or a combination of these as a result of slope failure. Landslides are very common along the stream and river banks and roads. Due to unstable slopes in Himalayan region, the occurrence of landslides is a serious problem during rainy season. Each year large scale damages to life and properties are caused by rock fall, especially landslides and creeps. Research findings have brought out that main causes of large scale landslide occurrence in the Himalayas are:

- Gravity force involving failure of the earth material under shear stress
- Road construction activities for civil, defence and tourism purposes
- Mismanagement of vegetal cover through unscientific removal, over grazing and forest fires

- Unstable geology due to weak formations, steep slopes and poor drainage
- Seismic disturbances by blasting for road, building activities, unscientific mining/quarrying, improper road alignments and toe cutting by hill torrents
- Excessive water discharge from upper catchment

**Control measures**

Recommended measures for the prevention and effective control of landslides are as follows:

- Arrangements for the proper drainage
- Construction of retaining wall which could be of gabion structure or of stone masonry
- Protection of bare slopes through planting with quick growing species such as *Eucalyptus*, *Populus spp, Robinia, Ipomea carnea, Arundo donax, Pennisetum purpureum, Vitex negundo etc.*
- Breaking slope by providing contour wattling at suitable intervals
- Enclosure of areas to control excessive grazing and exploitation of trees and shrubs

## Torrents/flash floods

Torrent (*choe*) erosion is a big menace in Shiwaliks. The main cause of the problem is high runoff down the hill slopes with heavy silt load that fills up the channel beds, thereby reducing their capacity to carry runoff and sediment. The flash floods in *choes* cause large scale despoliation in piedmonts and flood plains by inundating crops, eroding banks and spreading sand and gravels on fertile lands making them barren too. Recently, flash floods due to cloudbursts during heavy monsoons in high mountain peaks of Shimla, Kullu and Mandi districts of Himachal Pradesh have played havoc on life and property.

**Control measures**

- Provide proper drainage using check dams of boulders
- Construction of revetment cum retaining walls
- Erection of retards in front of eroding banks
- Construction of low cost boulder spurs reinforced with vegetation
- Afforestation of the river/stream banks and beds with site specific species which grow profusely in the stream bed *e.g. Acacia nilotica, Dalbergia sisoo, Populus* spp., *Robinia pseudocacia,* Bamboo, *Eucalyptus, Salix* spp., *Vitex negundo, Arundo donax, Ipomea carnea, Jatropha curcas, Pennisietum purpureum, Dodonaea viscoa, Saccharum munja, Eulaliopsis binata, etc.*

## Mining/quarrying

The fragile ecosystem in Himalayas has been greatly disturbed by mining and quarrying activities. Extraction of stones from the river/stream bed as construction material is also causing problem of stream bank erosion and disturbing/drying up of water resources. The mining activities especially for slates, limestone, sand, gravel *etc.* in Himachal Pradesh and for limestone, phosphorites *etc.* in Uttranchal have caused much denudation and degradation of land resources. Mountain slopes have been defaced and large percentage of area in hills has been scarified that has become barren and rugged. There is little vegetation left to support livestock. By this practice, existing vegetation is cleared exposing the soil to erosion. The debris from hill slopes having mining and quarrying activities fall into local streams, disrupt the flow and impair the quality of water downstream.

**Control measures**

The mechanical measures are the first line of defence and are very necessary to prevent further damage. However, being costly, these should be supplemented with vegetative measures. Areas highly degraded due to mining and where the establishment of vegetation is very difficult due to lack of moisture, movement of debris and rocks and absence of fertile soils, mechanical measures are the must for controlling erosion and helping the vegetation to establish. Following measures which involve both engineering and vegetative approaches are generally recommended (Barfield *et al.,* 1981; Dhruva Narayana *et al.,* 1987) for the stabilization and rehabilitation of the abandoned mine spoils:

- Enclosure of the area to control stone extraction and excessive grazing
- Construction of diversion drains to avoid runoff water going on weak zone such as slide face and loose mine spoil dumps
- Construction of continuous contour trenches on mine spoils and staggered contour trenches on denuded long slope
- Provision of road drains and culverts on mine land roads
- Terracing mine debris deposited in heaps on steep slopes which are more than the angle of repose
- Use of geo-jute, Nelton geo-grids, Excelsior matting, mulch anchoring *etc.* to avoid rain drop impact and to facilitate the revegetation of the area
- Construction of gabion drop structures in the main drainage channel upto 40% slope
- Construction of brushwood, logwood and loose rock filled check dams in the small tributaries (first order stream)
- Construction of stone filled log wood crib structures on steeply sloping loose areas especially on slide faces. These structures suit better than gabion drop structures where slope exceeds 40%

- Construction of retaining wall which could be of gabion structure or stone masonry
- Checking of indiscriminate and reckless removal of forests and other vegetation
- Rehabilitation of mined areas by quick growing species such as *Ipomea carnea*, *Pennisetum purpureum*, *Arundo donax, Vitex negudo* and *Salix tetrasperma.* Several grasses like *Eulaliopsis binata, Chrysopogon fulvus, Dactylus glomerata, Lolium perenne, Eragrostis curvula, Cenhrus spp.* are very promising. Such areas need not to be disturbed for exploitation in the form of grazing, however grass cutting after 2-3 years of establishment may be recommended.

The Central Mining Research Institute (CMRI, Dhanbad) has suggested that to prevent damage to ecology, mining should be allowed only where slope angles are more than 45 degrees and in case of mid slope, the mining foot wall should be of hard strata (Anonymous, 2000).

Some workers have suggested the following techniques to afforest the mined out areas, besides proper guidelines for granting lease for mining:

- Covering toxic or infertile material with soil or waste of better quality
- Neutralizing strong acid or alkaline soils by the use of lime, sulphur, peat, humus or clay having high exchange capacity
- Leaching of salts by means of rainwater, fertilizing with organic or green manure or with chemical fertilizers
- Use of mulches for stabilization
- Tree species such as *Acacia catechu, Dalbergia sisoo, Leucaena leucocephala, etc.* are considered promising for reforestation of limestone spoils

## Shifting cultivation

Shifting cultivation or rotational agro-forestry is the practice of clearing land and cultivating it for a short period of time until the soil is depleted and then abandoning it and clearing more land for cultivation. Mostly prevalent and practiced by the tribals in North-Eastern region, the practice is called as *'jhum'* and *'bun'* in local parlance. About 12% of the total geographical area in the region is affected with the practice (NEC, 1995). In *jhum,* the local farmers slash and burn a patch of forest land consisting mostly of thick growth of bamboo and wild vegetation while in *bun* farmers do not burn slashed vegetation. Whatever vegetation is cut, is ploughed back so that the biomass can be used as organic manure. This practice is considered as the primary cause of deforestation and was of some relevance when the population pressure was negligible. However, the situation has undergone a sea change today. Shortened *jhum* or *bun* cycles of two to five years owing to population pressure and paucity of cultivable land has led to large scale deforestation and denudation of hill slopes causing loss in soil fertility, occurrence of flash floods and silting of water reservoirs. This has resulted in total ecological degradation. The unsustainability of shifting cultivation begins with the reduction in shifting cycle, accelerating both on-site and off-site degradation due to erosion, runoff, nutrient losses, loss in biodiversity and watershed hydrology.

### Control measures/suggestions

- Since the problem is socio-economic in nature, the control measures should aim at improving the standard of living of the tribals at the first place
- The tribals should be educated to switch over to stable agriculture with modern management practices

- People should be involved in various rehabilitation schemes right from their formulation stage
- The rehabilitation schemes/projects should be thoroughly tested before implementing on larger scale
- Incentives be provided for developing a system of stable agriculture and the land should be used according to its capability

## Avalanche/Glaciers

An avalanche is a huge mass of snow on the surface of the earth, falling down a mountain while glacier is also large mass of snow but almost stationary in position. The avalanche while moving/falling along the slope, causes landslides/slips, damage to long stretches of land and infrastructural facilities, life and property. Long stretches of roads are washed out year after year. Large number of glaciers exists in Himalayas. These in North-Western Himalayan range descend to lower elevations as compared to that in North-Eastern. The altitude to which Himalayan glaciers may descend varies with the aspect, slope, total annual precipitation in the form of snow and latitude (Negi, 1982). These are the sources of fresh water and sustain the flow in rivers. But their retreat leaves behind unconsolidated debris which is very much prone to landslides/slips.

### Suggestions

Since avalanche/glaciers generally affect large areas, engineering measures involve huge cost in repair, construction and maintenance of infrastructure. Emphasis should be, therefore, on preventive measures like:

- Stabilizing affected or otherwise denuded areas with local, naturally occurring plant spp. which are site-specific. Plants like *Populus ciliata, Salix* spp.,

*Juniperous macropoda, etc.* occur naturally in cold deserts of Himalayas.

- Seabuckthorn *(Hippophae L)*, a multipurpose plant species has a great potential for greening and upgrading marginal mountain lands of cold deserts in our country after its great success in China (Rongsen, 1992). The plant is hardy and capable of providing adequate protection to the steeply sloping bare lands and also acts as an excellent wind break.
- In addition, a sound weather forecasting and warning system network could effectively reduce the loss to life and property.

## Land capability classification for soil and water conservation

Himalayan region is suitable for a variety of crops but these have to be grown with proper care, taking adequate soil and water conservation measures on priority basis. Each piece of land has to be used in accordance with its capability and limitations, *i.e.,* Himalayas have to be brought under rational land use plan. Out of eight land capability classes of USDA, Western Himalayan lands fit into five classes *viz.* III, IV, VI, VII and VIII (Gupta, 1977; Table 7). However, keeping in view the peculiar physiography, climate and socio-economic conditions of the region, some workers (Hudson, 1979; Khybri, 1979) have suggested modifications in the classification scheme of USDA (Table 8). Important inherent soil characteristics and land features which affect the yields of crops and the risk of erosion *viz.* soil depth, texture, soil: stone ratio, slope and climate prevailing in the Himalayan region have been taken into account. A modified classification scheme has been adopted by NBSS & LUP, wherein lands having 33 to 50% slope and very deep soils (>100 cm) are placed in class VI which have been earmarked for the

**Table 7 :** Land capability classification and proposed land uses in western Himalayas

| Present land use | Land capability class | Proposed land use | Treatment suggested |
|---|---|---|---|
| Wasteland, land unfit for agriculture | VIII | Steep rocky and precipitous land and slopes above 100 per cent or more | -Under present vegetation, no treatment |
| Area under cultivation | VII | Permanent vegetation cover of fuel and fodder trees, 35-60 per cent slopes | -Protection through fencing, soil conservation measures and improvement of existing vegetative cover |
| Cultivated at intervals (*Paspalum biculatum/Echinochloa/ coracana* | IV and VI | Orchards | -Terrace restoration through grass, planting of orchards, fuel and fodder trees *etc.* |
| Double cropped terraces: Mandua-wheat-barley,<br>Maize-wheat-mandua | IV | Orchards/crops where irrigation could be provided | -Restoration and improvement of existing system<br>-Water management through sprinkler/drip<br>-Changing cropping pattern<br>-Modeling of terraces |
| Triple cropped area ( well terraced) paddy-vegetable-cheena | III | Irrigated crops and application of improved practices | -Improved seeds, fertilizers and inputs, introduction of cash crops |

*Contd.*

*Table 7 Contd...*

| | | | |
|---|---|---|---|
| Forests:<br>No canopy forest (Open shrub/grass cover) | VI & VII | Community land improvement for fuel and fodder | -Enclosure and improvement of existing vegetation covers for fuel and grazing |
| Thin forest (Degraded forest/poor grass cover) | | " | -To be improved according to working plan of state forest department<br>-Water resource development and management for protective irrigation by construction of tanks, mulching, water harvesting *etc.* Improvement of existing stock |
| Moderately thin forest (Misc. spp./oak) | | " | |

**Table 8 :** Land capability class ratings for the Himalayan region

| Class | Texture | Soil: stone ratio | Soil depth (cm) | Slope range (%) | Erosion |
|---|---|---|---|---|---|
| I | l, sil, sicl, scl | >4 | >90 | 0-1 | — |
| II | cl, sic, cl | 2-4 | 45-90 | 1-3 | — |
| III | c, ls | 1-2 | 22.5-45 | 3-10 | — |
| IV | c, s | 0.5-1.0 | 7.5-22.5<br>22.5-45<br>45-90<br>>90 | 5-10<br>10-15<br>15-33<br>33-50 | — |
| V | — | 0.1-0.5 | — | 0-1 | — |
| VI | — | 0.1-0.5 | <7.5<br>7.5-22.5<br>22.5-45 | 1-10<br>10-33<br>33-100 | Gullied land, gullies < 5m deep |
| VII | — | 0.1-0.5 | <7.5<br>7.5-22.5<br>22.5-45 | 10-33<br>33-100<br>100-200 | Severely gullied land, gullies > 5m deep |
| VIII | — | <0.1 | <7.5<br><22.5<br>- | >33<br>>100<br>>200 | Landslide, torrent beds |

establishment of orchards. The objective of new capability classification is not merely to check soil erosion following soil and water conservation measures but also to increase the productivity of land in its different uses. The new classification is simpler, pragmatic and more relevant to the local conditions for mounting sustainable development plan.

## Conclusions

The unprecedented anthropogenic pressure and related developmental activities are exerting undue strain on natural resources in fragile Himalayan region, thus accentuating land degradation. Today, about half of the region is degraded. Much developmental activities, without the mandatory provisions for resource conservation, causing soil erosion and runoff loss (about 50% of annual rainfall), are the major causes of environmental degradation. The practice of shifting cultivation in North-Eastern region with shortened cycles has led to large scale deforestation and denudation of hill slopes causing excessive soil erosion (> 40 t $ha^{-1}$ $yr^{-1}$) and silting up of water reservoirs and is a serious threat to environment. Owing to biophysical and socio-economic constraints marked by marginality, fragility, inaccessibility, poor infrastructure and variations in agro-ecological conditions as contrasted to plains, the management of resources in the Himalayan region needs separate and specific developmental strategies with priority delineation. The answer lies in taking watershed as a unit of land-water resources conservation and development on sustainable basis. Effective planning for the management of resources on sustainable basis in the region needs priority delineation. Another important point to be considered while formulating developmental strategy is the inter relationship between upstream and down stream land users, as many rivers originate from Himalayas to generate hydropower, irrigate lands and feed reservoirs in the plains. The occurrence of flash floods due to creation of artificial lakes, siltation of reservoirs and quality of water in the plains are directly affected by exploitation and conservation of resources in the Himalayas. Thus, welfare of the people living in plains is, in a way, related to utilization and management of resources in the hills. Adoption of modified land capability classification scheme needs to be demonstrated and validated on larger scale according to the Himalayan conditions. Road side erosion, mining and torrent affected areas need to be managed and rehabilitated on priority basis using low cost technologies including traditionally utilizable species and skills, readily acceptable to the local community. Of course, all this is not possible without active involvement of local communities' right through the planning, formulation and implementation stages of any conservation programme.

## References

Anonymous (1998) Landuse Statistics–Part I. Directorate of Economics and Statistics, DAC, Ministry of Agriculture, Government of India, New Delhi, pp., 9.

Anonymous (2000) The Tribune, March 23, Vol. 120, pp., 7.

Barfield, B. J., Warner, R. C. and Haan, C. T. (1981) Applied Hydrology and Sedimentology for Disturbed Areas. Oklahoma Technical Press, 815 Hillcrest Stillwater, Oklahoma, USA.

Blaikie, P. and Brookfield, H. (1987) Land degradation and society. London , Metheun.

Darby, G. M. (1986) *In: Soil Erosion and Conservation*. Soil Conservation Society of America, pp. 649-653.

Dhruva Narayana, V. V., Katiyar, V. S. and Dadhwal, K. S. (1987) Mined area reclamation in Mussoorie hills. Indian J. Soil Cons., 15: 82-90.

Ghosh, S. P. and Ram Babu (1977) Effects of different fruit crops and their management on runoff and soil loss on slopping lands. Soil Conservation Digest, 5: 15-19.

Gupta, K. (1977) Alternate strategies for rural development in the Garhwal Himalayas. Paper presented at seminar on "Regional Development in the Himalayas" Garhwal University, Srinagar, Mimeo, pp. 1-13.

Gupta, M. P. (1974) Control of erosion on hill roads. Soil Conservation Digest, 2: 41-48.

Hudson, N. (1979) Report of the World Bank Identification Mission submitted to the Government of Uttar Pradesh, Hill Department, Lucknow.

Khybri, M. L. (1979) Suggestions for land capability classification for the Himalayan region. Indian J. Soil Cons., 7: 55-77.

Khybri, M. L. Prasad, S. N. and Sewa Ram (1980) Studies on the effect of removal of top soil on the yield of crop. Annual Report, CSWCRTI, Dehradun, Uttaranchal, pp. 140-144.

NBSSLUP (2004) Soil Resource Management Reports. National Bureau of Soil Survey and Land Use Planning, Nagpur, Maharastra, India.

NEC (1995) Basic Statistics of North–Eastern Region. North-Eastern Council, Ministry of Home Affairs, Government of India, pp. 297.

Negi, S. S. (1982) Environmental Problems in the Himalaya. BSMPS Publishers, Dehradun, pp., 86-103.

Rama Rao, M.S.V. (1962) *Soil Conservation in India.* ICAR, New Delhi.

Rongsen, L. (1992) A plant for upgrading marginal mountain lands. In: Seabuckthorn – A Multipurpose Plant Species for Fragile Mountains. ICIMOD Occasional Paper 20, Kathmandu, Nepal, pp. 25-34.

Sharma, C. K. (1987) The problem of sediment load in the development of water resources in Nepal. Mountain Research and Development, 20: 108-111.

Sharma, R. K. (2005) Impact of tillage and weed control methods on soil and crop productivity in pea-tomato systems in mid hills of North-Western Himalayas. J. Indian Soc. Soil Sci. (Accepted).

Singh, G., Ram Babu, Pratap Narain, Bhushan, L. S. and Abrol, I. P. (1997) Soil erosion rates in India. J. Soil & Water Cons., 47: 97-99.

## CHAPTER 4

# TECHNOLOGIES FOR RESTORATION OF DEGRADED ECOSYSTEMS

**Paromita Ghosh**

G. B. Pant Institute of Himalayan Environment & Development
Garhwal Unit, Upper Bhaktiyana, Srinagar–Garhwal -246174.

### ABSTRACT

The present chapter deals with the efficient technologies that have been developed for the rehabilitation of degraded ecosystems, so that the ecosystems can be rebuild and land productivity may be increased. Many causes of degradation, that has been identified, have also been discussed because they need to be understood and become the focus of considerable research aimed at minimizing ecological damage. The most commonly used popular management conservation and precautionary measures adopted as restoration technologies is discussed in detail with special reference to the successful technology package 'SWEET' (Sloping Watershed Environmental Engineering Technology) as an example.

**Key words:** Degradation, restoration, SWEET, rehabilitation, afforestation.

## Introduction

The problem of ecosystem damage is international and no country in the world is unaffected. To achieve sustainable development, it is essential to reverse current trends of environmental degradation by developing and using our knowledge of how to restore ecosystems. Further investigation and understanding of existing indigenous technologies are needed including compiling of available technologies. The aim of this chapter is to provide a scientifically sound basis for the reconstruction of degraded or destroyed ecosystems and to produce self-supporting systems, which are to some degree resilient to subsequent damage.

When ecosystems are degraded for whatever reason, either the vegetation or both vegetation and the soil suffer. The animals also suffer as their primary resource is lost. The soil holds some of the most important non-renewable resources of the ecosystem namely, the mineral nutrients and the soil organic matter. Soil is therefore, a critical controlling component of ecosystems. There are several components of land degradation associated with different degradative processes. They may be divided into those due to chemical, physical and biological processes (Fig. 1). Each of the processes creates typical symptoms, which can be helpful in assessing the degree of degradation that has occurred and the extent of degradation. Together they cause a marked loss of soil productivity, which is a function of the chemical, physical and biological properties of the soil. Fig. 1 summarizes the processes, components and causes of soil degradation. The restoration of soil degradation calls for the application of certain management, conservation and precautionary measures (Table 1). Measures such as contour cultivation, tied ridging, terracing, strip cropping, dense vegetation and planting cover crops, mulches, fast growing trees, selection of proper crop rotation, quick growing species and integrated cropping systems, provision of alternative fuel sources, check structures, protected watersheds, proper land preparation and ploughing, application of fertilizer, amendments and organic manures and drainage systems are some of the most applied techniques which help to protect and improve land.

**Table 1 :** The physical and chemical problems found in degraded terrestrial ecosystems and their short and long term treatments

| **Category** | **Problems** | **Immediate treatment** | **Long term treatment** |
|---|---|---|---|
| **Physical** | | | |
| Texture | coarse | organic matter or fines | vegetation |
| | fine | organic matter | vegetation |
| Structure | compact | rip or scarify | vegetation |
| | loose | compact | vegetation |
| Stability | unstable | stabilizer or nurse | regrade or vegetation |
| Moisture | wet | drain | drain |
| | dry | irrigate or mulch | tolerant species |
| **Nutrition** | | | |
| Macronutrients | nitrogen | fertilizer | legume |
| | others | fertilizer and lime | fertilizer and lime |
| Micronutrients | deficient | fertilizer | - |
| **Toxicity** | | | |
| pH | low | lime | lime or tolerant species |
| | high | pyretic wastes or organic matter | weathering |
| Heavy metals | high | organic matter or tolerant plants | inert covering or tolerant plants |
| Salinity | high | weathering or irrigate | tolerant species |

**Source :** Bradshaw, 1983

**LAND DEGRADATION**

- Vegetation degradation
- Water resources degradation
- Soil degradation
- Climate change
- Land alienation

| COMPONENTS | Chemical | Physical | Biological |
|---|---|---|---|
| PROCESSES | Leaching, volatilization | Compaction, erosion | Organic matter oxidation, biodiversity loss |
| SYMPTOMS Specific | Acidification<br>Low nutrient levels<br>Pollution<br>Salinization<br>Sodicity/alkalization | Crusting<br>Ponding<br>Poor water<br>Retention<br>Loss of topsoil<br>Pan formation | Less faunal activity<br>Delayed decomposition<br>Lower cation exchange capacity<br>Structural weakening |
| SYMPTOMS General | Low or declining yields<br>Poor responses to inputs | | |

**Fig. 1 :** Components of land degradation and components, processes and symptoms of soil degradation (Lal, 1997)

## Definitions

**Restoration:** The act of restoring to a former state or position or to an unimpaired or perfect condition. To restore is to bring back to the original state or to a healthy or vigorous state.

**Rehabilitation:** The action of restoring a thing to a previous condition or status. This appears similar to restoration but there is little or no implication of perfection.

For this reason this word is conveniently used to indicate any act of improvement from a degraded state (Box, 1978; Wall, 1992). Rehabilitation implies returning a habitat to a state in which it is more biologically acceptable to plants and animals. Rehabilitation may be used to imply assistance to a system to equilibrate to a new set of driving variables, if the habitat has changed irreversibly, then a system may be rehabilitated, but certainly not restored.

## Major causes of land degradation

In order to develop efficient technologies for restoration of degraded ecosystems, a thorough understanding of the major causes of degradation should be assessed. According to the International Soil Resources and Information Centre (ISRIC) under the aegis of UNEP four types of human interventions were identified as resulting in soil degradation: deforestation and removal of natural vegetation (579 million hectares); overgrazing of vegetation by livestock (679 million hectares); improper management of agricultural land (552 million) industrial activities leading to chemical pollution (22 million hectares). The processes causing soil degradation can be defined as follows:

(*a*) *Plant cover degradation and deforestation:* In rainfed agriculture many areas, particularly those in the lower rainfall areas in the tropics, are very fragile and the removal of the natural vegetation, growing different types of plants at a lower density than would be found under natural conditions and introducing more animals create conditions which are likely to lead to land degradation. Incorrect land use and bad land management (from the land being used in a manner incompatible with its capacity) are main factors causing deterioration of land cover and thus land degradation.

(b) *Wind erosion:* In (semi-) arid climates natural wind erosion is often aggravated by human activities. Wind erosion of topsoil is also a problem in flat lands even up to rainfalls of 750 or 800 mm.

(c) *Water erosion:* Water erosion is most likely to occur when the land is used for arable agriculture as the soil is then exposed without vegetative cover at certain times of the year. Loss of topsoil itself is often preceded by compaction or crusting causing a decrease in infiltration capacity of the soil and leading to accelerated runoff and soil erosion. Large areas of once productive river flats may become covered with a layer of fresh deposit, rivers and irrigation canals may become blocked while dams and lakes may fill with silt.

(d) *Soil crusting, sealing and compaction (physical deterioration):* Compaction, sealing and crusting occur in all continents, under nearly all climates and soil physical conditions. Soil crusting and compaction tend to increase runoff, decrease the infiltration of water into the soil, prevent or inhibit plant growth and leave the surface bare and subject to other forms of degradation. Compaction of the soil often arises from unsatisfactory cultivation practices, especially when mechanical cultivation methods are used, but can also arise from cultivation methods and by trampling by animals. Breakdown of aggregates at the surface causes a crust to form as the soil dries inhibiting water entry into the soil and preventing seedling emergence.

(e) *Reduction of soil organic matter and biological degradation:* Organic matter is important because of its indirect effect on plant growth. It feeds the soil animals and micro organisms which together breakdown and decompose organic matter so releasing in plant available forms of nitrogen, phosphorus, sulphur and microelements. It also increases cation exchange capacity of colloid compounds and improves soil physical properties. In the tropics, i.e., in warm or hot climates, oxidation of the organic matter is rapid and most of the soils are relatively low in organic matter. About 1.7 million hectares of tropical soils are low in organic matter and nutrient reserves. Under such conditions the fertility of the land declines and the soil becomes subject to other processes such as surface crusting, wind and water erosion.

(*f*) *Excessive toxic substances, other than salinization (chemical degradation) :* Soil toxicity can be brought about in a number of ways, but typical examples are from municipal and industrial wastes, oil spills, the excessive use of fertilizer, herbicides and insecticides, or the release of radioactive materials and acidification by airborne pollutants.

(*g*) The chemical processes mostly causing soil degradation occur in the form of removal of nutrients, which reduces the capacity of the soil to support plant growth and particularly crop production replenishment or recycling of nutrients by natural processes.

(*h*) Shifting cultivation is usually blamed for unproductive and serious cause of desertification.

## Restoration technologies popularly applied under various degradation conditions

**Degraded Land:** Conversion of tropical moist forest into farm or grazing land commonly results in rapid depletion of the soil's plant nutrient supply and accelerate soil erosion. In some places the degradation processes lead to takeover by persistent aggressive weed species of low nutritive value. Often the combined problems of low soil fertility and weed infestation become so great that the land is abandoned. Such lands are subject to frequent uncontrolled fires and are often covered by coarse grasses. Whenever the vegetation is burned erosion may increase and productivity may be reduced further.

In dry land farming, communities can build devices such as small dams to conserve water and can plant trees to protect the upper slopes of their land. Farmers should practice dry land farming techniques such as early ploughing, strip farming with the minimum soil disturbance (minimum tillage), conservation tillage as compared to clean tillage which promote the maintenance of soil structure and aggregates at the surface and thus reduce wind and water erosion. However, under specific conditions conventional tillage can promote water infiltration, control weeds and reduce mechanical impedance to root growth. Short season drought -tolerant cultivars should be used. Wind erosion can be reduced with fast growing trees and shrubs as windbreaks and shelterbelts, live fencing and roadside planting. Studies have shown that spacing of the shelterbelts can be 20 times the height of the tallest growing trees, this being the zone of protection. Narrow belts of 1-3 rows wide have considerable effect and improve the microclimate, prevent soil erosion, reduce the quantity of irrigation water used and protect the crop from desiccation. Integrating trees and livestock with arable farming, maintaining a good cover protects the soil. On flat farmland a good method of soil protection is to leave stubble and leaves on the surface after harvest and at planting. Maximum recycling of organic products should be encouraged from within and outside the farm (Crop residues, animal manure, composts and urban wastes) (Fig. 2). Improved land use systems including appropriate crop rotation, intercropping, agro forestry and related tree based farming systems, species that fix nitrogen should be considered.

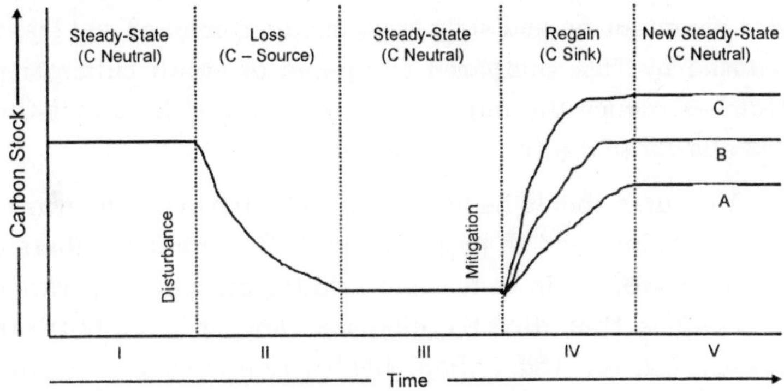


**Fig. 2 :** Conceptual model changes in ecosystem carbon stocks followng disturbance or degradation, and mitigation through reclamation : (A) stabilization at lower stocks than original, (B) stabilization at original stocks, and (C) stabilization at higher stocks (Johnson, 1995)

Dune stabilization measures include planting grasses followed by bushes and then trees. In several areas afforestation is started with mechanical fixation of dunes i.e. the surface of the dune is fenced with dry grasses and the like in a checkerboard system. Plant species used for afforestation must be able to withstand drought, salinity, low soil fertility and fluctuations in surface temperature and have deep root systems capable of reaching the moisture in deep layers or horizontal spread that allows for efficient use of surface rain and any dew. Chemical fixation using chemicals such as crude oil, asphalt and synthetic rubber latex is recommended when cost of labour is very high and the areas need to be stabilized in a short period.

Water erosion can be checked by many agronomic practices such as terraces to stop water erosion on steep slopes, level terraces to interrupt the rain flow and filter the water into the soil, water ways lined with concrete stone or even grass to direct the water down and ploughing along the contour of gentle slopes to check erosion. Studies have shown that if contouring and strip cropping are combined soil loss is reduced by 75% compared to up-and downhill cultivation. Mulches reduce the impact of raindrops and hold moisture and allow it to infiltrate into the soil.

Measures should be taken to avoid intensive local grazing and trampling and to propose a system to limit numbers of livestock, which can be feasible with the grazers' cooperation. Techniques that directly increase range productivity are disease control and animal health improvement; pasture regeneration through grass seedling and forage plantation.

All management plans must be site specific. There is need to adopt participative approach in which both the selection of solutions and their implementation are decided in cooperation with the beneficiary groups including farmers all land users and farmers. Identification, selection and farmer's adoption, through participatory approach, of improved and alternative packages of low-cost, low risk soil management and conservation practices are required therefore to address and control land degradation. In this regard integrated approach should be encouraged whenever feasible. Issues like changes in pricing policy, subsidy of inputs, market liberalization, land tenure reforms, infrastructural, policy and socio-economic aspects, environmental aspects should be considered in any restoration and land management plan.

**Mine spoil:** In mine spoils, one is confronted with a complete absence of soil in either pedological or a biological sense (Bradshaw, 1983). For restoring mine spoils emphasis is given first to build soil organic matter, nutrients and vegetation cover to accelerate natural recovery process. Establishment of vegetation on abandoned mined lands is hindered by physical factors such as high temperatures, low availability of soil moisture (Richardson and Greenwood, 1967), uncertain structure and unstable slopes due to hilly terrain (Brierly, 1956; Down, 1975) and compaction (Hall, 1957; Richardson, 1975). Artificial re-vegetation is often used to facilitate the generally slow natural rehabilitation process. Artificial seeding of grasses and legumes or both has been a commonly used method to stabilize unconsolidated mine tailings and to encourage natural invasion of tree and shrub seedlings. This ultimately improves site fertility and moisture retention capacity (Vogel, 1973). According to Harrington (1999), the first step to restoration of mine spoil should be stabilization of soil surface by contours, debris dams, mulch etc. Compaction of soil also needs to be reduced by mechanical disruption. If needed macro-porosity of the soil can be improved by incorporation of wood and shale. Soil toxicity in terms of pH, metals and salts has to be reduced by suitable amendments and plantation of resistant species and cultivars. Vegetation establishment and mulching with organic matter will increase soil organic matter. Nutrient limitations can be overcome by fertilization and other soil amendments. One aspect of vegetation plantation is to improve micro site conditions, which can be done by scalping, micro site preparation or by clump planting. Studies have shown that land rehabilitation benefits from plantations because it allows to jump-start succession (Ang, 1994). While most species appear to act as catalyst for ecosystem rehabilitation, broadleaf species seem to give better results than conifers (Parrotta *et al.*, 1997). Where phytotoxicity is suspected, it is particularly important to include plant material from populations growing naturally on mine sites and other areas likely to contain similar toxic factors (Piha *et al.*, 1995). In addition to their potential effects on soil fertility, species choice must be guided by seed and seedling availability, local uses for the species and economic aspects (Montagnini *et al.*, 1995). Many studies document the positive role of grass cover as a nurse crop (Vogel, 1973). They are useful in restoration of mined land because they stabilize soil, conserve soil moisture and may compete with weedy species. Tree plantations can be used as a tool for mine spoil restoration as they have ability to restore soil fertility and ameliorate microclimatic conditions. On mine spoils nitrogen is a major limiting nutrient and regular addition of fertilizer nitrogen may be required to maintain healthy growth and persistence of vegetation (Dancer, 1975). An alternative approach might be to introduce legumes and other nitrogen fixing species.

**Mountain ecosystem:** Deforestation in mountaineous regions is one of the most acute and serious ecological problems. Disturbance of vegetative cover on montane areas with thin soil and steep slopes result in land instability (landslides) and soil erosion. Excessive erosion not only impairs site productivity but also may adversely affect other sites or water bodies further down the watershed. A detailed restoration technology package (SWEET) developed indigenously is described later on in the chapter.

**Arid and semi-arid land:** In many arid and semi-arid open woodlands overgrazing and repeated fires have converted the vegetation to a degraded fire climax. Consequently, soil become dry and little woody plant regeneration occurs. Fire-tolerant vegetation-commonly unpalatable to animals-persists leading to a desert like state. Over 20.5 million ha of tropical arid lands become desertified every year (Wood *et al.*, 1982). The dimensions of conservation and restoration action in the arid and semi-arid lands are very varied, and need to be tackled according to local situations. The following approaches can be applied, some of which reinforce each other to attain objectives of sound land husbandry:

- Land use planning: zoning and integration of the various land uses to ensure optimal production of goods and services from the land resources.
- Preventive measures: to control grazing, deforestation and misuse of the biomass and to prevent fires and pests.
- Establishment of protected areas: For the *in situ* conservation of genetic resources, for national parks and recreation, for wildlife management, for scientific purposes.
- Management systems: Range and silvo-pasture management, watershed management, natural regeneration and forest management, wildlife ranching, fire control and use of controlled fires.
- Revegetation: Introduction of shrubs and trees for fuel wood and fodder production, to supply timber for rural needs and to enhance protection, air seeding, establishment of green belts around human settlements.
- Land rehabilitation: Watershed restoration, torrent and gully control, mechanical and biological measures to control run-off and promote infiltration in degraded land, control of sediments from bad lands and severely eroded areas, where these measures have an economic justification (protection of human settlements, infra-structure, water resources and valuable cropland).
- Forestry support to farmland: Wind breaks, shelterbelt, woodlots, agroforestry systems, introduction of multipurpose trees, fodder trees and

fuel wood species, introduction of nitrogen-fixing tree species.

- Land reclamation: stabilization of sand dunes (coastal and continental), reclamation of saline soils, and reclamation of marshland. Control of desert encroachment: stabilization of sand dunes affecting oases, cropland and infrastructure, establishment of large-scale shelterbelts.
- Water conservation and harvesting: Phreatophyte control, vegetation manipulation to increase water yield, water spreading, devices to promote ground water recharge and storage, dew harvesting techniques, mulching and other techniques to control evaporation losses in cropland and surface water.
- Saline ecosystem: A special form of land restoration is the rehabilitation of saline environments. It has been estimated that nearly 10% of the world's land area is salt affected. Each year over 500,000 ha of excessively irrigated land become saline or alkaline as a result of inadequate drainage or use of salty irrigation water. Capillary action draws moisture to the soil surface where it evaporates, leaving salts in or on the topsoil. In some cases, salts can be leached from upland soil and bedrock raising the salinity of runoff from deforested slopes. The increased runoff harms agricultural soil in lowland areas by causing temporary or lasting water logging and salinization. These salt affected lands can be transformed from sources of erosion and desertification to areas producing valuable forage, fuel and other products by growing plants possessing sufficient salt or alkali tolerance (halophytes) to withstand the existing conditions without reclamation. Salt tolerant plants need to be cultivated extensively in salt-affected soils

or for irrigation with saline water. The rehabilitation of saline environments is dependent on successful establishment of a vegetative cover depending on the site conditions; grasses, shrubs or trees may be suitable. There is often need of using a "pioneer" species to ameliorate the site sufficiently for other more desirable plants to become established. For all situations, a careful screening of plants against suitability criteria is a pre-requisite.

- Use of global satellite surveillance systems and powerful computer based GIS's for evaluating land use and preventing ecosystem degradation: Analysis of digital information from satellites and aerial photography allows us to accurately monitor land conditions over large areas and increases the value of traditional ground-based surveys of soil properties, land use, crop productivity and mineral resources.

## Basic mechanics of reforestation

The steps involved in the development of a successful reclamation scheme are presented in Fig. 3.

***Land preparation:*** Many degraded sites need some type of preplanting preparation, such as clearing stumps and competing weedy vegetation. Under some circumstances site cultivation controls weeds and improves soil aeration, soil biochemical activity, percolation of water, pH regulation, nutrient application and surface evenness. The degree and type of land preparation depends on several factors: site and soil conditions, vegetative cover, species to be planted and available capital and labour. Land preparation can be done by hand or by machine.

Ploughing the soil surface to increase water infiltration, ripping across the slope to retain water, plus construction of

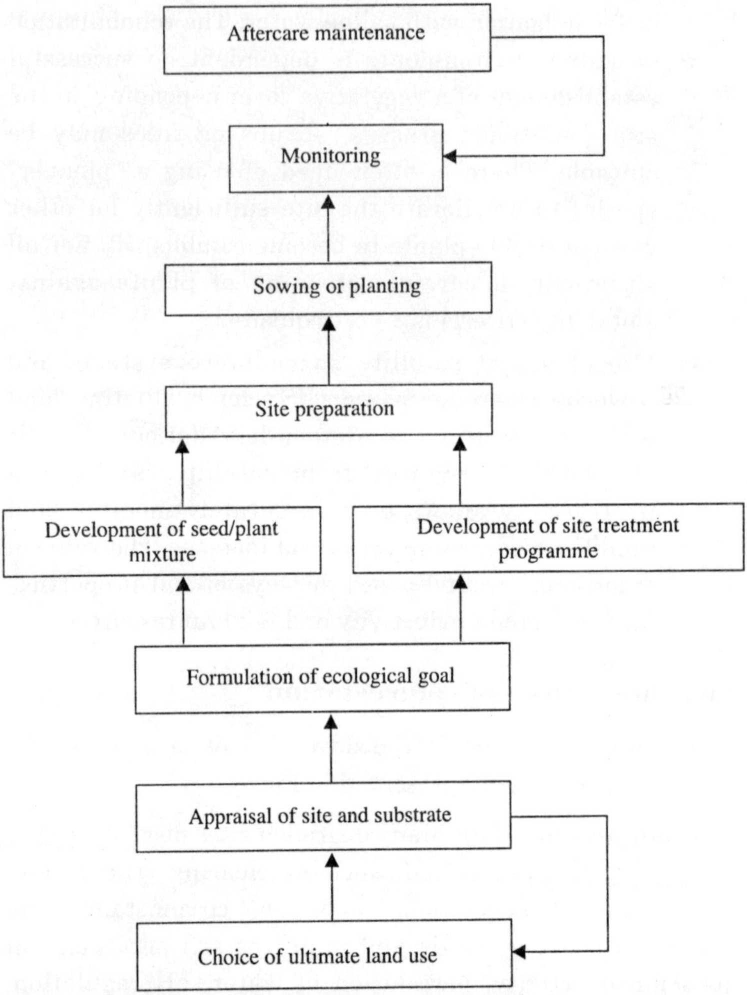


**Fig. 3 :** The steps involved in the development of a successful reclamation scheme. At a number of stages feedback may lead to alterations in programme (Bradshaw and Chadwick, 1980)

bench terraces on steeper slopes and funneling moisture onto a smaller area are all conservation measures used to maximize planting success. Minicatchments built to concentrate water into rooting zones of individual trees are a particularly important technique in arid zones.

It may be necessary to add nutrients during land preparation. Several techniques exist including mulching with organic matter, planting nitrogen-fixing trees, applying green manure (especially herbaceous legumes), and commercial fertilizers. Mulching suppresses weeds, improves soil moisture conditions and augments soil organic matter, but it may increase problems with rodents or other pests. Nitrogen-fixing trees can improve soil with their ability to produce nitrogen fertilizers. Foliage dropped by legumes is nitrogen-rich and will augment soil fertility as it decays. Other measures such as addition of commercial fertilizers and amendments also improves soil fertility. Nutrient levels and fluxes in plantations should be monitored to determine the prospective benefits and cost effectiveness of soil amendments. Another deficiency that occurs in eroded soils in drier climate is the lack of necessary micro-organisms. An ancient and effective method to add micro-organisms is to inoculate either nursery soils or planting holes in the field with a few grams of topsoil from well-established plantations or healthy forests.

***Species selection.*** Tree species selection is important for plantation success. When a tree is grown under unsuitable soil or site conditions, it will be stressed and thus become susceptible to attacks from insects or competition from weeds. Several factors influence species selection, including the objectives of reforestation, seed availability and costs associated with reforestation alternatives. For many degraded sites the species need to be those that can add nitrogen to the soil as well as provide products wanted by local communities. The species suitability to a particular site also depends on the races used. Increases in yield and resistances to disease can be achieved through selection and use of appropriate seeds.

Only by planting species and races on the sites for which they are adapted can maximum yields be obtained.

Plantations cannot substitute wholly for natural forests as reservoirs of germplasm or as components of the natural environments-they are really agricultural crops. Plantations contribute to preservation of the natural environment because they concentrate wood, food and forage production within a minimum area thus relieving some demands on natural forests. However, where plantations are established on land with good potential for annual agricultural crops, the effect actually is to increase pressure on the natural forests.

## Planting material

To reforest lands, seeds of various species must be available in great quantities. The seed supply for multipurpose agro forestry species is small. The customary way of raising planting stock in the tropics is to grow seedlings in a forest nursery either in open beds for bare root planting or in containers. Good nursery practices are essential to produce a hardy plant with a well-balanced straight root system. Bare rooted seedlings are susceptible to desiccation. Containerized seedlings are more costly and bulky to handle in the field and are subject to root coiling if closed-bottom containers are used. Therefore, containers with open bottom and suspended aboveground should be used.

Another technique for producing planting material is vegetative propagation-reproduction of planting stock without the use of seed. Vegetative propagation is widely used in tree crops such as rubber, coconut, tea, coffee, cocoa and oil palm. Methods include cuttings, air layering, budding, grafting and tissue culture. Vegetative propagation has the advantage of hastening massive reproduction of genetically superior plants ensuring that all are of the desired genetic type.

Seedling survival and growth rates in the nursery and at the planting site sometimes can be improved by special kinds of fungi and bacteria. For most tropical trees, associations between tree roots and mycorrhizal fungi are essential for healthy growth.

Legume trees can grow well on degraded land because their root can be a symbiotic host for rhizobium bacteria, which produce nitrogen fertilizer, and essential nutrient for plant growth.

An alternative to using seedlings in nurseries is to plant or sow the seed directly at the reforestation site. This method is feasible where seed is plentiful and where seed and seedling mortality is low. Direct sowing of drought resistant species is sometimes preferred especially for species that have long and fast growing taproots that may be damaged in a nursery or in transfer to the field. The advantage is that no nursery is required and planting costs are low. On the other hand, seeding survival may be low because of weed competition, lack of the tending, poor weather or animal damage.

## Tree care and maintenance

Proper care and maintenance of the planted site is essential to ensure that trees survive to maturity. Once grown, there is the problem of monitoring timber harvests and of systematic replanting. The main causes of reforestation failure other than inappropriate technologies are uncontrolled grazing and fires, competition from weeds and uncontrolled cutting for fuel, fodder, poles and lumber.

Direct protection through fencing or guards tends to be expensive. Other less costly methods include planting unpalatable trees (e.g. *Cassia siamea)* or thorny trees (e.g., *Parkinsonid)* as barriers around the plantation. The use of living fences is becoming a more widespread practice because they provide a number of auxiliary benefits including shade, fodder, windbreak, fuel and wildlife habitat. Another alternative is subsidizing farmers with livestock feed or with cash to purchase feed during the period when trees are most susceptible to animal damage. Grazing beneath the tree canopy sometimes can be beneficial as a means of weeding. However, livestock grazing on recently reforested watersheds can be harmful because animals compact the topsoil, leading to poor tree growth and increased runoff.

Weeding is an important aspect of plantation establishment and maintenance. Weeds compete directly with seedlings for light, soil nutrients and water. Their shade can smother and eventually kill young trees. There are three main methods of weeding -manual, mechanical and chemical. The manual method is the most common and requires little skill or capital. Mechanical methods may be used in large plantations projects but generally are not considered profitable in the tropics. In many tropical countries chemical weed control techniques have been tested and found successful, but because of safety and cost problem they are not used extensively.

Whatever the type and location of tree planting, the cooperation of local people is essential if newly planted trees are to survive. Because most trees do not yield much benefit for several years the options offered must demonstrate explicit benefits to the people. Tree planting programmes are most successful when local communities are involved and when the people perceive clearly that success is in their self-interest. In local communities, support can be generated through local involvement in project design, demonstration plantings, commercial plantings by entrepreneurs with larger working directly with farmers or labourers and direct financial assistance or provision of substitutes.

Successful reforestation requires sufficient funds, strong political will, massive popular support and cooperation among all involved parties.

## Rehabilitation of Degraded Mountain Ecosystem Using SWEET Technology

The terrain and altitudinal characteristics of mountain areas require a distinct treatment of space in rehabilitation planning methodology as different elevation and altitude ranges coincide with different agro climatic and resource zones. It was observed that the mid altitude zone ranging from 500 m to 1500m above main sea level was most thickly populated and was damaged severely. The population pressure was very high; families were fragmented which resulted in small land holdings. Resource exploitation beyond the regenerative capacity from smallholdings led the farmers migrate in search of off-farm livelihood. Therefore, the SWEET package was designed in such a way so as to address the degraded land which included abandoned agricultural land owned by individual farmers as well as land owned collectively by the villagers. The geographical location, Mountain farmers around the world practice traditional terracing techniques to control soil erosion. In parts of western Hindukush Himalaya, where soils are shallow and gravelly, farmers have devised a technology to collect eroded soil from floodwater to make fertile arable land. The technologies for prevention of soil erosion and fertility are constantly under experimentation in order to improve the efficiency. In Burkina Faso, land degradation and soil erosion have been halted by sculpting scalloped patterns of half moons into land. A novel solution developed in Japan, called the 'Effective Micro-organism Technology' involves the addition of liquid culture of bacteria to soil which, helps to revive soil fertility, improve yields and suppresses the soil borne pathogens and pests. An effective technology was developed in the Phillippines based on the traditional terracing of mountain land and was called the 'Sloping Agricultural Land Technology (SALT).' It involves planting nitrogen fixing plants along contour lines to form hedge grows. Food or cash crops are grown in between the alleys. The hedge grows act as barriers to soil erosion while pruned leaves provide green manure and fodder for livestock. Some of the trial results from China, Bangladesh, Nepal, India, Myanmar and Pakistan showed a significant fall in soil loss and improvements in soil fertility and crop yields. Trials in China showed that planting leguminous hedge grows on upland terrain can reduce soil loss by up to 94 to 99%. However, the major hindrance were high labour requirements and returns were not sufficient to compete with other higher paying off-farm employment opportunities. The cost of traditional terracing techniques is rising with the increase in market value of wage labour, example it costs US $ 4,800 to create one hectare of terraced land in northern Pakistan.

The scientists of G. B. Pant Institute of Himalayan Environment & Development conceived a rehabilitation technology based on behavioral ecological approach. The technology was christened as Sloping Watershed Environmental Engineering Technology (SWEET) in 1994, by the then Chairman of the Governing body of the institute, Mr. R. Rajamani. It was realized that in contrast to much of ecological research, restoration ecology has a social and economic aspect embedded in it.

The SWEET technology is an integrated approach through scientific, social economic and cultural ingredients for achieving socioeconomic development along with rehabilitation. Basic characteristics of the technology is in its flexibility. The technology can be devised/designed/

implemented based on the behavioral ecological approach, which is now considered as the most important factor governing the success of any rehabilitation programme. Five general principles were adopted for designing a suitable package for a given location.

It was realized that society has expectations and they often questioned what to expect from restoration. Any restoration site was initially restricted to access and the initial appearance was unsightly, which gave rise to general notion that money is being wasted. Therefore, a restoration ecologist needs to explain the consequences of the work first. Thus, the first principle of SWEET states: Win the confidence of the people after close interaction and make them agree to protect the area from open grazing. It is now being recognized that, rehabilitation programmes should address issues concerning not only improvement in production of scarce resources but also on realization and appropriation of monetary benefits from the produce. This would reduce cost of rehabilitation in the long run and would mobilize local initiatives. It is now being recognized that rehabilitated or restored sites are not only scientifically interesting or attractive places of recreation but they are highly important in terms of providing ecosystem services upon which we all depend, e.g. flood control, clean air and water.

A restoration ecologist has to convince the society on how the rehabilitated site is important with regard to its function as an ecosystem service provider, the benefits of which is not yet valued in financial terms and also the cost in terms of environmental damage if remedial measures are not taken. Therefore, the second point to be kept in mind while designing a rehabilitation project was to device a combination of interventions for providing benefits in short as well as long term, blending the local and regional interests.

The tenet of SWEET goes on to explain and stresses that the most important intervention, which will provide immediate benefit to most of the people should be started first and only after observing the response of the people the next intervention should be started. In other words, adaptive management as a restoration strategy is essential, because what happens at one stage in restoration dictates what needs to happen next. The restoration plan must contain in-built flexibility. If reconnaissance or monitoring reveal that objectives are not being met, then alternative interventions may have to be attempted.

'Man, by experience, finds where his difficulties lies. Perception of problems in time and cultural context is prerequisite for finding solution to this problem' (Purohit, 1995). The above statement by the then director of G. B. Pant Institute of Himalayan Environment & Development, Almora, led to the formulation of the next tenet of SWEET, which envisaged that local knowledge and skill of resource management should be supplemented / complemented with science/technology inputs rather than replacement by alien systems. It was observed that local knowledge on biological production systems is extremely rich and provides scope for improvement through conventional science and technology. Building on local knowledge minimizes the risk of failure of interventions and investments.

The fifth and last principle of SWEET envisages participation of entire village community, particularly, women for any resource management programme. Decision making on specificities and organization of work elements in an open forum with all the inhabitants rather than a group of selected or elected individual is more rewarding. Logically, by doing so the participants develop a feeling of ownership and they will be more likely to assume a stewardship role for the completed project. Apart from this, volunteer labour by local residents may reduce overall project costs. However, such labour also requires coordination, special supervision and additional liability insurance.

Thus, with the above principles to be followed SWEET had three goals. The primary goal was to reestablish a functional ecosystem that contained sufficient biodiversity to continue its maturation by natural processes and to evolve over longer time span in response to changing environmental conditions.

Social and cultural goals were also envisaged as long as they were congruent with the primary goal. The social goal was largely economic and consisted of production of goods such as timber, forage and fisheries at restored site. They may also comprise of natural services like protection of recharge areas, potable water supply, detention of flood water, attenuation of erosion and sedimentation, noise reduction, immobilization of contaminants, transformation of excess soil nutrients, generation of pollinators for crops, generation of predators for crop pests, provision of recreational opportunities and tourism, conservation of germplasm of economic species and serve as refuge for wildlife and rare species. Cultural goals included aesthetic amenities and revival of historical environments as aspects of preserving cultural heritage.

**ELEMENTS OF TECHNOLOGY PACKAGE** *The eightfold pathway to SWEET*

## Land Use History

*A systematic knowledge of the land use history, past and/or existing vegetation, physico-cultural settings and factors leading to land degradation should be ascertained before considering appropriate interventions.*

This aspect is very important as project evaluation depends in part upon being able to contrast the project site before and after restoration. With advancement in technology, it is now very important to have properly labeled and archived photographs. Camera locations should be recorded so that before and after photos can be compared. Disturbance features should be photographed.

The years in which impacts occurred should be recorded. Soils and other physical site conditions should be described. Species composition need **to be listed** and species abundance estimated.

The structure of all components should be described in sufficient detail to permit objective means of evaluating the performance of projects subsequent to their implementation.

## Protection

*Prevention of open grazing and other biotic interference is one of the important elements of the proposed technology package. Biofencing or stone walls are to be preferred over barbed wire enclosures to bring fragmented land under one workable unit. Plugging of gullies with biological/physical means is also carried out.* The project site should be staked or marked conspicuously in the field. Fencing and fire lanes should be installed as needed. This guideline is often ignored until it results in a contingency, such as neighbour's cattle escaping into a freshly planted project site. The site also needs to be protected against vandals and herbivory.

## Waste water harvesting

Alleviation of water stress is a prerequisite for enhancing the pace of regeneration of natural or introduced productive processes. Rainfall regime is highly variable, depending upon the location, surface/lows are harvested by constructing water tanks. Size, number and distribution of tanks is decided depending upon the rainfall regime, water balance, soil properties, topography of the watershed and size of the area to be reclaimed. Surface runoff should be diverted through V—shaped temporary channels to siltation pits and finally to underground tank whose inner walls should slightly slope outwards. UV stabilized polythene lining (black) of 250-300 micron thickness is used to minimize seepage. Wastewater from perennial sources can be diverted through PVC/GI pipes, placed at a depth of atleast 30 cm below soil surface to guard against biotic disturbances/forest fires.

## Selection of Tree Species

Species differ in respect of their utility and ecological values and growth rates. Mixed planting is undertaken but the selection is made on the basis of villagers' needs and ecological realities. In high altitudes temperate bamboos preferred by villagers are most promising for plantation on common lands. The promising species for mid altitude are *Ainus nepalansis, A. nitida, Albizzia* spp., *Bauhinia spp., Celtis australis, Dalbergia sissoo, Ficus* spp. *Grewia optiva, prunus cerasoides, Quercus* spp., etc.

## Nursery

Success of introduction of trees on terrace margins in abandoned agricultural land or degraded community land depends upon the physiological vigour of transplants. Establishment through seeds is slow. Polyethylene tunnels, resting on bamboo framework (polyhouse), is gainfully utilized to reduce nursery time and for protection from frost. Trays have been designed for raising vigorous transplants as well as for minimizing likely damage during transport/ transplantation. Since, these trays can be reused, the cost of seedling is much lower than that of the traditional polyethylene bag method.

## Plantation and soil management

Physical as well as biological treatments of degraded lands are essential for enhancing their productive potential. Transplantation should be done in pits (60cm x 60cm x 60cm) filled with gravel free soil, mixed with well composted farmyard manure *(FYM: 3, 2 or 1 kg/pt for fast growing, moderately fast growing and slow growing species respectively).*

*Biocomposting of weeds and agricultural wastes can be utilized to supplement FYM. In case of abandoned terraces, these should be tilled to a depth of 30 cm leaving aside a 50 cm strip on the terrace margins. FYM@ 10 tonnes/ha should be applied at the time of tillage in the first year.*

## Green fodder

Surface irrigation, once fortnight during dry spells, together with periodic harvest (rather than open grazing) would increase fodder yield by 5-10 fold, depending upon the level of existing degradation. Plantation of thysanolaena, Arundinaria, Crotolaria, etc., on the margins of terraces and along risers prevents erosion and provides quality green fodder and / or green manure. Maggar bamboo can also be planted as windbreaks and for fodder/culms.

## Crop diversity and value addition to raw material

Over emphasis on cash crops has been one of the reasons of degradation of arable land. Farmers are encouraged to raise diverse crops/practice crop rotations and earn cash benefits by way of organized marketing and value addition locally.

The success of ecosystem reconstruction depends on a) a basic environment without toxicity or other serious limiting factors, b) adequate supplies of nutrient elements, which would contribute to the ecosystem. The importance of appreciating the underlying soil processes involved in accumulation, cycling and release of both nutrient and toxic elements in the soil has become apparent and a lot of fundamental understanding is required.

Some ecosystems in the Himalayan states are still managed by traditional, sustainable cultural practices. However, these ecosystems have suffered from demographic growth and external pressures of various kinds and are in need of restoration. The restoration of such ecosystems needs a concomitant recovery of indigenous ecological management practices, including support for the cultural survival of indigenous people and their lifestyle as living libraries of traditional ecological knowledge.

## Conclusions

There is a need to lead the community in weaving together traditional know-how and new technology resulting in creation of tradition in modernity.

The keystone or system-directing species need to be identified and protected because ecologically they have large effects on the overall system diversity.

The initiation of rehabilitation therefore should involve control and eradication of alien species, both plant and animals, and the protection of the more seriously impacted native species.

A serious paradox is happening with reference to information management. There is too much information but not enough to start a rehabilitation project. All rehabilitation programmes must start with an inventory and a map. Information also needs to be shared.

Any rehabilitation project should be based on scientific knowledge about the health and dynamics of that landscape. In order to arrive on such scientific knowledge, extensive ecological monitoring programmes need to be developed so that information on changes to the systems will be available.

Research will be necessary where there is a need to know why changes are happening.

Each mountain state in India faces a unique set of challenges, constraints and opportunities, therefore the recommendations will need to be adapted, amended and combined to meet the specific needs of a particular region.

## References

Ang, L. H. (1994) Problems and prospects of afforestation on sandy tailings in Peninsular Malaysia. J. Tropical Forest Sci., 7: 87 – 105.

Box, T. W. (1978) The significance and responsibility of rehabilitation of drastically disturbed land. In *Reclamation of drastically disturbed lands.* (Eds. F. W. Schaller and P. Sutton ) Madison, WI : American Society of Agronomy, pp. 1-10.

Bradshaw, A. D. (1983) The reconstruction of ecosystems. (Presidential address to the British Ecological Society). J. Applied Ecology, 20 : 1 – 27.

Bradshaw, A. D. and Chadwick, M. J. (1980) *The Restoration of Land.* Oxford, Blackwell.

Brierley, J. K. (1956) Some preliminary observations on the ecology of pit heaps. Journal of Ecology, 44:383 – 390.

Dancer, W. S. (1975) Leaching losses of ammonium and nitrate in the reclamation of sand spoils on Cornwall. J. Environ. Qual., 4: 499 – 504.

Down, C. G. (1975) Soil development on colliery waste tips in relation to age. 1. Introduction and physical factors. J. Applied Ecology, 12: 613 – 622.

Hall, I. G. (1957) The ecology of disused pit heaps in England. J. Ecol., 45: 689 – 720.

Harrington, C. A. (1999) Forests planted for ecosystem restoration or conservation. New Forests, 17: 175 – 190.

Johnson, M. G. (1995) The role of soil management in sequestering soil carbon. *In : Soil Management and the Greenhouse Effect* (Eds. R. Lal, J. M. Kimble, R. F. Follet, and B. A. Stewart), Lewis Publishers, Boca Raton, FL, pp. 351 – 363.

Lal, R. (1997) Residue management, conservation tillage and soil restoration for mitigating greenhouse effect by $CO_2$ enrichment. Soil and Tillage Research, 43: 81 – 107.

Montagnini, F., Fanzeres, A. and da Vinha, S. G. J. (1995) The potential of twenty indigenous tree species for reforestation and soil restoration in the Atlantic forest region of Bahia. J. Applied Ecology, 32: 841 – 856.

Parrota, J. A., Knowles, O. H. and Wunderle, Jr., J. M. (1997) Development of floristic diversity in 10-year old restoration forests on a bauxite mined site in Amazonia. Forest Ecology and Management, 99: 21-42.

Piha, M. I., Vallack, H. W., Reeler, B. M. and Michael, N. (1995) A low input approach to vegetation establishment on mine and coal ash wastes in semi arid regions. I. Tin mine tailings in Zimbabwe. J. Applied Ecology, 31: 372 – 381.

Purohit, A. N. (1995) The murmuring man: Man in search of environmentally sound development. Bishen Singh Mahendra Pal Singh, Dehradun, pp. 80.

Richardson, J. A. (1975) Physical problems of growing plants on colliery wastes. *In* : *The Ecology of resource degradation and renewal.* (Eds. M.J. Chadwick and G.T. Goodman) Oxford Blackwell Scientific publications, pp., 275 – 285.

Richardson, J. A. and Greenwood, E. F. (1967). Soil moisture tension in relation to plant colonization of pit heaps. Proceedings of University of New Castle Philosophical Society, Vol 1. pp. 129 – 136.

Vogel, W. G. (1973) The effect of herbaceous vegetation on survival and growth of trees planted on coal mined spoils. In : Proceedings of the Research and Applied Technology Symposium in Mined-land Reclamation, National Coal Association, Bituminous Coal Research, Inc. Monroeville, Pittsburgh, Pennsylvania, pp. 197 – 207.

Wali, M. K. (1992) *Environmental Rehabilitation*, Vol.2. Ecosystem Analysis and Synthesis (Ed. S. P. Bakker), Publishers, The Hague, The Netherlands, pp. 396.

Wood, P. J., Burley, J. and Grainger, A. (1982) Technologies and technology systems for reforestation of degraded tropical lands, OTA Commissioned paper.

CHAPTER 5

# WATERSHED DEVELOPMENT FOR LAND AND WATER MANAGEMENT IN ARID ECOSYSTEM

**K.K.Singh[1], Alka Tomar[2], Vinod Singh[3] and Mahadevi Singh[4]**

[1]Project Directorate (Research), Agriculture & Soil Survey, Krishi Bhawan, Bikaner (Raj.)-334001, India.

[2]CMS Environment, Research House, Saket, New Delhi-110017.

[3]Department of Geography, Govt. Dungar College, Bikaner (Raj.)-334001.

[4]Sophia Sr. Secondary School, Bikaner (Raj.)-334002.

## ABSTRACT

The approach to watershed management calls for an integrated effort on many counts, viz. area development, resource identification and management programme-planning, implementation and evaluation and also the disciplines involved. It is devised basically to deal with water resources, its quantification and distribution in time and space, so as to formulate strategic schemes, to use water more judiciously matching its availability against the needs.

**Key Words :** Watershed, Land and Water Management, arid ecosystem

## Introduction

Our very own survival on earth essentially depends on two basic resources viz., soil and water, nature's two valuable gifts to mankind. Mother nature gives protection to these resources through natural vegetation. This protective shield of land is disturbed by our interference, making the soil susceptible to detachment and transportation – a vicious process called 'soil erosion'. A no-care attitude and gross negligence coupled with our ever-increasing needs and demands over the years have taken the problem to a threatening dimension (average annual soil erosive loss in India – 16.35 tonnes $ha^{-1}$ of which 20% is lost to the sea – an estimation given by Dhruv Narayana *et al.*, 1993).

Water in its natural form being the basic constituent for agriculture, livestock, forestry and various other activities that people choose to pursue life patterns and survival, its imbalance creates corresponding imbalances. Thus, water has been regarded as ample and copious to support all these activities. Its shortage, felt only in recent times, compels one to take a cautious, circulated and concerted approach to use it judiciously and in a sustainable manner.

The dryland or rainfed areas constitute 68% of the cultivable land (143.7 million ha) contributing about 45% of the total foodgrains production in the country. Even, after full exploitation of the irrigation potential, about 50% of the cultivable land will still continue to depend on erratic rainfall for production. The country have to depend for most of its requirements of coarse cereals, pulses, oilseeds and cotton on this land. If the estimated requirement of food are to be met in future, the productivity of drylands has to be increased by at least 72% (Singh and Shekhawat, 2000). To ensure sufficient supply of food for the growing population, the production of food will need to be doubled by 2025, against the present level of food grains production at about 203.9 million tonnes during 1999-2000 (Sanio, 1998 and Kanwar, 1997).

On the water front, India is blessed with one of the highest annual precipitation (400 M ha mm) in any country of this size, but because of its wide space and time variation, agricultural production suffers a lot and also, our country is affected greatly by recurrent floods and droughts of high magnitude. The acute shortage of water, even in places of good rains and the people's anger and rage over it, clearly show the morning of the day (Chakraborty and Mukherjee, 2001).

"Soil without water is desert and water without soil is useless". Here comes the adoption of soil and water conservation methods and technology, combining together, in agricultural development plans for treating these two resources, for achieving the long and sustained use of them towards increasing production.

Hence, it is imperative to develop suitable technology for increasing production of food, fibre and fuel to meet our increasing demands, since horizontal expansion of cultivable land is not possible, vertical increase in production is to be the only alternative.

## Some Definitions

### *Dry Farming*

It can be defined as a programme of soil and crop management, improved cultural practices designed to conserve all available rainwater in the areas of low and uncertain rainfall for better production. At the same time, it is the best measure for controlling floods.

### *Water Harvesting*

Water Harvesting in its broadest sense will be defined as the "collection of runoff for its productive use". Runoff may be harvested from roofs and ground surfaces as well as from intermittent or ephemeral water courses. A wide variety of water harvesting techniques for many different applications were known. Productive uses include provision of domestic and stock water, conservation of runoff for crops, fodder and tree production and less frequently water supply for fish and duck ponds.

Water harvesting, an age-old practice, has been variously defined "the practice of collecting water from an area treated to increase runoff from rainfall and snow melt". Water harvesting is "the process of collecting natural precipitation from prepared watersheds, for beneficial use" (Singh, 1994).

### *Watershed*

It is a geographical unit that drains into a common point. This natural unit carved out through the interaction of rain water with landmass and typically comprises arable and non-arable lands and natural drainage line. Watershed is a self-defined area which does not allow any water from outside the catchment to enter into it and allows its excess water to discharge to a common point in a stream. Essentially, watershed based natural resource development involves the optimum use of the watershed precipitation through improved water, soil and crop management and it is a complex long-term task and includes the integrated development of all types of lands-agricultural, grasslands, forest lands and uncultivated lands as integral part of the system.

Various definitions have been proposed over recent years for the term 'watershed'. While the definitions use a wide variety of words, they all mean practically the same thing. Since, large watersheds consists of many smaller watersheds. It is necessary to define the watershed in terms of a point. The point is usually referred to as the watershed 'outlet'. With respect to the outlet, the watershed consists of all land area that sheds water to the outlet during a rain storm (McCuen, 1989).

A watershed is a topographically delineated area that is drained by a stream system, i.e., the total land area that is drained to some point on a stream or river. A watershed is a hydrological unit that has been described and used as a physical biological unit and also, on many occasions, as a socio-economic-political unit for planning and management of natural resources (Sheng, 1990).

Generally, a watershed can be defined as an area from which runoff resulting from precipitation flows from a single point into a stream, river, lake or an ocean. The terms watershed, catchment area or drainage basin are used synonymously. The watershed boundary is called drainage divide. Rains received on opposite sides of drainage divide, do not contribute runoff and reach to the adjoining areas.

## Western Dry Region

It covers as many as 9 districts of Rajasthan. The main characteristics of the region are : hot sandy desert, erratic rainfall, high evaporation, no perennial river and scanty vegetation, deep ground water and often brackish, famine and drought conditions, land-man ratio high (1.73 ha/person), average rainfall only 395 mm, forest cover 1.2%, land under pasture low (1.3%), net irrigated area 6.3% of net sown area (44.4%), cropping intensity 1-5%. Bajra, guar and moth are main crops in kharif and wheat and gram in Rabi. Density of livestock is 1.08 animal $ha^{-1}$ and 1.56 animal per person.

| **Thrust area** | **Strategy** |
|---|---|
| Desert land development | Develop silvi-pastoral and energy plantation, sand dune stabilization |
| Water conservation and land use | Integrated watershed development programme, *In situ* moisture conservation practices. |

## Problems of dryland agriculture

The primary problem of dryland agriculture is an effective storage of rain water in the soil. Watershed approach may prove beneficial in such a dry agro-climatic condition. Only safely stored water within the reach of root zone can be used in crop production. The major problems in dry farming are : rainfall variability and problems of cropping system management, problem of germination, characteristics of soils, constraints in fuelwood and fodder production, problem of fertilizer application, mechanical and implement needs, environmental changes such as water logging and the increase in salinity and socio-economic problems.

## Conventional Approach

In the conventional approaches to water resources development, the required quantity of water is abstracted from a locally available source, a river, a reservoir or a well for the purpose of drinking, irrigation or industrial water supply. The water supply system is regarded as a device to solve a specific water demand. One is not concerned therefore to keep an account of the input-output balancing of the water resources system with a mechanism of depletion and replenishment within the limits of its hydrologic cycle. This was basically due to the fact that water is regarded as a capacious resource if not infinite, hence, probing into its system or 'hydrologic cycle' for the purpose of creating a local water source is considered superfluous. For designing an isolated water supply system on the basis of ground water source, similarly, the capacity of the well (a single well or a battery of wells) to yield the necessary quantity is the only consideration. Thereafter, it is assumed that the system will continue to run perpetually though, the yield of a well changes when more people share from the common ground waterbody. Even the chemical quality of well water may change if ground water system is not properly treated in respect of sinking of wells and pumping practices.

Water resources system is universally accessible. More facilities are being created continually and extensively to cope up with the increasing demand for water. The feasibility for an individual water supply system is often not considered from the point of view of the broader water resources system and its capacity to cope.

- It follows a simple demand supply relationship. If agricultural situation is favourable and irrigation demand exists the project is considered feasible. Similarly, if the urban or industrial authority is willing to find, a source is identified and the project is formulated without considering its position in the total water resources system and its basic strength to sustain.
- The project ensures protecting interests of the command area that benefits. Often, large irrigation projects are implemented to benefit people of the valley or plains at the expense of people or the community occupying high slopes (Fig. 3). At times, the catchment and command area fall in two different water regimes.
- It is not realistic to assess sustainability of a water supply system and potential environmental threats if it is unrelated to the natural water resources system. In a watershed approach, the basic water supply source would be created strategically for the entire water regime-the watershed-keeping in mind the interest of the people who occupy it.

## Concept of Watershed

Water is a vital natural resource. It is the life-line for efficient crop production. Thus, rainwater should be utilized as much as possible from the hill sides, rocky areas, sloppy and degraded wastelands as well as watersheds, generating maximum possible runoff. For the optimal use of the rainfall resource for increased crop production from rainfed agricultural lands, it has been recognized that runoff recycling should form an integral part of the agricultural management system. The recycling of runoff water necessitates efficient collection and storage of runoff water in the farm ponds. Thus, the stored water can be used for crop life saving irrigation at critical stages of crop growth to stabilize agricultural production in the rainfed farming areas (Singh, 1994).

The basic concept of watershed management is to conserve all the basic natural resources of the watershed and to plan, for their optimal utilization, the approach and strategy are primarily based on the twin concepts of (i) integrated watershed management, and (ii) sustainable farming system.

A watershed consists of 3 physical sectors : (i) arable or cultivated land, (ii) non arable land - village pastures and grazing land, culturable wastelands, and (iii) network of natural drainage lines. These sub-sectors are hydrologically interspersed. Watershed being a manageable hydrologic unit, conceptually and in practice, these sub-sectors should be treated as one geo-hydrological entity for project planning and implementation. Thus, sustainability of natural resources of land and water can be ensured.

A rainfed farmer derives his subsistence from his own cultivated land and partly from common property resources and community lands. His income is supplemented by off-farm activities, wages and subsidiary occupation. The landless labourer meets his fuel and fodder requirements from common property resources. The following component in household farming systems are required to be considered : (i) feed sub-component, (ii) fodder sub-component, (iii) fuel sub-component, (iv) income generation component, and (v) household production systems. These various components are inter-related and interlinked. Therefore, these components should be treated as a part of one organic unit.

The Ministry of Agriculture in the Eighth Plan has accepted the following key objectives for the National Watershed Development Project :

- Production of biomass on a sustainable basis
- Restoration of ecological balance
- Reduction of regional disparity
- Generation of employment
- Increasing income levels.

During the Seventh Plan, the Government of India had launched a national development programme of rainfed agriculture on a watershed basis. The Indian Council of Agricultural Research pioneered the field-level implementation of 47 model watersheds in collaboration with state governments. Based on the experiences gained from 4400 micro-watersheds, it is summarized that unless rain water conservation, harvesting, recycling and efficient use become the focal point in watershed management research, it cannot create a significant impact on rainfed agriculture. Unless, the rainfed farmer is given an alternative option to increase the net income and reduce risks of rainfed/dryland farming, he will not be motivated for change. Thus, water is the key to change.

The river system is hierarchical. Rainwater on a ridge is divided in the direction of its slopes. The ridge acts as a 'water divide', meaning that the rain water diverges from here in two or more direction following land slopes (Fig.1). Within the area surrounded by the ridge the surface flow of water converges to feed the drainage system. The area within the ridges, i.e., the catchment area of the drainage system is defined as the watershed. The rainfall draining the uplands follow slopes to converge into small gullies and, streams which, in turn, meets large tributaries and finally the main river course. Any of the constituents of a river - a tributary, a stream or a gully - has a defined catchment. This catchment is identifiable on the ground or on a topographical map as the watershed. Each watershed has a network of streams - the 'drainage system', occupying an area surrounded by a continuous ridgeline. The rainfall in the watershed turns into surface and ground water flows to pass through its drainage and groundwater system tending to exit the area through the lowest part of the trunk stream (McCuen, 1989).

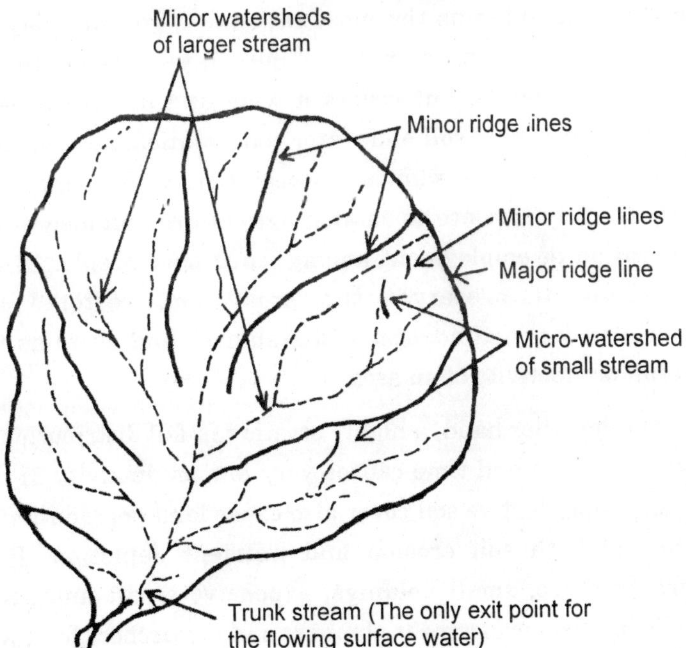


**Fig. 1 :** Watershed hierarchy and identification of geographical boundaries

From land management point of view, a convenient size of watershed may vary from 500 ha to 1000 ha. However, these limits should not be taken as rigidity. On an average, a size of 2000 ha is considered optimum for agricultural development with regard to ease of surveys, investigation and effective planning keeping in view the local conditions and completion of the project within a reasonably short time (Tideman, 1996). Watershed is marked by an elevated line that forms a division between two areas drained by separate streams, systems or bodies of water. A watershed may be of any size but it must be manageable, hydrologically.

It is very much 'natural' and it allows planners to focus on all the effects of downfall runoff in a given area and to plan accordingly to control or contain it. Watershed management has been accepted as the most rational approach today. In this approach, development is not only confined to the agricultural lands, but covers a wide and diverse area of activities including soil and water conservation, development of degraded and wastelands, afforestation, water harvesting with special reference to rainfed agriculture and also to the generation of employment among rural poor people. In the long run, it preserves the ecosystem, restores the environmental degradation and stabilizes and sustains the overall productivity of an area.

On the other hand, a highly erratic rainfall distribution in terms of space and time causes very low productivity in dry areas. Unproductive soil cover also cause land degradation in terms of both soil erosion and nutrient depletion. Poor infrastructure, small holdings, expensive credit and gross negligence by development planners and researchers for many years made the situation more pathetic. The soil and water conservation activities (if called so) were confined to only contour bunding or terracing on individual or a group of farm holdings. These failed to achieve success because it could not take account of the natural hydrological cycle. With the establishment of a chain of soil conservation research demonstration and training centers in different regions of the country in 50's during the first and second five years plans, the concept of integrated land use planning on watershed basis was introduced. The essence of this concept is a set of principles. These are as follows :

(1) Land use planning and utilization based on its potential.

(2) Rain water harvesting.

(3) Maintaining good vegetative cover over the ground to minimize erosion of soil and water and maximize water retention in soil.

(4) Draining out excess water to pond/reservoir for future use.

(5) Putting some relevant soil and water conservation structures to control erosion.

(6) Maximizing productivity per unit area, per unit time and per unit of water and increasing cropping intensity.

(7) Utilization of marginal lands to its maximum potential use.

(8) Maximizing and stabilizing income of the people of the areas through integrated crop-livestock-tree-labour complex over years and to cut down risks due to aberrant weather conditions.

(9) Developing rural energy management systems, infrastructural facility and improving health,

education and other socio-economic conditions of local residents.

(10) Finally, restoration of the ecosystem towards achieving sustainability.

Based on these principles, the following components were identified which need immediate attention :

(1) Hardware or core components.

(i) Conservation measures (engineering) like bunds, terraces, waterways, etc.

(ii) Water storage structures (surplusing structures).

(iii) Afforestation and plantation.

(2) Software or shell components : Crop and cropping systems (agronomic practices) including pond use and conservation agronomy, etc.

## Benefits of Watershed Management

Mahnot and Singh (1993) outlined the following benefits of watershed management :

(*i*) Sound watershed management means controlling floods and reducing erosion and sediment production.

(*ii*) Maximizing productivity per unit area, per unit time and per unit of water.

(*iii*) Increasing cropping intensity.

(*iv*) Proper utilization of marginal or wastelands through alternate land use systems.

(*v*) Ensuring ecological balance.

(*vi*) Maximizing the combined income from the inter-related crop-livestock-tree-labour complex over years, and

(*vii*) Stabilizing income even under unfavourable weather conditions.

## Factors influencing watershed operations

### A. *Physiography*

#### (*i*) Size

The size or area of watershed, determines the peak runoff rates, which usually increases, as watershed size increases. Peak runoff rate give an idea for designing erosion control structures and channels to carry maximum runoff. The planning and implementation of watershed development plan over a large area (say river basin) is very difficult to manage; hence, small watershed with an area not exceeding 4000 ha should be taken as basic natural planning unit.

#### (*ii*) Shape

Time of concentration (time required for water to flow from the most remote point of the area to the outlet) is more for a long and narrow watershed resulting in lower runoff rates than square shaped watersheds of the same size. Form factor, compactness, coefficients, shape index are some of the indices to characterize shape of a watershed.

#### (*iii*) Relief

Both speed and extent of runoff depends on the slope of the land. The greater the slope, the greater will be the velocity of flow of the runoff water. Flow velocity varies as square root of the velocity drop and consequently, the erosive or cutting capacity is increased by four times of the velocity. The quantity of material that can be carried is increased about 32 times and the size of the particles that can be transported by pushing or rolling is increased by about 64 times if the velocity is doubled. Hence, relief is of prime importance for treatment details and other operational designing.

### (*iv*) Drainage morphometry

Several parameters, like drainage density, bifurcation ratio, stream order, drainage pattern, etc. characterize the basin morphometry. For example, a high drainage density [drainage density = Total length of all streams (km)/catchment area ($km^2$)] drains runoff water rapidly, decreases the lag-time and increases the peak of hydrograph. Interpretation and quantitative analysis of various drainage parameters are needed for quantitative evaluation of surface run-off, infiltration and susceptibility to erosion within the watershed.

## *B. Soils and geology*

Soils and geology of a watershed determine the runoff and sedimentation potential of a watershed, ground water recharge. Geology also determines the availability of material for constructing structures. Geological parameters include type of rocks, stratigraphy.

Soils of a watershed also determine the production potential for which soil survey is essential. Soil data on soil texture, structure, depth, water holding capacity, soil moisture regime, degree of erosion and other soil physical, and chemical properties need to be gathered for a successful watershed planning.

## *C. Land use*

A detailed land use planning aims at utilizing all kinds of resources of the watershed (land, water, vegetation, animals, micro-climate and man) to their fullest potential and capabilities.

## *D. Climatological and meteorological information*

It includes not only precipitation, but also peak time of precipitation, duration and its intensity, apart from other parameters like temperature (mean monthly and annual temperature and their ranges), evaporation, sunshine hours, etc. These data are essential for drainage peak runoff rate and for determining cropping pattern.

### *E. Design peak runoff rate*

Designing of peak runoff rate is very essential for soil and water conservation of a watershed area. There are a number of methods used to estimate runoff. They are rational method, Cook's method, hydrologic soil cover complex number method, table method, etc.

### *F. Socio-economic factors*

The ultimate objective of water development programme is to increase and stabilize socio-economic condition of local people. A detailed record as per capita income, social status, local interest must be collected before implementing any watershed development programme. A socio-economic survey should be carried out before any other activities are undertaken.

## Components of Watershed Management Projects

Based on the objectives, the watershed management programmes have the two major components as under (Mahnot and Singh, 1993) :

(a) **Foundation practices** of engineering and biological measures for soil and water conservation include the following :

  (*i*) Treatment of land and water resources mainly on agricultural lands, such as contour farming, diversion bunds, graded and vegetative bunds, terracing, check dams, vegetative barriers and grassed water ways.

(*ii*) Water storage structures including *nullah* bunds, gully plugs, bunds, anicuts, *khadins* and percolation tanks for efficient utilization of rain water.

(*iii*) Mainly in non-arable lands, alternate land uses like afforestation and plantation of fodder and fuel trees, pasture development supported by rain water conservation measures such as contour trenches, contour furrows, sub-soiling and vegetative and mechanical barriers.

(b) **Improved production practices** such as *In-situ* water conservation practices like contour farming and stubble mulching, improved crop and cropping systems, use of short duration improved crop varieties, fertilizers, plant protection measures and improved implements. It also includes horticulture, plantations, aquaculture, animal husbandry and other practices.

The foundation practices are usually cost-intensive for which the financial assistance is provided by the government. On the other hand, production practices are generally undertaken only by the people themselves and a part of financial assistance is given by the government. People's participation and application of improved soil and water conservation measures will assist in higher production from cultivated, grazing and forest lands and other plant and animal resources on a sustainable basis. Small ponds, check dams and gully plugs will help to mitigate the droughts, conserve and restore soil health and prevent flooding down stream.

## Deterioration of Watershed

Due to changes in the broader system of people and environment, the balance of replenished and consumable resources gets disturbed over time. The flow diagram below (Fig. 2) indicates a problem chain which is rather easy to comprehend. In actual situation, the problem chains are normally complex requiring in-depth investigation to reveal the picture.

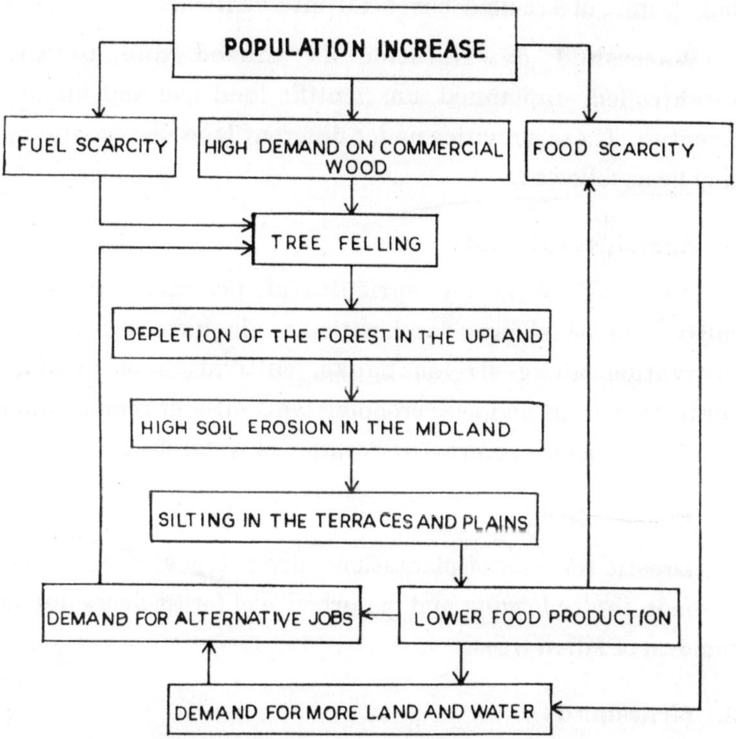


**Fig. 2 :** Problem chain of watershed degradation as excess demand breaks balancing mechanism of the renewable resources

In watershed treatment, land use and cropping patterns are often changed to promote high yielding commercial crop or to provide better opportunities in terms of food security to the deprived sections. Commonly, one notices changes in cropping from dryland crops to high water-intensive sugarcane or irrigated wheat. These changes often pave the way for degradation of land and soil in due course of time. The soil conservation activity serving as the source of gully formation augmenting soil erosion is rather a common feature. This is how the good effects of the watershed treatment fail to last long despite of so called 'beneficial' interventions.

Watershed deterioration is caused due to the uncontrolled, unplanned, unscientific land use and human activities. These activities under different land use conditions may be as follows :

### 1. Agricultural land

Adoption of faulty agricultural practices such as cultivation on sloping land without adequate precaution, cultivation along stream banks, cultivation of erosion-permitting crops and over cropping land without replenishing soil fertility cause severe deterioration of watershed.

### 2. Forest lands

Drastic removal of plantations along slopes, construction of roads, faulty logging and disturbance of forest floors due to removal of fallen trees.

### 3. Grasslands

Disappearance of protective cover due to excessive grazing, compaction of soil reduces infiltration rates and development of tracts into channels and gullies during rainy season.

### 4. Fire

Accidental or intermittent fire results in loss of organic matter (O.M.), vegetation and micro-organisms. Fire also disturbs the hydrological behaviour considerably for a very long period.

**5. Shifting Cultivation**

Shifting cultivation is practised in north-east region of India. Shifting cultivation destroys protective vegetative cover from the soil surface. It also results in soil loss and other consequential damages. Shifting cultivation can cause destruction in the watershed to a greater extent.

**6. Unscientific mining and quarrying**

Unscientific mining and quarrying cause considerable damage to the landscape by destroying the vegetation. The practice of digging up of slopes results in exposure of protective cover. Haphazard disposal of mine, spoils blocks drainage channels and transportation network. It also spreads over agricultural and pasture lands.

**7. Bad Road Alignment and Construction**

This is a major problem in hilly areas. Construction of roads causes dislocation of sediments which contribute to the blockage of flow in drainage channels.

**8. Extension of Industrial Activities**

Haphazard growth of industries destroys protective cover from the land surface of a watershed. Industrial activities also affect the hydrological behaviour of the watershed.

**9. People's Apathy**

Without the people's participation, watershed development programme can not be implemented. People's participation is the key to success of any programme. People's apathy hampers the development activities in a watershed.

In a watershed development approach, it is imperative to assume that each watershed is unique. It is therefore, necessary that the primary step to watershed development should be the proper assessment of its problems, influences, resources and opportunities. The investigation, formulation of the concepts and action to treat must be laid in a logical sequence. Straight action through bypassing essential preparatory steps is likely to show negative results sooner or later.

## Consequences of Watershed Deterioration

Das (1977) has reported that area of 23.85 million of west-central Rajasthan is desertic having annual rainfall of 150-500 mm. Desertic area extends in some parts of Haryana, and Runn of Kutchha. This area mainly suffers from following problems (i) shifting of sand dunes, (ii) wind erosion hazard, (iii) extreme moisture stress, (iv) recurring drought, (v) overgrazing, and (vi) improper land management leading to denuded forest cover and degraded and waste lands.

## Desert Development Programme

The Desert Development Programme (DDP) was initiated in 1977-78 with the objectives of (i) controlling desertification of the desert area through integrating and developing other related state/central/govt. programmes, and (ii) to conserve, develop and harness land, water and other natural resources including rainfall for restoration of ecological balance in the long-term, (iii) The aims of sand dune stabilization, shelter belt plantation and grassland development, (iv) soil and moisture conservation and water resources development.

The programme covers 131 blocks of 21 districts in five states namely, Rajasthan, Haryana, Gujarat (hot arid region), Jammu & Kashmir and Himachal Pradesh (cold arid region).

The total area covered by DDP is about 36.2 million ha. This programme is implemented with 100% central financial assistance.

## Suitable crops and their varieties for drylands

Some important crops and their varieties recommended for dryland conditions are as under :

| | |
|---|---|
| Safflower | - A300, N 62-8 |
| Taramira | - T27, IISA |
| Til or Sesame | - T13, N32 |
| Guar | - Durgapura safed, FS 277 |
| Maize | - Ganga 2, Ganga 5, Vikram |
| Soybean | - Bragg, Ankur |
| Sorghum | - CSH1, CSH2, M35-1, CSH5, JS 20 (fodder) |
| Pearl millet | - PHB 10, Mamupur |
| Groundnut | - TMV1, MI13, T64, S206 |
| Pigeonpea | - Pusa Ageti, Sharada, Prabhat, T21 |
| Castor | - Aruna, GCH3 |
| Cowpea | - C132, FS68, Pusa Barsati, IC10 |
| Wheat | - Pratap, C-306, K-65, WH 410 |
| Sunflower | - EC 68414, EC 68415 |
| Gram | - G24, G130 |
| Linseed | - Neelam, Mukta |
| Mustard | - T-59, BSH1 |
| Lahi/Toria | - T9 |
| Mungbean | - Pusa Baisakhi, S5, S8, Jawahar 45, RS4 |
| Urdbean | - T9 |
| Setaria | - H1, K221-1 |

## Watershed Characteristics

Landform with its slope variation, undulations and land erosion features, soil characteristics and thickness, and rock types (geology) determines the water retention capacity of the watershed. If the land slopes are steep, surface and ground water will have the tendency to flow downwards and exit the watershed quicker. If the soil is thin and porous its capacity to hold water will be low. On the other hand, if the soil is thick and less permeable it can maintain soil moisture for a longer time.

Exposed rocks help quicker draining of water, if the basement (compact, impermeable, basic rock mass) lies deeper, the watershed can hold a higher quantity of ground water.

## Land Slopes

In the plain and valley areas, sources of water are normally active and reliable. The reason being in a river system slopes from all directions converge in the valleys (Fig. 3). In other words, highlands will have a common tendency to lose water from its surface and ground water bodies while in the valley region the same will constantly be enriched and saturated.

Portion of rainwater retained in the upper slopes in soil, rocks and vegetation is released gradually in form of surface flow. It maintains flow in the main river and its tributary systems occupying the valley. Ground water held in the upper slopes maintains a perched groundwater body with a steeper gradient. The groundwater body thus hanging on a high slope is prone to get drained out sooner. This process of the nature retaining rainwater temporarily in the ground water bodies in high slopes helps maintaining the water flow in perennial and semi-perennial streams. The streams flowing for a part of the

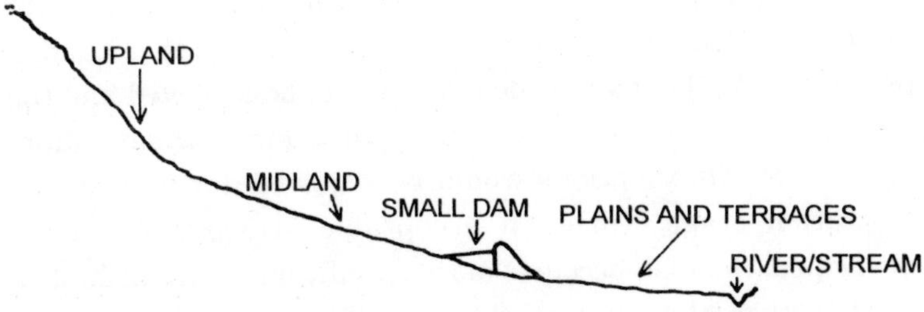


*The Land-Forms : For creating small surface water based irrigation systems, upland is considered as the provider, midland the host while the lowland is the consumer. This is how the water resources is being shared presently. For ground water schemes the vision is yet shortsighted. If well digging is feasible at a point, ground water schemes are passed. In a watershed approach, there is a scope to view the total water resource regime rather than targeting the plot of an individual farmer or for that matter, a larger command area.*

**Fig. 3 :** Land slopes and landform characteristics

year or throughout till the next monsoon play useful role in water management within the watershed (Fouzdar, 1999).

Commonly, the lower slopes and the valley area of the watershed are rich in soil that can hold moisture within for a longer time. Due to high agricultural potential in the valleys and plains, smaller as well as the larger irrigation systems are well developed in these areas. Still, the demand for irrigation in the valley and plains are high and its potential and utility are well known among farmers.

## Watershed Management Strategies and Responses to Problems

Watershed management is concerned with the control of water from upstream to downstream. Once the objectives for watershed management have been established, a general strategy for action requires to be formulated. The distinction between strategy and a plan is subtle and more a matter of scale. Usually, the term strategy refers to the general direction taken to achieve the objectives. On the other hand, a plan refers to the magnitude of targets to be achieved and the timing of the action to be taken to achieve them. Many preliminary informations would be required during strategy formation stage. Once an acceptable strategy has been developed, the task becomes more specific and more technical. At this stage, there is a need to identify different actions that could be used to implement the strategy and produce desired results.

Watershed management involves employment of non-structural (vegetation management) and structural (engineering) activities when conditions warrant them. Soil conservation measures and land use planning activities can be the tools employed in watershed management. The activities employed may be water harvesting structures, establishing protected reserves and developing regulations to guide road building, timber harvesting and agro-forestry practices. The ultimate focus in all cases is on how these activities affect the relationship between water and other natural resources in a watershed. The integrating factor is water. The focus on water and its interrelationship with other natural resources and their use distinguishes watershed management from other natural resource management strategies.

In practice, activities using natural resources are carried out by individuals, local administrations, and different groups that control land in a political framework that has little relationships to the boundaries of a watershed. Activities are carried out independently, usually with little regard to how these activities affect other areas. However, in spite of independent or political and economic activities, it remains a fact that water and its constituents flow downhill and ignore political boundaries. Activities undertaken at upstream can affect the welfare of those people living downstream. It is necessary that the physical facts of watershed and the political realities be brought together. This is the aim of integrated watershed management.

Watershed management activities are employed in preventive strategies aimed at preserving existing sustainable land use practices. Restorative strategies are also designed to overcome identified problems or to restore conditions in a watershed to a desirable level. Desirable level is used both in environmental and in political terms. The aim of preventive strategies is to prevent a problem in a watershed. The objective of restorative strategies is to restore conditions once problem has occurred in a watershed.

In real situations, a continuum is followed going from regulatory support and reinforcement of existing sustainable land use practices (preventing strategy) to emergency relief, building of temporary gully control structures, removing cattle, or restricting land use on fragile, eroded lands (restorative strategy). In most of the cases of watershed management things are between the two extremes. Routine preventive strategies and activities are fully as essential as the more dramatic and visible restorative activities, losses avoided (through preventive strategies) can be just as important to people as gains from solving a problem. In economic terms, the cost of preventing losses of productivity may be much lower than the cost of achieving the same advantages through more dramatic activities to restore productivity on problem lands that have already been damaged.

Table 1 presents the most common situations encountered and alternative solutions (preventive or restorative) for overcoming them as they relate to watershed management objectives (Brooks *et al.*, 1997).

**Table 1 :** The role of watershed management in developing solution to natural resource problems

| Problem | Possible alternative solutions | Associated watershed management objectives |
|---|---|---|
| Deficient water supplies | Reservoir storage and water transport | Minimize sediment delivery to reservoir site, maintain watershed vegetative cover |
| | Water harvesting | Develop localized collection and storage facilities |
| | Vegetation manipulation, evapo-transpiration reduction | Convert from deep-rooted to shallow rooted species or from conifers to deciduous trees |
| | Cloud seeding | Maintain vegetative cover to minimize erosion |
| | Desalinization of ocean water | Not applicable |
| | Pumping of deep ground water and irrigation | Management of recharge areas |
| Flooding | Reservoir storage | Minimize sediment delivery to reservoir site, maintain watershed vegetative cover |
| | Construct levees, channelization etc. | Minimize sediment delivery to downstream channels |
| | Flood plain management | Zoning of lands to minimize human activities in flood prone areas, minimize sedimentation of channels |
| | Revegetate disturbed and denuded areas | Plant and manage appropriate vegetative cover |

*Contd....*

| | | |
|---|---|---|
| Energy shortages | Utilize wood for fuel | Plant perpetual fast growing tree species, maintain productivity of sites, minimize erosion |
| | Develop hydroelectric power project | Minimize sediment delivery to reservoirs and river channels, sustain water yield |
| Food shortages | Develop agroforestry | Maintain site productivity, minimize erosion, promote species compatible with soils and climate of area |
| | Increase cultivation | Restructure hill slopes and other areas susceptible to erosion, utilize contour ploughing, terraces, etc. |
| | Increase livestock production | Develop herding-grazing systems for sustained yield and productivity |
| | Import food from outside watershed | Develop forest resource for pulp, wood and wildlife products etc. to provide economic base |
| Erosion/ sedimentation from denuded landscapes | Erosion control structures | Maintain life of structures by revegetation and management |
| | Contour terracing | Revegetate, mulch, stabilise slopes and institute land use guidelines |
| | Revegetate | Establish, protect and manage vegetative cover until site recovers |

*Contd....*

| | | |
|---|---|---|
| Poor quality drinking water | Develop alternative supplies from wells and pumps | Protect ground water from contamination |
| | Treat water supplies | Filter through wetlands and uplands forests |
| Polluted streams/ reduced fishery production | Control pollutants entering streams | Develop buffer strips along stream channels, maintain vegetative cover on watershed, develop guidelines for riparian zones |
| | Treat waste water | Use forests and wetlands as secondary treatment systems for waste water |

**Source :** Brooks *et al.*, 1997

## Preventive Strategies : The Key to Watershed Management

There is a general impression that watershed management most often involves the restoration of degraded lands. Problems of soil erosion, gully formation, flooding or water deficit resulting from abusive land use require action, generally in the form of engineering structures and revegetation in the problem areas. The natural disasters and problem of human suffering associated with resource depletion and degradation generally get more attention than quiet successes. Similarly, the mobilization of people and equipment to renovate devastated areas receives public attention. It is an effective way to get attention to serious problem. However, it is not always true that watershed management comes into play only when problems arise.

An important feature of watershed management is that of establishing and sustaining preventive measures which include implementing land use practices on a day to day basis that result in long-term, sustainable resource development and productivity without causing land degradation. Usually, land and natural resource management agencies have established policies that embody sound watershed management principles. The preventive practices represent the ultimate objective of watershed management.

The role of watershed managers should be to achieve the required goods and services desired by society without adversely affecting long-term productivity and without causing unwanted environmental change. People who occupy watersheds should be an integral part of any watershed management programme.

The dilemma in watershed management is that the land use required to sustain the survival of society over the long term can be at cross purposes with what is important to the survival of the individual over the short term. Food and natural resources requirements of the present should not be met at the expense of future generations. It is essential that sustainable natural resource development should consider watershed boundaries, the linkages between uplands and downstream areas, and the effects of land use practices on the long-term productivity. Land use practices that are at cross purposes with environmental capabilities can not be sustained on long-term basis. However, sustainable productivity and environmental protection can be achieved by following integrated and holistic approach for management of watersheds.

## Techniques of harvesting rain water

The increasing population and urbanization are having effects on the availability and quality of water. In this situation the activity of artificial recharge to ground water through rain water harvesting is an indispensable measure. Rain water harvesting is the technique of collection and storage of rain water at surface or in sub-surface aquifer before it is lost.

Now-a-days rain water harvesting and artificial recharging of ground water technology have come as a bonanza for urban lives to remove drinking water problem to the maximum extent possible with minimum cost effect. This technology involves the process of augmenting the natural infiltration of rain water or surface runoff into underground formation by some artificial methods. The augmented resource can be harvested in the time of need. Its advantages are many. For instance, the cost of recharge to sub-surface reservoir is low. The aquifer serves as a distribution system also. No land is wasted for storage purpose and no population displacement is involved. Ground water is not directly exposed to evaporation and pollution. Storing water under ground is environment friendly. It increases the productivity of aquifer. It reduces flood havoc, mitigates effects of drought, reduces soil erosion and raises ground water table. It is common and community duty that every citizen in India should adopt this programme and help to improve the environment (Yadav, 2003).

## Methods and Techniques

The methods of ground water recharge are :

(*i*) **Urban areas** : Roof top rain water/storm runoff harvesting through recharge pit, recharge trench, tube-well and recharge well.

(*ii*) **Rural areas** : Rain water harvesting through gully plug, contour bund, Gabion structure, percolation tank, check dam/cement plug/nala bund, recharge shaft, dug well recharge and ground water, dams/ subsurface dyke, *khadeens*, anicuts, etc.

In urban areas, rain water available from roof tops of buildings, paved and unpaved areas goes waste. This water can be recharged to aquifer and can be utilized gainfully at the time of need. The rain water harvesting system needs to be designed in a way that it does not occupy large space for collection and recharge system. It can be as follows :

(*i*) In alluvial areas where permeable rocks are exposed on the land surface or at very shallow depths, roof top rain water harvesting can be done through Recharge Pits.

(*ii*) Recharge trenches can be used for buildings with roof area of 200/300 $km^2$.

(*iii*) In areas where the shallow aquifers have dried up and existing tube-wells are tapping deeper aquifer, roof top rain water harvesting through existing tube wells can be adopted to recharge the deeper aquifers.

(*iv*) In areas where the surface soil is impervious and large quantities of roof water or surface runoff is available within a very short period of heavy rainfall, the use of trench/pits is made to store the water in a filter media and subsequently recharge to groundwater through specially constructed Recharge wells.

In rural areas, rain water harvesting is taken up considering watershed as a unit. Surface spreading techniques are common since space for such system is available in plenty and quantity of recharged water is also large. Following techniques may be adopted to save water going waste through slopes, rivers, rivulets and *nalas* :

(*i*) Rain water harvesting can be done through gully plug using local stone, clay and bushes across small gullies and streams.

(*ii*) The Contour Bund technique is effective method to conserve soil moisture in a watershed.

(*iii*) Rain water harvesting through Gabion structure is a kind of check dam commonly constructed across small streams to conserve stream flows with practically no submergence beyond stream course.

(*iv*) Rain water harvesting through Check Dams/Cement Plugs/Nala bunds constructed across small streams having gentle slope is very useful. The site selected should have sufficient thickness of permeable bed or weathered formation to facilitate recharge of stored water within short span of time.

(*v*) Rainwater harvesting through Recharge Shaft is the most efficient and cost effective technique to recharge unconfined aquifer overlain by poorly permeable strata.

(*vi*) In another technique, that is, rainwater harvesting through dugwell recharge, the existing and abandoned dug wells may be utilized as recharge structures after cleaning and desilting the same.

(*vii*) Another important technique is groundwater dams or sub-surface dykes technique. Sub-surface dyke or underground dam is a sub-surface barrier across stream which retards the base flow and stores water upstream below ground surface. By doing so, the water levels in upstream part of ground water dam rises saturating otherwise dry part of aquifer.

## Traditional Methods of Water Harvesting in Rajasthan

Water is the most precious commodity in Rajasthan due to unfavourable environmental situations. In most part of

Rajasthan, the quantities of water available from surface and ground water are not sufficient to meet the requirements for agriculture, domestic and industrial purposes. The history of Rajasthan reveals that the rain water harvesting had been practiced since time immemorial. The traditional methods of rain water harvesting include (i) anicut (ii) *khadeen* (iii) *nadi*, and (v) *tanka* (Singh *et al.*, 2003). A brief description of these techniques is as under :

### *(i) Anicut*

Anicut is a weir structure constructed across the natural drain for impounding of water in the drain. It is basically constructed on hilly regions where hilly streams carry large amount of runoff during monsoon. The stored water behind the anicut is used for supplemental irrigation besides providing the drinking water for human beings and livestock. Anicut also serves the purpose of recharging of ground water (Laddha *et al.*, 1996). Hence, anicut plays an important role in conservation and management of groundwater to ensure sustained agriculture production. Anicut reduces erosive velocity of run-off and thus prevents the formation of gullies.

Suitability of site for construction of anicut depends upon both technical and economical considerations. The slope of the drain at the construction site of anicut should be <3.0%. The catchment are of anicut differs from region to region depending upon the rainfall pattern. For 750 mm annual rainfall, the catchment area may be kept from 25 tc 100 ha.

### *(ii) Khadeen*

*Khadeens* are water harvesting structures on low lying lands where crops are raised by conserving rain water received from the relatively impervious uplands. *Khadeen* is a land use system developed centuries ago in Jaisalmer area of Rajasthan. It is practiced where rocky catchments and valley plain occur in proximity. The water is harvested during monsoon months and allowed to stand in the low lying farm lands during major period of rainy season. The soils in the *khadeens* are extremely fertile because of the frequent deposition of fine sediment.

*Khadeen* also helps in recharging the ground water thus increasing the discharge of surrounding wells. It reduces the soil erosion because of reducing the total length of travel. In arid zone, by construction of *khadeen* migration during dry season may be stopped by assured water supply and increased vegetation. It saves labour and time for fetching water for animals.

### *(iii) Nadi*

Dug out embankment pond is called *Nadi*. *Nadi* is a water harvesting structure. These are the principal source of drinking water in the arid zone of Rajasthan. The depth of *Nadi* may vary from 1.5 to 12 m. The capacity may range from 400 $m^3$ to 70000 $m^3$. *Nadis* have a drainage basins of various shapes and sizes (8 to 2000 ha). *Nadi* consists an earthen embankment. It collects water from relatively impervious reaches of the watershed. *Nadi* is constructed in low lying area and slope of watershed is maintained for maximum discharge of water.

### *(iv) Tanka*

*Tanka* is a local name given to a covered underground tank in western Rajasthan. Tanka is a low cost water harvesting structure for providing safe domestic water supply in western Rajasthan. It is made of masonary or concrete for collection and storage of surface runoff. Rain water harvesting in a *tanka* offers the advantages of private ownership. *Tankas* exist on village common land and the catchment area is often used for grazing livestock as well.

The shape of the *tanka* is usually kept as circular or rectangular. The circular *tanka* is most economical structure. The capacity of the *tanka* depends on the consumption of water for domestic purpose. Generally, a two hectare catchment of compact size, 3 to 6% slope, gravelly soils and free from vegetation is quite sufficient for a *tanka* of 200 $m^3$ capacity in western Rajasthan. Yearly disilting of *tanka* is essential before onset of the monsoon.

## Benefits of Artificial Recharge & Water Harvesting

The benefits are many in number and various in nature, most important are :

(*i*) Improvement in infiltration and reduction in run-off,

(*ii*) increase in ground water levels and yields,

(*iii*) reduces strain on municipal water supply, and

(*iv*) increase in ground water quality, etc.

Taking 800 mm as an average rainfall in Chennai city, for a plot of $150m^2$, the total volume of rainfall recharge would be 75 $m^3$ which works to 75000 litres of water. This will meet the water requirement of a family of 5 members for about 10 days in a year (Ganesan, 1999).

## Integrated Water Management

The basic aim of integrated water management (IWM) is saving of irrigation water as well as increasing water use efficiency. These can be achieved by developing efficient irrigation schedules in terms of volume and time of application, optimization of designs for irrigation methods, better crop planning and judicious agronomic management. Micro-irrigation systems can save irrigation water upto 20-50% in horticultural crops. Where irrigation efficiency of traditional methods is merely 30-50%, it is upto 70-75% and 90-95% for sprinklers and drip methods, respectively. Development of multi-irrigation system will further help in optimal allocation and utilization of water resources (Singh *et al.*, 2002).

Watershed, a natural hydrological unit is a good device for water harvesting. Proper watershed management can check not only further deterioration of ecosystem, but degraded lands can also be restored. In India, 68% (92 million ha) cropped area is still rainfed, where productivity can just be doubled if irrigation facility is provided. For rainfed agriculture, both *in situ* conservation as well as water harvesting are equally important measures to ensure efficient water management. Present strategy for rainfed agriculture should be based on integrated management of watershed and promotion of farming system approach with a view to evolve methods for sustainable agriculture in these areas.

Providing good drainage facility is also a basic component of efficient water use system (Priyanka, 2000).

## Issues to be addressed

The conceptualization of integrated treatment of lands on watershed basis dates back to the year 1949 when, an interdisciplinary department of soil conservation of the then Damodar Valley Corporation adopted and implemented the programme. Being an isolated programme, it could not produce any impact at the national level. This idea consolidated during 1957 in a meeting at Hazaribagh (organized jointly by the FAO and Govt. of India). Consequently, different major watershed management projects were taken up in different parts of the country. In the early seventies, the major objective was to reduce the sediment load and siltation in reservoirs (and also in catchments of selected flood prone rivers); and river valley projects were launched in 1962-63. But these projects failed to achieve the target. It has been reported that Tungabhadra reservoir is left with 24% of its designed life, Nizam Sagar with 6% and Bhakra with 68%. Subsequently, Drought Prone Area Programme (DPAP) (1972-73) and Desert Development Programme (1977-78) were started with the objectives of drought management and for improving desert areas, respectively. Recently, National Watershed Development Programme for Rainfed Areas (NWDPRA) was initiated in 1986-87 for development of the rainfed/dryland areas. The primary objective of this programme is to stabilize agricultural production in rainfed areas, which constitute nearly 68% of total geographical area of our country comprising 33% in the low rainfall region (<750 mm) and 35% under medium rainfall region (750-1175 mm). Till date, no appreciable improvement was found out (Anonymous, 1994).

Integrated Watershed Development Programme (IWDP) has come up as an excellent national approach. Though government, NGOs, financial agencies provided a strong support in terms of money and efforts, the achievements are more close to the imagination and far from the actual goal. Piecemeal approaches to address particular problems; inadequacy of organization for planning, organizing and implementing the programmes; inefficient skills needed for collecting and interpreting data; lack of proper coordination among research and development departments; technologies being mostly sectorial and addressed to specific problems; lack of identification and appreciation of the grass root problems and overall lack of people's participation made the story quite disappointing.

For getting quick success the development strategies, which are somewhat foreign to the respective natural system were adopted, while the traditional knowledge and experience were many times neglected. On ground, there are a few success stories of watershed development, which include traditional wisdom. For a programme, which aims at sustainability, people's participation must be an essential component, as it is the local inhabitants, who should be the main authority. Grass root democracy is the first and preliminary requirement before starting any watershed development project. Such projects have been included in the schedule of subjects to be handled by the 'Gram Panchayats' after the 73$^{rd}$ Amendment. People of the area must have a feeling that it is their development programme and hence, land and water conservation programmes should originate from the actual need of them. In fact, the indigenous and traditional wisdom and knowledge must be considered first and then should be reinforced with the advanced science and technologies. At the same time, the adopted technologies must not be very costly and should be based on the existing natural resources. Agronomic practices are always preferable to the engineering structures. There should not be any dogmatic stand in favour of the low cost technologies, but a rational approach towards integrating the hard and soft components of a watershed is essential. So far, the watershed management programmes were aimed mostly at soil and water conservation practices. This approach could minimize the detachment and transportation of soil to reservoirs, thus increasing the life of the reservoir, but it neglected the production aspect, which is of prime importance to the farmers and village community of that area. According to many scientists, too much emphasis has been given to the quantification of soil loss and land degradation. The other side, i.e., the agricultural production in terms of monetary return to the farmers was grossly overlooked.

Another crucial issue, which needs to be addressed immediately, is the lack of documentation, which could provide systematic data/information base for planning integrated watershed management. The approach is to gather, in a systematic way, basic information of the process occurring in a watershed (like rainfall, data related to various aspects and parameters of crop production, status of natural vegetation and forests, ground water status, water level in the ponds and other reservoirs, water use and other relevant data) involving the watershed community. The information may be divided into several components like general (total area, stream length, soil types, water holding capacity of soils, cultivated and uncultivated area, irrigated/unirrigated land, etc.), climate (agro-climate set up, annual rainfall, number of rainy days, average humidity, etc.), water resources (drainage lines, drainage orders, ground water status, peak runoff flow, etc.) and socio-economic information of local people. They should be encouraged to form a 'Resource Management Society' to take up these activities in future. These data will be of immense value for the researchers for identifying and solving the problems (Singh and Shekhawat, 2000).

Resource mobilization is another important issue. A number of scientists are working in different institutes and organizations for the cause of development of agricultural production keeping in view the sustainability and stability of the system. The human resources should be mobilized to take up the task and lead from the front. The research, extension and development must be integrated in a single capsule to achieve the target of integrated watershed development.

## Conclusions

In arid and semi-arid regions, uncertain, erratic and scanty rains, coupled with meager irrigation facilities, lead to low and unstable crop yields. Low and erratic rainfall, high evaporation rate and low water holding capacity of surface soils constitute the principal natural resource constraints in agricultural production in these regions. Therefore, success in rainfed agriculture depends upon the efficient utilization of rain water. The question arises how and when this available water can be utilized to best advantage? An appropriate solution seems to lie in the collection of runoff water and application at critical stages of crop growth during long spell of dry days as part of *In-situ* management of harvested water. In addition to irrigation, the harvested water can be used for drinking purposes for livestock and human beings.

A projection of the needs of food, fodder and fibre (3Fs) for increasing population by the 2010 A.D. reveals a very alarming demand. If the food production is to be doubled by 2025, against the present level of food grains production at about 203.9 million tonnes during 1999-2000, it is to be achieved without sacrificing the precious forest lands, which are already dwindling and without upsetting ecological balance. Adoption of sound land use planning, as a method of scientific upgradation is must. In order to obtain maximum sustained benefits from technological advancements for optimizing production, it is imperative that the precious natural resources of soil and water should be judiciously used. Watershed development is a holistic approach aimed at optimizing the use of land, water and vegetation in an area, so as to provide an answer to alleviate drought, moderate floods, prevent soil erosion, improve water availability and increase fuel, fodder and agricultural production on a sustained basis.

Dr. M.S. Swaminathan has rightly pointed out ".....It is through the protection of our life support systems and working for the conservation of the environment - the prime requisites for sustainable development - that we can ensure to build a "National Ecological Security system". The watershed based development approach is undoubtedly an agreeable concept to be set as the goal. But this approach demands a massive people's movement - a decentralized bottom up participatory management system, to make the village community self-reliant. Or in other words, these ecologically sound development programmes are much economically viable and can provide employment opportunities for the people.

The world conservation strategy adopted for India, has one major component in the programme, that is, management of natural resources, the soil and water on watershed basis. Thus, watershed management has become the corner stone of planning and development in agricultural sector. Watershed management in dryland agriculture is an integration of technologies, within the natural boundaries of a development area, for optimum development of land, water and plant resources to meet the basic minimum needs of people in a sustained manner. This programme must be taken up on priority basis in a big way. In the words of Dr. M.S. Swaminathan, "for the future welfare of dryland farmers and for the conservation and development of our land and water resources, scientific management of watersheds needs to become a mass movement".

## References

Anonymous (1994) *Guidelines for Watershed Development*. Ministry of Rural Development, Government of India, New Delhi, pp. 90.

Brooks, K.N., Fflolliott, P.F., Gragersen and DeBano, L.F. (1997) *Hydrology and Management of Watersheds*, 2nd edn. Iowa State University Press, Ames, pp. 502.

Chakraborty, D. and Mukherjee, J. (2001) Watershed management. *Employment News*, 25(51): 1-2.

Das, D.C. (1977) Soil conservation practices and erosion control in India : A case study of soils. FAO bulletin, Rome, 33:11.

Dhruv Narayan, V.V., Shashtri, G. and Patnaik, U.S. (1993) *Watershed Management*, Publication and Information Division, ICAR, Krishi Anusandhan Bhawan, New Delhi, pp. 454.

Fouzdar, D. (1999) Watershed development concept and strategic land water management options. Yojna, 43(10) : 26-30 and 49.

Ganesan, G. (1999) Harvesting rain water. Environment and People, July, 1999, pp. 21-23.

Kanwar, J.S. (1997) Fertilizer policy issues (2000-2025) National Academy of Agriculture Science, India. 3rd Agriculture Science Congress, March, 12-15, 1997.

Laddha, R., Singh, P.K. and Singh, R.V. (1996) Effect of soil and water conservation measures on ground water recharge, Proc. 3rd Int. Agril. Engg. Conference held at Pune, Dec. 9-12, pp. 7.

Mahnot, S.C. and Singh, P.K. (1993) *Soil and Water Conservation*. Inter Co-operation Co-ordination Office, Jaipur, pp. 90.

Mc Cuen, R.N. (1989) Hydrologic analysis and Design. Prentice Hall, New Jersey, pp. 876.

Priyanka,K.(2000) Natural resource management : Towards sustainable agriculture in 21st century. Employment News, 24(46) : 1-3.

Sanio, M. (1998) Waste not, want not. Urban age. Summer, pp. 18-20.

Sheng, T.C. (1990) *Watershed Management Field Manual*. Watershed survey and planning FAO conservation guide, 13/6, Food and Agriculture Organization of the United Nations, Rome, pp. 170.

Singh, K.K. and Shekhawat, M.S. (2000) Watershed approach to dryland agriculture. Indian Farming, 50(5) : 4-8 and 44.

Singh, K.K., Swami, B.L. and Kapoor, B.B.S. (2002) Techniques of soil conservation and water harvesting for arable lands. Chapter 3, *In : Current Environmental Issues* (Eds.

B.B.S.Kapoor, Ahmed Ali, K.K.Singh and Chandrakanta), Madhu Publications, Bikaner, pp. 53-76.

Singh, R.P. (1994) Management and recycling of run-off water in the Indian arid zone. *In Sustainable Development of the Indian Arid Zone : A Research Perspective* (Eds. R.P.Singh and Surendra Singh), Scientific Publishers, Jodhpur, pp. 232-239.

Tideman, E.M. (1996) *Watershed Management : Guidelines for Indian Conditions*. Omega Scientific Publishers, New Delhi, pp. 372.

Yadav, S. (ed.) (2003) *Water Problem and Its Management*. Hope Indian Publications, Gurgaon - 122017, pp. 142-144.

# CHAPTER 6

# INDUSTRIAL PARTICULATE POLLUTION AND AGRO-ECODEGRADATION IN KASHMIR HIMALAYAN VALLEY

**F.A. Lone and M.A. Khan**
Division of Environmental Sciences,
S.K. University of Agricultural Sciences and Technology of Kashmir
Shalimar Campus, Srinagar - 191121

## ABSTRACT

A study was carried out to investigate the impact of cement dust on crocin content, floristic characteristics and yield of saffron (*Crocus sativus*) along with its impact on soils. The effect of cement dust on *Phaseolus vulgaris* and *Brassica oleracea* and other vegetation are discussed in detail.

**Key Words :** Cement Dust, Saffron, Pollution

## Introduction

The atmosphere which makes up the largest fraction of the biosphere, is a dynamic system that continuously absorbs a wide range of solids, liquids and gases from both natural and man made sources. These substances travel through air, disperse and react with one another and with other substances both physically and chemically. Most of the constituents eventually find their way into a depository such as the ocean, or to a receptor such as man.

In general, the actions of people are the primary causes of pollution and as the population increases, the pollution problems also increase proportionately. The first significant change in man's effect on nature came with his discovery of fire. Pre-historic man built a fire in his cave for cooking, heating and to provide light. The problems of air pollution came into existence at this time.

It was for the first time in 1273 A.D. that the British Parliament passed an Act in 1273, forbidding the burning of coal in London because it was beginning to choke the atmosphere. In 1300 A.D. King Edward I issued a royal proclamation, "whosoever shall be found guilty of burning coal shall suffer the loss of his head". In 1306, a man was executed for violating this regulation. Later, the law fell into disuse as the industrial revolution took place in England (Rao and Rao, 1999).

Kashmir valley, popularly known as the paradise on earth, presents no less hellish picture than any other polluted area of the country. Its serene and refreshing environs, its placid waters and its mesmerisingly tranquil atmosphere all used to be free from any pollution till recent times. For the last two decades, the atmosphere of Kashmir valley has shown signs of deterioration due to the growing number of vehicles, establishment of cement factories, stone crushers, brick kilns, coal burning in hardcoke stoves, burning of garbage and fallen leaves for charcoal making, bomb blasts, firing and land mines, etc. In the following text a review of work carried out related to the ecological impact of cement industries (particulate pollution) in Kashmir valley is discussed in detail.

## Cement Industries and Agro-Ecodegradation

The cement industries are one of the basic industries on which industrial development of a country depends. It is manufactured from a suitable mixture of lime stone and clay or from marls which are first crushed and ground, either in the dry state or with water. The raw mixture is thereafter burnt at a sintering temperature and the clinker thus obtained is ground to a fine powder with the addition of gypsum, to give cement. The cement produced by the Khrew cement factory (JK Minerals) usually contains Lime stone = 78%, Clay = 22.5%, Iron ore = 1.5% and Gypsum = 5%. The chemical composition of the cement is as follows :

| Constituent | | % by weight |
|---|---|---|
| CaO | | 61.53 |
| $SiO_2$ | | 22.75 |
| $Al_2O_3$ | | 6.90 |
| MgO | | 4.20 |
| $Fe_2O_3$ | | 3.10 |
| $SO_3$ | | 0.27 |
| Insoluble residue | | 0.53 |
| Alkalies | (*a*) $Na_2O$ | 0.22 |
| | (*b*) $K_2O$ | 0.66 |
| Ignition loss | | 0.62 |

In Kashmir valley there is a great potential for cement production as the main raw material (lime stone) is available in plenty in the hillocks adjoining Khunmoh (district Srinagar), Wuyan, Khrew (district Pulwama) and several other places. Presently, around six factories are operational in these areas and many more are on anvil. These factories, according to recent estimates, produce about 1500 tonnes of cement per day and release an enormous amount of cement dust in the atmosphere causing severe ecological damage to all life forms including flora, fauna and humans. The dust settles on the vegetation in the form of hard crust blocking stomata and bringing about changes in the morphology and physiology of the various metabolic processes. Since, plants are being constantly exposed to the environment, they absorb and accumulate pollutants on the foliar surfaces. Consequently, they undergo changes which if properly quantified can serve as measure of pollution affecting plants.

The dust fall measures at a distance of 1 and 2 km from the Khrew cement factory (district Pulwama) have been found to be 2.08 and 1.19 g $m^{-2}$ $day^{-1}$ respectively (Lone, 2004). The dust emanating from the factories has virtually transformed the entire agricultural land (near the vicinity of the factory) into barren land and many agricultural crops including saffron have suffered severe losses due to dust pollution.

## IMPACT OF CEMENT DUST ON SAFFRON

### Economic Important and Plant Characteristics of Saffron

Saffron is an important cash crop of Kashmir and in the valley it is mainly grown in the Karewas of Pampore (district Pulwama) where around six factories are operational in the areas adjoining saffron fields. The details of the saffron growing areas in different districts of Jammu and Kashmir and the production, productivity and the land under its cultivation are given in tables 1-3. Saffron, also called the golden condiment, is the nature's best food flowering and coloring substance with reputed medicinal properties. In Kashmir valley it is the legendary crop and has been grown since very ancient times. The recorded account of saffron cultivation in Kashmir dates back to 550 A.D., nearly four centuries earlier than its recorded cultivation in Spain by Arabs around 961 A.D. In India, commercial saffron production is exclusive to Kashmir which has the worlds largest saffron acreage. The commercial saffron is the dried carpellary portion (stigma) of the flower of *Crocus sativus*. The best known spice of family Iridaceae. The chief pigment of the saffron is its yellowish red glycoside crocin. Picrocrocin is the bitter testing pigment and it too is a glycoside. The average percentage composition of saffron is water (15.6%), starch and sugar (13.55%), essential oil (0.60), fixed oil (5.63%), Total N free extract (43.64%), crude fibre (4.48%), Ash (4.27%) (Kannan, 2002). It is rich in potassium and phosphorus with traces of boron. The aroma is accredited to volatile oils. The coloring agent is crocin ($CH_4H_{64}O_{26}.H_2O$). The coloring component of Kashmir saffron is 13-14.5%.

**Table 1 :** Saffron growing areas in different districts of Jammu and Kashmir

| District | Areas under saffron cultivation |
|---|---|
| Pulwama | Quil, Gooso, Malangpora, Chursoo, Tral, Awantipora, Barso, Leitpora, Pattalbagh, Chandhoor, Kramchoo, Indroos, Mandikpal, Drusu*, Konibal, Gundbal*, Ladoo*, Khrew*, Wuyan* |
| Budgam | Kokoring, Chrawni, Hayatpur, Dardpora, Nawgam, Badipora, Chadoora, Gopalpora, Nowbug |
| Srinagar | Khunmoh*, Zawoora*, Zawoosa, Zewan*, Balhama*, Ganderbal |
| Baramulla | Wanigam, Pattam, Kreeri, Palhalan, Taper, Waripora, Safapora |
| Anantnag | Bijbehara |
| Doda | Poochal, Hular, Chahard, Bandakoot, Sangrambata, Podyarana, Nayal, Hata |

* The areas under the impact of cement dust pollution

**Table 2 :** District-wise distribution of area, production and productivity of saffron

| District | Year | Area (ha) | Production (q) | Productivity (kg $ha^{-1}$) |
|---|---|---|---|---|
| Pulwama | 1996-97 | 4987 | 141.13 | 2.83 |
| | 1999 | 3428 | 62.04 | 1.81 |
| | 2000 | 2325 | 29.20 | 1.26 |
| | 2001 | 2161 | 1.42 | 0.07 |
| Budgam | 1996-97 | 439 | 10.93 | 2.49 |
| | 1999 | 350 | 8.15 | 2.32 |
| | 2000 | 291 | 3.93 | 1.35 |
| | 2001 | 362 | 0.97 | 0.26 |
| Srinagar | 1996-97 | 210 | 5.18 | 2.47 |
| | 1999 | 211 | 5.15 | 2.45 |
| | 2000 | 210 | 2.66 | 1.27 |
| | 2001 | 210 | 0.20 | 0.09 |
| Anantnag | 1996-97 | 27 | 0.72 | 2.67 |
| | 1999 | 8 | 0.16 | 2.00 |
| | 2000 | 5 | 0.12 | 2.40 |
| | 2001 | 0 | 0.0 | 0.0 |
| Doda | 1996-97 | 44 | 1.55 | 3.52 |
| | 1999 | 45 | 2.18 | 4.84 |
| | 2000 | 45 | - | - |
| | 2001 | 46 | 0.044 | 0.009 |

**Source** : Planning and Statistics, Financial Commissioner Office, J&K Govt., Srinagar

**Table 3 :** Data on the area under cultivation of saffron production and productivity in Jammu and Kashmir State from 1982-2001

| Year | Area under cultivation (ha) | Production of commercial saffron (q) | Productivity (kg $ha^{-1}$) |
|---|---|---|---|
| 1982 | 3185 | 44.00 | 1.38 |
| 1983 | 3699 | 90.00 | 2.43 |
| 1984 | 3848 | 88.00 | 2.28 |
| 1985 | 3566 | 46.00 | 1.28 |
| 1986 | 3655 | 85.00 | 2.32 |
| 1987 | 3798 | 85.00 | 2.23 |
| 1988 | 3713 | 87.00 | 2.34 |
| 1989 | 4000 | 90.00 | 2.25 |
| 1990 | 4050 | 130.00 | 3.20 |
| 1991 | 4050 | 130.00 | 3.20 |
| 1992 | 4496 | 130.65 | 2.906 |
| 1993 | 4496 | 134.25 | 2.986 |
| 1994 | 4496 | 141.28 | 3.142 |
| 1995 | 5707 | 159.52 | 2.79 |
| 1996 | 5707 | 159.52 | 2.79 |
| 1997 | 5361 | 173.82 | 3.24 |
| 1998 | 4161 | 130.21 | 3.13 |
| 1999 | 4042 | 77.68 | 1.92 |
| 2000 | 2876 | 35.91 | 1.25 |
| 2001 | 2779 | 2.63 | 0.094 |

**Source**: Financial Commissioner Office, Jammu and Kashmir Govt., Srinagar

## Plant Characteristics

The saffron (*Crocus sativus*) belongs to family Iridaceae. It is a perennial low growing herb with globulus corm ranging from 0.5 to 5.0 cm in diameter. The corms produce 6-15 narrow needle like channeled leaves about 10-15 cm long surrounded in the lower region by 4-5 scales. The flowers are borne singly or in twos and threes. They are funnel shaped about 7-8 cm long. The parianth is made up of six segments in two series and are violet or reddish purple in colour. Androecium consists of three stamens with short filaments and long yellow anthers. Pistil bears elongated pale yellow existed filiform styles, divided at the top into brilliant orange red, trifid stigma 25 to 30 mm in length. The stigma alongwith the style, when dried, constitute the pure saffron of commerce. The cultivated saffron is auto-triploid and is sterile with 2n=3x24 chromosomes.

## Growth performance of saffron under alkaline dust pollution

A study was carried out to assess the impact of cement dust on the growth performance of saffron growing under ambient field condition around the cement factory situated at Khrew (Lone, 2004). This factory being the largest in Kashmir valley produces almost 12000 tonnes of cement per day and releases enormous amount of cement dust in the surrounding atmosphere. The dust fall measured at a distance of 1 and 2 km from the Khrew cement factory (district Pulwama) has been found to be 2.08 and 1.19 g $m^{-2}$ $day^{-1}$ respectively in the year 2002 (Lone, 2004). However, after the installation of electrostatic precipitator the dust emission has significantly reduced. Mature corms of saffron were sown 20 cm apart in rows spaced 25 cm in 1.5x3 $m^2$ plots in September, 2002 in the selected plots at sites S-1 and S-2 situated, at 1 and 2 km from the Khrew cement factory, respectively, in combined

Randomized Block Design. Another, plot which served as control (site-C) was established at 5 km distance from the cement factory in a cross wind direction and was free of any dust pollution.

In a similar way one more study was carried out at Konibal Saffron sub-station of SKUAST-K near Pampore (Lone, 2005). In this experiment cement dust was sprayed on selected T-1 and T-2 plots at the rate of 1 and 2 g $m^{-2}$ $day^{-1}$ (5 days/week) for a period of seven months for two consequent growth years (Sept, 2002 to March, 2003 and September, 2003 to March, 2004). A comparative study of the two experiments (table-4) have revealed that apart from photosynthetic pigments (Chlorophyll a, b, total chlorophyll) and leaf morphology and biomass, the floristic characteristics of saffron suffered severe loses both under ambient field conditions as well as in the plots treated/sprayed with cement dust under control conditions.

**Table 4 :** Percent reductions of various floristic characteristics, crocin content and yield of saffron affected by cement dust under ambient field conditions and various dust treatment

| Parameters | Ambient field conditions | | Dust treatment | |
|---|---|---|---|---|
| | S-1 | S-2 | T-1 | T-2 |
| Length of whole flower (cm) | 10.02* | 6.16* | 10.75* | 11.39* |
| Length of parianth (cm) | 5.30$^{NS}$ | 3.61 $^{NS}$ | 4.81* | 24.57* |
| Width of parianth (cm) | 11.23 | 9.55* | 9.55* | 28.00* |
| Length of stigma (mm) | 16.32* | 10.10* | 13.03* | 25.69* |

*Contd.*

| | | | | |
|---|---|---|---|---|
| Length of style (mm) | 5.0 NS | 3.33 NS | 13.86* | 24.96* |
| Total length of pistil (Stigma and style) (mm) | 11.00* | 6.48* | 13.49* | 25.28* |
| Fresh weight of whole flower (g) (10 flower basis) | 25.20* | 16.40* | 19.76* | 28.21* |
| Dry weight of whole flower (g) 10 flower basis | 24.41* | 13.95* | 13.95* | 24.41* |
| Fresh weight of stigma (g) 10 flower basis | 17.64* | 11.76* | 11.76* | 26.47* |
| Dry weight of stigma (g) 10 flower basis | 11.76* | 5.88* | 11.49* | 17.24* |
| Fresh weight of pistil (g) 10 flower basis | 12.50* | 10.0* | 18.75* | 35.41* |
| Dry weight of pistil (g)10 flower basis | 12.12* | 8.08* | 8.08* | 12.12* |
| Crocin content of stigma (%) | 2.96 NS | 1.54 NS | 1.53 NS | 2.96 NS |
| Yield of saffron(kg ha$^{-1}$) | 24.32* | 20.12* | 12.92* | 19.66* |

**S-1** Experimental site situated at 1 km from cement factory

**S-2** Experimental site situated at 2 km from cement factory

**T-1** Plots treated with cement dust at the rate of 1 g m$^{-2}$ day$^{-1}$

**T-2** Plots treated with cement dust at the rate of 2 g m$^{-2}$ day$^{-1}$

*Significant at $p<0.01$ and $p=0.05$ level NS = Non-significant

**Source** : Lone (2004, 2005)

The data reveals that cement dust adversely affected the size of stigma (saffron of commerce), style as well as their fresh and dry biomass in both the experiments. However, the percent losses were higher in the plots treated with cement dust than those growing under ambient field conditions. The experimentation also revealed that the yield of saffron (kg $ha^{-1}$) suffered significant losses in the plots though higher under ambient field conditions rather than in the treated ones. In all the parameters it was observed that cement dust affected the plant to higher level near the factory as well as in the plots sprayed with higher concentration of dust. Further, losses were observed more in the second year of growth rather than in the first year.

## Impact of Particulate Pollution on Saffron Soils

The soil analysis of the polluted sites and experimental plots (Lone, 2004, 2005) have revealed that the values for soil pH, conductivity as well as exchangeable Ca and Mg was higher compared to the control (Table 5). The increase in soil pH in the polluted soil might have been caused by the hydroxides of Ca and Al formed during hydration (Stratman and Vant Haut, 1956; Panjenkemp, 1961; Czaja, 1966) which may impair the various metabolic processes in the plants indirectly. Also, changes in the soil pH due to cement dust in the polluted plots might have affected the growth of the foliage (Schonbeck, 1960; Scheffer *et al.*, 1961; Czaja, 1962) as has also been observed in the present studies. On the other hand, exchangeable NPK was reduced. In general, the alkalization of soil might complicate the mineral nutrition process of the plants and unbalance the mineral composition of the foliage (Mandre *et al.*, 1992) and, subsequently, may be responsible for the decrease of pigment concentration and might affect the various biochemical processes in the plants.

**Table 5 :** Mean values of various soil characteristics of the saffron field affected by cement dust at the end of second year of growth

| Parameters | Mean control | Ambient field conditions | | Dust treatment | |
|---|---|---|---|---|---|
| | | S-1 | S-2 | T-1 | T-2 |
| pH | 7.94 | 8.36 | 8.10 | 8.10 | 8.36 |
| EC (d $Sm^{-1}$) | 0.15 | 0.18 | 0.17 | 0.19 | 0.25 |
| Exch. Ca Cmol (p+) $kg^{-1}$ | 15.00 | 18.0 | 16.0 | 20.0 | 26.0 |
| Exch. Mg Cmol (p+) $kg^{-1}$ | 1.5 | 1.8 | 1.7 | 1.75 | 1.9 |
| Available N kg $ha^{-1}$ | 439.04 | - | - | 313.60 | 282.2 |
| Available P kg $ha^{-1}$ | 18.58 | - | - | 14.52 | 10.80 |
| Available K kg $ha^{-1}$ | 296.00 | - | - | 264.00 | 261.00 |

**S-1** Experimental site situated at 1 km from cement factory
**S-2** Experimental site situated at 2 km from cement factory
**T-1** Plots treated with cement dust at the rate of 1 g $m^{-2}$ $day^{-1}$
**T-2** Plots treated with cement dust at the rate of 2 g $m^{-2}$ $day^{-1}$
**Source** : Lone, 2004 & 2005

## Response of *Phaseolus vulgaris* to cement dust pollution

*Phaseolus vulgaris* commonly called as Kidney bean is cultivated in all parts of the valley and is considered as stable source of protein by the people of all classes. An experiment was carried out by Zargar *et al.* (2002) to assess impact of cement dust pollution on this pulse crop under laboratory conditions, where soils were amended with FYM (Farm Yard Manure), DDW (Decomposed Dal Weed), Mycorrhizae + Azotobacter and Mycorrhizae + Azospirillum. The pots were sprayed with cement dust at the rate of 1.5, 3.0, 4.5 and 6.0 g $m^{-1}$ $day^{-1}$ upto the bloom of the crop. Results have shown that DDW when amended with soil was able to mitigate the effect of cement dust to a greater extent as maximum plant height was observed in this treatment. This was followed by mycorrhizal application along with Azospirillum. It seems that high fertility state of the soil as a result of organic amendments and biofertilizers have ameliorated the adverse effects of cement dust. Moreover, similar trends were also observed with respect to the yield of French beans. Minimum yield was recorded at 6 g cement dust $m^{-2}$ $d^{-1}$.

The study also revealed that the application of cement dust at the rate of 3 g $m^{-2}$ $d^{-1}$ and doses higher than that reduced the yield significantly as compared to the lower doses of cement. All the organic amendments and biofertilizers increased the yield as compared to the control. DDW and FYM were preferable amendments as they could ameliorate the adverse effects of cement dust better than other amendments.

## Effect of Cement Dust on *Brassica oleracea*

*Brassica oleracea* locally called as Haak is widely grown and is the most consumed leafy vegetable in Kashmir valley. Due to the rapid growth of cement industries in Kashmir valley, the growth and yield of this vegetable crop seem to be likely affected by particulate pollution. In view of this a laboratory pot experiment was carried out by Zargar *et al.* (1999) to assess the impact of cement dust on the growth and biomass yield of Haak grown on low and high fertile soils. In this experiment 35 days old seedlings were sprayed with cement dust at the rate of 0.5, 1.0, 1.5, 2.0, 2.5, 3.0, 3,5, 4.0 and 4.5 g $m^{-2}$ $d^{-1}$. At the end of the experiment they reported that leaf wash pH and leaf extract pH were significantly higher in dusted plants than their respective controls, the maximum being observed in samples wherein 4.5 g $m^{-2}$ $d^{-1}$ cement was sprayed. The study also revealed that there was a significant reduction in plant height, number of leaves and biomass at cement dust levels of 2.5 $g^{-2}$ $d^{-1}$ and beyond. They also reported that the adverse effects of cement dust was lesser on plants raised in high fertile than in low fertile soils.

## Mechanism of Action of Cement Dust on Vegetation

Cement dust emanating from industries falls on vegetative organs of the plant and forms a crust when it becomes moist due to dew, fog or light rain. This phenomenon creates changes in the light, temperature and water regimes of the plant tissues (Borka, 1980). The losses in the photosynthetic pigments has also been observed in the studies carried out in Kashmir valley. It might have been caused by the highly alkaline nature of cement dust which might have degraded the chlorophyll molecules and/or by shading (Pajenkamp, 1961; Borka,1980). Lerman (1972) suggested that continuous application of cement logs the stomata, thus interfering with the gaseous exchange. This may lead to increased leaf temperature which may retard chlorophyll synthesis (Mark, 1963; Singh and Rao, 1981). Mandre and Thulmets (1977) have also opined that decrease in light availability caused due to dust pollution may lead to decreased elemental uptake and hold the view that inhibition of the absorption of the active parts of the solar radiation spectrum participating in photosynthetic process might have directly contributed to the low concentration of chlorophyll in Norway spruce needles, under the influence of high level of dust pollution. The reduction in chlorophyll in vegetation due to cement dust has also been earlier reported by several authors (Shukla *et al.*, 1990; Mandre *et al.*, 1992; Mishra *et al.*, 1993; Mandre and Tuulmets, 1997; Cesar and Lepedus, 2001; Lone, 2004, 2005)

It is an established fact that the length of the foliage of the plants is determined by genetic constitution and also, by the edaphic and weather conditions especially temperature and water regimes, but it also depends on the dust load, the duration of its effect and the tolerance of the plants. Cement dust may cause essential negative changes and inhibit the growth of the plants, reduce the dimension of their leaves and decrease their biomass (Shukla *et al.*, 1990; Mandre and Ots, 1999). The studies carried out on the impact of cement dust on saffron have also shown greater reduction in the phytomass as well as in the size of the foliage. Such reduction may be due to the reduced photosynthesis, through a combination of factors such as reduced interference with the gaseous exchange of foliage due to clogging of stomata, interception in the incident light due to cement encrustation on the leaf surface, pigment degradation and intra or inter cellular changes in the leaves (Shukla *et al.,* 1990).

The results of the studies carried on saffron also show that various floristic characteristics like length and biomass of stigma (saffron of commerce) also suffered significant losses both under natural ambient field conditions and in the plots treated with cement dust. These losses might be due to the less accumulation of photosynthates in the cormels, which might have also proved detrimental so far as their vegetative multiplication is concerned. Losses in the flower production and subsequent yield in the fruits has also been reported by many workers (Singh and Rao,1981; Misra *et al.*, 1993, Pandey *et al.*, 1996; Shukla *et al.*, 1990, Zargar *et al.*, 1999, 2002, Deepali and Khan, 2002).

## Conclusions

The long-term research studies to investigate particulate pollution emanating from industrial establishments in the Kashmir valley and their impact on various agricultural crops and ecosystems deserves adequate environmental attention.

## References

Borka, G. (1980) The effect of cement dust pollution on the growth and metabolism of *Helianthus annus*. Environ. Pollut. Ser. (A), 22 : 75-92.

Cesar, V. and Lepedus, H. (2001) Peroxidase activity, soluble proteins and chlorophyll content in spruce (*Picea abies* L. Karst.) needles affected by cement dust. Acta Botanica Croatica, 60(2) : 227-235.

Czaja, A.T. (1962) *Uber das problem der Zementstaub-wirkungen and pflanzen*. Staub, 22 : 228-32.

Czaja, A.T. (1966) The effect of dust, especially cement dust upon plants. Angew Bot, 40 : 106-120.

Deepali, R. and Khan, A.A. (2002) Impact of industrial particulate pollutants applied to soil on the growth and yield of tomato. Thai J. Agric. Sci., 35(2) : 187-194.

Kannan, S. (2002) Current status of saffron production export in the world. Proc. Natl. Seminar-cum-workshop "Development of Saffron in Kashmir", SKUASTK-K and Spice Bd. Minist. Comm. Industr. Govt. India, 67-73.

Lerman, S. (1972) Cement - Kiln dust and the bean plant (*Phaseolus vulgaris* L. Black Valentine var.) : Indepth investigations into plant morphology, physiology and pathology. Ph.D. Dissertation, Univ. of California, Riverside.

Lone, F.A. (2004) Effect of cement dust on the growth and yield of saffron (*Crocus sativus* L.) under ambient field conditions. Proc. Natl. Seminar on Conservation of Biodiversity in India and particular reference to Himalaya Univ., Kash. March, 22-24, 2004 (in press).

Lone, F.A. (2005) Effect of cement dust on foliar growth, flower morphology, crocin content and yield of saffron (*Crocus sativus* L.) Ind. J. Bot. Soc. (in press).

Mandre, M. and Ots, K. (1999) Growth and biomass partitioning of 6 year old spruces under alkaline dust impact. Wat. Air Soil Pollut., 114 : 13-25.

Mandre, M. and Tuulmets, L. (1997) Pigment changes in Norway spruce induced by dust pollution. Water, Air and Soil Pollution, 94 : 247-258.

Mandre, M., Annuka, E. and Tuulmets, L. (1992) Response reaction of conifers to alkaline dust pollution : Changes in the pigment system. Eesti-Teaduste Alladeemia-Toimetised Okloogia, 2(4) : 19-56.

Mark, L. T. (1963) Temperature inhibition of carotene synthesis in tomato. Bot. Gaz., 124 : 180-185.

Misra, J., Pandey, V., Singh, S.N., Singh, N., Yunus, M. and Ahmad, K.J. (1993) Growth responses of *Lycopersicon esculentum* to cement dust treatment. J. Environ. Sci. & Health (A), 280 : 1771-1780.

Pajenkamp, H. (1961) *Einwirkung des Zementofenstaubes auf pflanze und tiere*. Zem-Kalk-Gips., 14 : 88-95.

Pandey, D.D., Sanjeev, K. and Kumar, S. (1996) Impact of cement dust pollution on biomass, chlorophyll, nutrients and grain characteristics of wheat. Environ. Ecol., 14(4) : 872-875.

Rao, M.N. and Rao, H.V.N. (1999) *Air pollution*. Tata McGraw Hill Publishing Company Limited, New Delhi.

Scheffer, F., Przemeck, E. and Wilms, W. (1961) *Untersuchungen uber den Einfluss Von Zementofen - Flugsstaub auf Boden und Pflange. Staub.*, 21 : 251-254.

Schonbeck, H. (1960) *Beobachtungen zur Frage des Einflusses von industriellen Immissionen anf die Krankbereitschaft der pflanze-Ber*. Landesanstalt Bodennutzungsschutz (Boechum), 1 : 89-98.

Shukla, J.V., Pandey, S.N., Singh, M., Yunus, M., Singh, N. and Ahmad, K.J. (1990) Effect of cement dust on growth and yield of *Brassica campestris* L. Environ. Pollut., 66 : 81-88.

Singh, S.N. and Rao, D.N. (1981) Certain responses of wheat plants to cement dust pollution. Environ. Pollut. Ser. (A), 24 : 75-81.

Stratmann H. and Van Haut H. (1956) *Vegetation versuche-mit Zement flugsstaub* (Unpublished investigations of Kohlen stoff-Biologischen Forschungs station). Essen German.

Zargar, A.H., Zargar, M.Y. and Khan, M.A. (2002) Cement dust pollution in Kashmir, Response of *Phaseolus vulgaris* to cement dust treatment under soil amendments. J. Curr. Sci., 2(1) : 15-18.

Zargar, A.H., Zargar, M.Y., Dar, D.H. and Ganai, B.A. (1999) Impact of cement dust on growth and biomass yield of Haak (*Brassica oleracea*). Applied Biological Research, 1 : 179-181.

## CHAPTER 7

# EQUIPMENTS: OPERATION AND MAINTENANCE FOR POLLUTION LEVEL ASSESSMENT

**G.H. Pandya, V.M. Shinde, G.S. Kanade and V.K. Kondwar**

National Environmental Engineering Research Institute (NEERI), Nehru Marg, Nagpur – 440 020, India

**ABSTRACT**

Over the years demand has been increasing in determining concentration of pollutants at ppb and sub-ppb levels. This has put a severe load on equipments that detect pollutants at trace levels. Management of equipments in an environmental laboratory requires planning, involving drafting of specification for the purchase of equipment, creation of infrastructure for installation and testing of the equipment. Optimization of analysis conditions and development of in-house operation and maintenance procedures forms a major part of Instrumentation and R & D.

The chapter reports the results of such an analysis carried to support all those interested in this area for environmental analysis.

**Key words:** Equipments, Selection, Procurement, QC, Electronic workshop, Maintenance.

## Introduction

Since last over three decades, we have been involved in developing capability for analysing environmental pollutants at trace levels (Acoustics, 1989). Prior to this, a variety of samples were being collected and analysed but not in an organised way. It became apparent that budget justifications, facility planning, manpower requirement and other actions could have been facilitated if information on laboratory objectives, its structure, the instrument requirement based on parameter to be determined, the preventive maintenance and quality checks to be performed were available. A general overview was, thus, undertaken on the operating structure of an environmental laboratory involved in measurement and analysis of various parameters for air, water and land components. Each parameter requires some sort of equipment for its determination. With the advancement of electronics and data processing facilities, the equipments have become quite expensive and their characteristics also vary from manufacturer to manufacturer.

The essential equipment required for the laboratory is governed directly by the variety of analysis being performed and by whether these are rapid measurements of routine determinants or specialized, in depth analysis involving sophisticated instruments for special problems (CPCB, 2000 and Kadiayali, 1978).

Management of equipment for an environmental analysis laboratory involves:

Assessing the work load for arriving at the operational structure of the laboratory, Establishment of criteria and specification for the purchase of equipment, Checking and testing of the equipment against specification before putting it in operational use, Development of a preventive maintenance program for each type of equipment, Development of and maintenance of supply of spares, chemicals, gases, reference standards, Maintenance of a history sheet of the equipment received above a minimum price level, Keeping a list of vendors of local/imported instruments used for environmental applications, Regular audit checks with reference standards. The paper considers the above aspects so as to develop an information for management of equipment supplies for an environmental laboratory engaged in R&D work, or Serving as an Industrial laboratory or as an Govt. Analysis laboratory.

The design of an environmental laboratory depends upon the primary tasks it has to undertake. These may be analysis of potable water, wastewater from industries, sewage, sludge and solid waste, gaseous and particulates, and biological samples.

The laboratory can serve as an operation and process-controlling laboratory of a treatment plant, or as an government support laboratory with specific tasks, or as an research and development laboratory with flexibility to work on emerging areas of research. The floor space required for the laboratory depends on the volume of work, the diversity and complexity of different analysis, and the staff. For an average laboratory approximate space would be 30-35 $m^2$. The allocation of laboratory space depends mainly on the number of samples to be analysed, number of determinants per sample, nature of determinants, frequency of the individual determinants, number of replicates required, preliminary requirement for sample preparation, the requirement of preservation and storage of samples, and availability of existing equipment. The structure also depends upon whether the samples come from large groups or as single samples. It also depends on whether the analysis is done by different workers consequently or all done by one group of workers or even one person. In large laboratories, automated and mechanized instruments are used saving space and time.

The requirement of sampling instruments for collection and analysis for some common parameters to be chosen for analysing air, water and soil samples are illustrated in Tables 1-2. Only a few basic parameters are considered so that a simple environmental laboratory can plan its operational requirements.

**Table 1 :** Sample Collection Devices for Soil, Water and Air Matrices

| Environmental Matrix | Sample Collection Device |
|---|---|
| Soil | Shovel, Scoop, Auger, Corer, Trier,<br>Rigid Glass or Plastic jar.<br>Nonrigid plastic or paper bag |
| Water | Rigid glass or Plastic jar or bottle.<br>Non rigid reseable plastic bag.<br>Thief tube, Coliwasa tube, Bacon bomb,Bailor, Vacuum or Peristaltic pump. |
| Air | High-Volume samplers with filters of suspended particulates.<br>Dust fall bucket for settleable particulates.<br>Air sampling pumps with solid adsorbents.<br>Air sampling pumps with liquid absorbent.<br>Evacuated rigid glass or stainless cannisters for gases and vapours.<br>Direct reading instantaneous sampling and analysis of gases, vapours and particulates. |

**Table 2 :** Sample Analysis Devices for Common Parameters Measured in Soil, Water and Air Matrices

| Environmental Matrix | Parameter | Sample Collection Device |
|---|---|---|
| Soil and water | pH | pH Meter |
| Soil and water | Conductivity | Conductivity meter |
| Soil | Solids (Texture) | Stacked sieves and Electro Balance |

*Contd.*

| | | |
|---|---|---|
| Soil and water | Total Solids | Porcelain crucible, Oven and Electro Balance |
| Soil | Volatile Solids | Porcelain crucible, Oven, Furnace and Electro Balance |
| Water | Suspended and Dissolved solids | Porcelain crucible, Membrane Filter Assembly, Oven and Electro Balance |
| Soil and Water | Microorganisms | Membrane Filter Apparatus, Nutrient Growth Media, Thermal Incubator, Microscope |
| Water | DO | DO Meter |
| Water | BOD | BOD Bottle, DO Meter, Refrigerated Incubator |
| Soil, Water and Air | Organic Chemicals | UV-VIS Spectrophotometer, GC, HPLC, GC-MS, LC-MS |
| Soil, Water and Air | Inorganic Chemicals (Non Metals) | UV-VIS Spectrophotometer |
| Soil, Water and Air | Inorganic Chemicals (Metals) | AAS, ICP |
| Air | Total and Respirable Particulate | Electro Balance |

Depending on the objectives of the laboratory one can plan the requirement of the equipments in an R&D laboratory. The major analytical load is in the determination of metals in various types of samples. As an illustration, the widely used technique for heavy metal estimation in an environmental laboratory is Inductively Coupled Plasma (ICP) spectrometer. The number of samples analysed per year is 6213.

Fig. 1 depicts the analytical workload on a typical instrument ICP in terms of samples analysed per year for heavy metals in air, water, wastewater, soil, solid wastes, and other typical samples. The number of samples were comparatively more for drinking water. On an average 60% were water, 15% wastewater, 11% dust, 4% solid wastes, 2% soil and rest 8% comprise of specific determinants.

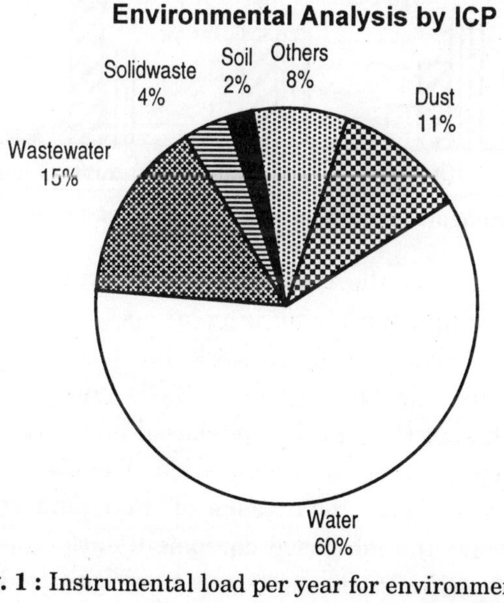


**Fig. 1 :** Instrumental load per year for environmental analysis

On the other hand, environmental laboratory attached to Government departments or to Industries will have a different requirement. An analysis was also carried out for assessing the various instrumental requirements for a environmental laboratory engaged in R&D work, committed to Government Tasks and engaged in maintenance of Industrial plants. Assuming their demand of basic equipment for field work (Requirement more than 50 each of particular type), Laboratory Analysis (requirement of 20-50 units of each type), and Sophisticated Equipments (requirement of 5 - 20 units of each type), and some Specific Analysis requiring special Equipments (less than 5 units of each type) was considered.

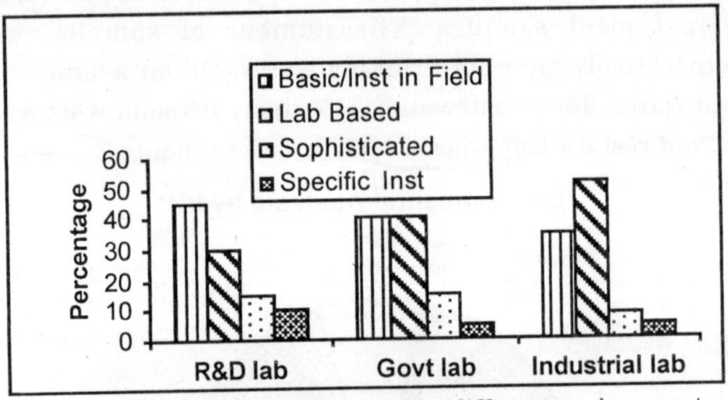


**Fig. 2 :** Instrumental requirement for different environment

It is observed that the R&D lab requirement has more flexibility to change with emerging areas and also has opportunity to carry out field work for environmental monitoring. Thus, the percentage of Basic equipments is comparatively higher (Fig. 2). The lab-based instruments are based on the objectives of the organization. The Government labs and Industrial labs have tasks of analysing specific parameters. Hence the lab-based equipments are more. The percentage of Specific Instruments are more with R&D labs due to their requirement of low level, precise and shorter analysis time.

## Selection and procurement

The procurement of instrument is an important task. Hence, care is necessary in formulating the specification for its purchase, its selection, and installation. In addition to cost and performance characteristics, some factors like conditions of warranties, availability of spares, costs involved, training and testing as per the specifications are of growing importance. If the suppliers give demonstration at customer's lab or at their own facility it becomes advantageous for understanding the salient features of the techniques. Eventually, the purchase made on reliable information and good comparative evaluation of various available models is advantageous in the long run. Other terms for considering during negotiation is a fixed date of delivery, complete installation, adequate training for day-to-day operation and maintenance. Further, extended warranties/service contracts, copies of operating and service manuals, and sufficient availability of spare parts for solving urgent breakdown problems must also be considered.

## Site preparation and installation

Prior to purchase of equipment, a thought must be given to its location and installation. For most instruments, it is better to locate a permanent place so as to avoid realignment, calibration, electrical and gaseous fittings. The pre-installation details are normally obtained from the vendors such as bench height, floor space required, utility needs such as water, electricity, compressed gases, safety and a compatible environment. The installation requires check against the specification and performance requirements. If the item/equipment does not perform as required, it cannot be placed into service and, therefore, should not be given final approval. In such a case, consideration may be given for withholding final payment until a correction is made by the supplier. It is always advisable to put a condition of supplying operational as well as service manual of the equipments while placing the order. When obtained, the diagrams, manual and charts should be studied and kept in a safe place for reference.

During installation, the manufacturer's instructions should be followed. If the installation is made properly, many hours of the maintenance work may be saved.

## Preventive maintenance

Preventive maintenance is an integral part of equipment management. It reduces malfunctions, permits adjustments on a time basis and ensures fewer equipment breakdowns and increases the measurement system's reliability. Preventive maintenance includes specification checks, calibration, cleaning, lubricating, reconditioning and testing. It is essential that calibration standards are maintained and the performance record is compared.

A permanent inventory record of each piece of instrument costing more than a lakh of rupees must be kept. The record should include, name of the item, model number, serial number, vendor's name and address, date of receipt, date of physical verification, specification and date of installation. If the inventory is kept in computer file along with the essential spares' cost, it becomes useful in retrieving the information incase of breakdown, replying to audits and system replacements. This also serves a service record for downtime, repairs and performance problems. It will also help in deciding whether or not to order similar models and the services of vendors when additional units are to be purchased.

One important consideration in management of preventive maintenance is to see that the task assigned to the personnel is performed as scheduled. A regular training, exposure to various seminars and exhibition of analytical instruments, and a periodic reference of current journals and other literature will go a long way in improving the measurement methodology in the competence of data generation capacity of the institute. Besides the equipments, environmental monitoring also involves use of quality reagents, glasswares and other sullies like gases. A good inventory procedure ensures the specification and the purity of reagents to be used in analysis. Some reagents act as primary standards/reference standards and can be used directly without further testing.

## Development of infrastructure facilities

Repair and service of equipment should be done with proper tools and testing instruments available in the electronic workshop. Use of improper tools can damage the equipment. Recommended spare parts as specified by the manufacturer should replace the defective components or subassembly. The equivalent spare parts should only be replaced in case of non-availability of original spare parts.

## Infrastructure of electronic workshop

The workshop should be developed in such a way that it contains elements of facilities as highlighted in Fig. 3 and the essential accessories summarised in Table 3. The electronic repair and measuring instruments are essential for attending to some urgent breakdown problems. The equipments listed are specific and could be kept as per the repair and maintenance workload of the laboratory.

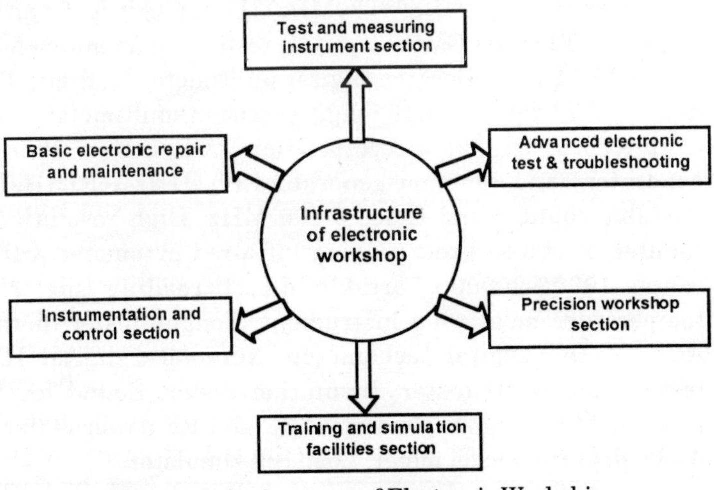


**Fig. 3 :** Infrastructure of Electronic Workshop

**Table 3 :** Organization of Electronic repair, maintenance, testing, calibration and control facilities

| **Electronic repair and maintenance section** |
|---|
| Soldering tools, Desoldering tools, IC extractors and inserters, 8-40 pin ,Precision tools: pliers, cutters, nippers, tweezers, screwdrivers (slot head and Philips head): Allen keys, Wire and cable stripper, Crimping tools, Manual and battery operated wire wrapping and unwrapping tool (wire size24-30 SWG), Antistatic mat, tray and wrist strap, Precision electronic tool kit for field service (e.g. Xcelite TC-100),Power supplies: Fixed voltage (regulated) 5V, 5-amp, Multiple output (regulated) 5V, 2-amp, ±15V, 1-amp: 0-30V variable DC, 1 amp., Multimeters: Pen type 3_ digit hand-held digital multimeter, Analogue multimeter, sensitivity 20 k volt. |
| **Test and measuring instruments section** |
| Universal dual trace oscilloscopes, 35 MHz B&W and standard facilities.<br>1OOMHz/150MHz dual trace/ four trace oscilloscopes with delay triggering and slope selection facility, Digital storage oscilloscopes (B&W: 20MHz),Digital logic probe and pulser for TTL and CMOS logic, IC tester clip (monitor) for 8 pins to 64 pins, Desktop digital multimeter 3_ digit, 4_ digit and 6_ digit types, 6_ digit precision multimeter (for calibration), Digital direct reading LCR meter, Pulse generators and function generators (O.O1Hz-1OOMHz), Portable counter and timer 0-100 MHz, High resolution counter, Portable direct reading infra-red pyrometer with range 10000-20000, Portable direct reading surface temperature measuring instrument, Tongue tester (both AC and DC),Digital tachometer, Automatic digital IC tester, Linear IC tester, Insulation tester, Sound level meter, AM/FM signal generator, AF and RF power meter, Audio distortion level meter, Load cell simulator. |

*Contd....*

**Advanced electronic test and troubleshooting section**

Curve tracer for semiconductor devices, Logic analyser, Microprocessor troubleshooter, Signature analyser, Intelligent terminal and keyboard, Personal computer with standard interfaces (RS232. IEEE 488 Serial and Centronics Parallel), Logic comparator and current tracer, Power line disturbance analyser, Signal memory recorder, 2 to 4-channel chart recorder with pen frequency response up to 100 MHz, RS232 breakout boxes, X-Y recorder, Radio telephone tester, Programmable sweep generator.

**Instrumentation and control section**

Voltage and current calibrators, Dead weight testers, Electro-pneumatic calibrator panel, Hand operated pressure generator, Over pressure protection valve, Electro-pneumatic portable calibrator, P/I converter, U-tube water and mercury manometer, Precision pressure gauges of various ranges, Standard size nipples, connectors and adapters of various types, Environmental chamber with temperature and RH control.

**Precision workshop section**

PCB inspection accessories like bench magnifier and PCB inspection glass, Ultrasonic cleaning tank for PCBs, Printed circuit drilling machine stand mounted (with precision chuck 0-2-4mm), Hand-held electric mini drill (with accessories like grinding wheel, brushes, cut-off wheels etc), Bench guillotine, Precision

Hex key driver and nut driver set, Watchmaker's lathe with standard accessories, Jeweler's screwdriver set, Mini grinder, Adjustable multipurpose bench vice, Contact cleaning and burnishing tool, Adjustable torque wrenches and screwdrivers, Drive socket and spanner set 6.35mm (MM/AF/WW/BA),Tap and die set (M/BA/BSF/UN), Circlip pliers set, Vernier caliper sand screw gauges, Engineer's wire and tread gauges, Thyristor commissioning kit.

## Calibration Of Equipments

Many times questions are raised about the quality of data being generated through various types of equipments such as Spectrophotometers, AAS, GCs, etc. as well as the supporting equipments as electronic balances, distillation units. A checklist was prepared based on our own experience in the laboratory.

The calibration of environmental analysis equipments covers a wide range of disciplines and requires a well-established infrastructure and trained manpower with an understanding of various environmental monitoring and sampling principles. It has been observed that the already established labs have developed in-house facilities for testing, calibration of their daily use equipments. The initiation of building up such facilities required considerable effort in identifying the parameter and the measuring instrument and procuring or developing the reference source required for standardization. Some of the identified parameters, frequency of checks, and the standards to be used for tool are summarised in Table 4.

**Table 4 :** Operational Checks for Quality Control Management

| Sr. No. | Instrument | Frequency of checks | Parameters to be checked | Standards to be used |
|---|---|---|---|---|
| 1 | AAS | When used | Sensitivity<br>Detection Limits | Standard solvent of specific element to be determined using standard solvent<br>Determine response of twice the base line at highest attenuation |
| | | Quarterly | General maintenance check | To be performed by staff specialized in maintenance |

*Contd.*

| | | | | |
|---|---|---|---|---|
| 2 | GC | Quarterly<br><br>Quarterly | Temperature of the column oven<br>Gain, damping linearity & chart speeds of recorders/printers<br>Septum, Glass Liners<br>Electrometer, FID, ECD etc | Portable indicating reference pyrometer<br>Adjust gain & Chart speeds<br>Replace septum, Clean or replace liners.<br>Reference standard<br>Check column efficiency, clean detectors |
| 3 | IR | Monthly or depending on use | Resolution<br><br>Wave number accuracy | Polystyrene film peaks & scan total range<br>Polystyrene peaks at 2851.5, 1601.8, 1028.3 |
| 4 | General Analytical balances | When used<br><br>Quarterly | Level of the balance, Zero point & Cleanliness<br><br>Accuracy | Level bottle indicator & adjust balancing legs<br><br>Use Reference weights |
| 5 | Incubator | Each Day<br>Weekly | Temperature<br>Temperature | Recording Thermometer<br>Thermometer with 0.1 C Divisions |
| 6 | Ovens | Quarterly | Temperature | Indicating rerefence pyrometer |
| 7 | PH meters | When in use | Accuracy and Linearity | Use Standard buffers<br>Wash electrodes carefully after use |
| 8 | Distillation units | Weekly<br>Weekly<br>Weekly | Cleanliness<br>Conductivity<br>PH, Heavy metals, Organic quality | Visual<br>Conductivity meter<br>PH meter, AAS, TOC |

*Contd.*

| 9 | UV – VIS Spectrometer | Twice a month | Wavelengh accuracy & Reproducibility | Holmium Filter & Didymium Filter. Check Wavelengh over entire range by SRM glass filters, standard solutions |
|---|---|---|---|---|

## Conclusions

The increasing use of solid state devices and computing system, places problem for analysts when troubleshooting starts. Generally, an instrument repair experts are called which means delay in analysis and considerable expense if some components are to be imported. The only solution is to keep a stock of essential spares that are likely to need periodic replacement. One must also make deal with the supplier when a purchase is to be made that sufficient spares would accompany the equipment at no extra cost. This will help in maintaining the equipment and extend its life in case the model of the equipment undergoes a change.

## Acknowledgements

The authors would like to thank Dr. Sukumar Devotta, Director, NEERI for the encouragement in above work and permission to publish the work.

## References

Acoustics (1989) Attenuation of sound during propagation outdoors, Part 2. "A general method of calculation", ISO/DP 9613-2. International Organization for Standardization, CH-1211, Geneva, Switzerland.

Central Pollution Control Board (CPCB), New Delhi (2000) *Ambient Air Quality Standards in respect of Noise, Schedule-III. Gazette 643.*

Kadiayali L.R. (1978) *Traffic Engineering and Transport Planning.* Khanna Publications, Delhi.

Pandya G.H. (1995) Requirements of an Average Environmental Laboratory. Indian Journal of Environmental Health, Vol. 37(3) : 179-187.

Pandya G.H. (1997) Investigation of the Quality of GC Performance for analysis of Environmental samples. Indian Journal Of Environmental Health, Vol. 39(4) : 274-280.

Pandya G.H. and Kondawar V.K. (2000) Environmental laboratories in the millennium. Journal of Indian Association of Environmental Management, Vol. 27(3) : 208-209.

Pandya G.H. and Verma Ravi, (1997) Characterization and Measurement of Noise Levels in an Urban Environment. Indian Journal Environmental Health. 39(2). 274-280.

Rau, J.G. and Wooten D.C., (1980) *Environmental Impact Analysis Handbook*, McGraw Hill Book Company, USA.

Stevens, S.S., (1961) Procedure for calculating Loadness : mark VI. Journal Acoustical Society of America, 33 (1).

Webster, J.C. (1968) Effect of Noise on Speech Intelligibility. Proceedings of conference on Noise as a Public Health Hazard, Washington DC, June 13-14.

CHAPTER 8

# RAPID ASSAYS IN POLLUTION ANALYSIS : IMMUNOCHEMICAL TECHNIQUES

**Eline Meulenberg**

ELTI Support VOF
Drieskensacker 12-10
6546 MH Nijmegen
The Netherlands.

## ABSTRACT

With regard to wide spread occurrence of pollutants in the environment and adverse effects on humans, animals and ecosystems, it is highly desirable to dispose of analytical methods that allow for a rapid detection and optionally quantification of these substances in order to track sources and then lower concentrations or even eliminate these. A description is given of existing assays with emphasis on immunochemical techniques, including immunoassays, immunoaffinity chromatography, immunosensors. Target substances comprise micro-organisms, toxins, pesticides, industrial chemicals, pharmaceuticals and hormone disrupting compounds. Each of these classes is illustrated by literature references and examples are described.

**Key words:** Pollution, detection, rapid assays, immunoassay, immunoaffinity, chromatography and immunosensors.

## Introduction

Our environment consists of air, water and soil. The air we breath, water we drink, and soil we use to generate food. Each compartment may be polluted by undesired or toxic substances. Since the industrial revolution, industry has been booming and, consequently, millions of anthropogenic compounds have entered our environment. Persistent organic pollutants have been found even in remote areas of the world (Ballschmiter *et al.,* 2002). In addition, natural substances may also be toxic such as the cyanobacterial microcystines and marine toxins, bacteria, viruses, etc. In some instances, potentially toxic chemicals have been or are still being used for the production of food, e.g. pesticides in agriculture and food preservation. Pollution may be defined as the presence of undesired natural or anthropogenic substances in our environment. In order to ensure human and animal health and balance ecosystems, there have been developed methods to detect and monitor the presence of pollutants in the environment and to take measure to reduce or eliminate levels of pollutants by establishing norms, acts and regulations. As a consequence, advanced analytical methods, wastewater treatment plants (WWTP), water purification plants for the production of drinking water, industrial emission control systems, soil remediation programs, etc. have been established. In addition, in the course of time certain chemicals and pesticides, in particular highly toxic and persistent ones, have been banned from use, especially in Western countries.

Conventional methods are defined as highly advanced analytical methods used in specialized laboratories and include GC, HPLC, MS, MALDI-TOF, CE, TLC, etc. Generally, these require expensive equipment and highly educated practitioners. Most of the methods start with collection of sufficient sample, processing using appropriate solvents for liquid-liquid extraction, pretreatment, e.g., by SPE or SPME, optionally a derivation step and analysis of the constituent compounds. For each of these methods review articles have been published (Bruzzonoti *et al.* 2000; Hogendoorn & van Zoonen 2000; Jeannot and Sauvard 2000; Motohashi *et al.* 2000; Sasano *et al.* 2000; Waterval *et al.* 2001; Richardson 2001, 2004; Larsson *et al.* 2000; Dabek-Zlotorzynska *et al.* 2003; Eeeltink *et al.* 2003; Flurer, 2003; Imbenotte *et al.* 2003; Poisnot *et al.* 2003; Schmitt-Kopplin and Frommberger, 2003). Advantages are that many compounds can be determined simultaneously in each sample and currently automated apparatuses are commercially available, including the required software for identification and quantification of individual compounds. Moreover, MS allows for the identification of unknown compounds. Complementary methods for screening and analytical purposes comprise bioassays and immunoassays and the following is directed to such methods.

## Effects of pollution

Pollution may have an effect on ecosystems, plants, animal and human health. These effects may be exerted at several levels: populations, individuals, organs, cells, genes, DNA, enzymes. Uptake or intake of pollutants may lead to poisoning, disturbance of biochemical or physiological processes, mutagenesis, genotoxicity and the like, by which properties cells and organs are altered and individual cells and organs loose their viability, with consequences for individuals, populations and optionally ecosystems. The wide distrubution of pollutants may be evidenced by the presence of persistent organic substances in the fats of arctic animals and in human blood or breast milk. To date, various test methods have been developed to assess one or more of these effects.

Results of toxicity tests and bioassays and of analytical detection methods provide the tools for establishing norms, regulation and legislation in order to lower or even eliminate pollutants from the environment. In general, for this purpose quality control programs are established, including monitoring and early warning programs. In practice, this means that regularly samples are taken and analyzed for a broad range of polluting substances, in particular nutrients and priority compounds. Lists of priority compounds have been established in various countries, e.g., in the US by the US EPA, the European Union, the WHO, and national priority lists. Such lists are regularly adjusted based on recent findings. Frequently, new compounds are detected, for example, in surface waters and an example is given in a Dutch RIZA report (Schrap *et al.* 2004). Herein a survey of perfluorinated compounds is described. Perfluorinated compounds have since long been used to render textiles water and stain-resistant, in food packing materials and as additives in fire fighting foams. From the 1990s, concern about the presence of these compounds in the environment has been expressed in Canada, the United States, in Western Europe and now also in Asian countries. Control starts as soon as analytical methods become available and from the above survey perfluorinated compounds have been detected in fresh water, sea, sediment and some organisms at nanogram levels. Once new compounds of interest have been determined, rapid assays are needed for monitoring purposes in order to be able to optionally trace their sources and reduce their levels.

Various priority compounds such as certain herbicides are present in surface waters at increased levels only in restricted times of the year, especially in spring time and autumn after large scale application in agriculture. As the emission into surface water highly depends on weather conditions, peak levels can hardly be predicted and in such cases an early warning program is desirable to be alert on increases, in particular for water used for the production of drinking water. These situations require rapid cost-effective assays both to allow for the screening of a large number of samples and to obtain results within a short time. Hereinafter, first an overview of rapid assays is given, followed by possible pollutants that may be detected by the various tests. It should be noted that the references cited are by no way exhaustive, only exemplary.

## Rapid assays

For large scale monitoring and in early warning programs as well as during calamities, rapid assays are highly suitable when known compounds and organisms are to be detected in a large number of samples. Suitable assays may be divided into bioassays and immunochemical assays. Bioassays measure the presence and toxicity of substances present in environmental samples. As examples of commercially available toxicity tests mention may be made of the Ames test (gene mutations), SOS, UmuC, Mutatox (DNA damage), Microtox$^{TM}$ (luminescent marine bacterium Vibrio fisheri), CALUX (PCBs/dioxins), E-Screen (EDCs), Two-hybrid Yeast assay (EDCs), VITOTOX (genotoxicity) and Biomet (heavy metals). For literature references see Palmer *et al.* (1998); Volpi Ghiradini *et al.* (1998); Köhler *et al.* (2000); van der Lelie *et al.* (2000); Fochtman *et al.* (2000); Blaise *et al.* (2000) ; Koppen *et al.* (2001); Doherty (2001); Suzuki *et al.* (2004) ; Gizzi *et al.* (2005).

Drawback of such assays is the non-specificity of the assay. Any substance, micro-organism or compound having an effect leads to a detection signal. Identification should be performed using different methods. A review of bioassay technology especially for dioxins and dioxin-like compounds is given by Behmisch *et al.* (2001). The applicability of immunochemical assays for identification and quantification of such pollutants depends on the characteristics of the particular assay. If an immunochemical assay meets the definition of, e.g., the EPA, AOAC, DIN or ISO norms, they are comparable to conventional analytical methods. In the following an overview of immunochemical methods is given. In the last decade several reviews have been published containing lists of pesticides, organics, toxins for which assays, in particular immunoassays, have been developed (see below).

## Immunochemical Techniques

Immunochemical techniques involve by definition an immunoreagent, the antibody. Antibodies or immunoglobulines are glycoprotein constituents of the immune systems as defense proteins against intruding foreign substances in the body. A more detailed description of antibodies is given below. These proteins can be used in semi-analytical, analytical and preparative methods for the detection, analysis or capture/purification of target compounds. The most well-known application is in immunoassays. In addition, antibodies are used in immuno affinity chromatography (IAC) when coupled onto a solid phase column, and recently in immunosensors for real-time assay. Each item will be discussed below.

## Immunoassays (IA)

As mentioned above, the main component of an immunoassay is the antibody. Antibodies originate from the immune system as a response to intruding foreign substances. Prerequisite for the immune system to initiate the synthesis of antibody specific for the foreign substance, referred to as antigen, is a size exceeding about 500 Daltons and preferentially a three-dimensional structure. In the case an antigen is presented to B-lymphocytes, it binds to specific receptors on the cell surface which triggers the differentiation of the particular B-lymphocyte to a clone for the production and secretion of antigen-specific antibodies. Complex formation between antibody and antigen leads to the activation of a cascade of serum proteins responsible for dissociation, degradation and elimination of the antigen. The living body is capable to generate an infinite number of different antibodies.

An antibody is composed of 4 peptide chains, 2 identical heavy chains and 2 identical light chains, connected hydrogen bonds and disulfide bonds. A schematic diagram of an antibody is given in Fig. 1. Antigen binding occurs at the N-terminus of the chains and is determined by the variable regions of the heavy and light chains. The constant, C-terminal part defines the species specificity of the antibody. It will be appreciated that small compounds fit into the binding site of the antibody, but larger compounds or micro-organisms only show binding of part of their structure or surface. The binding part of an antigen is called epitope. It can be imagined that larger compounds or micro-organisms possess more than one epitope for presentation to B-lymphocytes and as a consequence may lead to several populations of diverse antibodies in the body. On the other hand, smaller antigens such as pesticides, will not elicit an immune response and in that case the antigen, also called hapten, has to be coupled to a carrier protein for experimental production of antibody.

Design of an immunoassay starts with the production of antibody against a target substance (immunogen/hapten conjugate) by eliciting an immune response in an experimental animal using a whole or part of the antigen or an immunogenic conjugate, generally in the presence of an adjuvant to enhance the immune response. Most commonly used adjuvants are Freunds adjuvants (complete and incomplete) and aluminium compounds such as aluminiumphosphate and hydroxide. Alternative adjuvants are Ribi, Adjuvax, TiterMax, Quil A and synthetic lipopeptides. After a certain period of time the aimed antibody is collected from the blood of the animal as immune serum. Purification of the desired antibody from the blood can be performed in several ways: salting-out using ammonium or sodium sulfate, isolation by affinity chromatography using protein A or G coupled to the solid support, or even the target compound coupled to the support. Such antibodies are called polyclonal antibodies. Monoclonal antibodies and production methods will be discussed below. Once the antibody is obtained in relatively pure form, it has to be characterized for its intended use. Each of the steps for the generation of antibody and the design of immunoassay will be explained hereinafter.

## Immunogen

Immunogen is defined as the antigen or part of the antigen or optionally the hapten-carrier conjugate that acts or is used to elicit an immune response in an organism for the generation of antibodies. Starting point is the structure and nature of the antigen to which the antibody should be raised. The antigen may be an organism such as a bacterium or virus, or a single compound or even mixture of compounds. Furthermore, the possible toxicity of the antigen should be taken into account. For example, when a bacterium or virus is known to be toxic for the animal to be used, an epitope of the micro-organism may selected, e.g., a membrane component. For toxins there may be used non-toxic derivatives, if possible. Smaller compounds that do not elicit an immune response as such, should be conjugated to a carrier protein. Carriers that may be used for conjugation to an antigen or hapten are generally selected from albumines such as bovine serum albumin (BSA), OVA (egg albumin), keyhole limpet hemocyanin (KLH), thyroglobulin (TG), toxins such as diphteria, tetanus, cholera, and chicken immunoglobuline (IgY). Procedures for conjugation of proteins for enzyme or fluorescent immunoassays are described by Gosling (1996).

In case a compound possesses one or more functional groups such as amine, carboxylic, SH groups, etc. the conventional coupling chemistry may be used (Lemieux and Bertozzi, 1998; Ponsati *et al.,* 1989; Finet, 1998). It will be appreciated that conjugation of a compound to a carrier may alter the physico-chemical properties of the starting compound, which is especially important with regard to the recognition site of the compound for the antibody. Effects of hapten design and of the coupling site on the specificity of the antibody produced have been described. Pesticides generally are produced as classes of similar compounds consisting of a core structure with various substituents and side-groups. The choice of the hapten for antibody production depends on the intended use, single-compound specific or group-specific. Antibodies that recognize the core structure of a group of pesticides can be used for group-specific immunoassys, and in contrast, antibodies that recognize a specific unique part of a pesticide compound can be used for single-compound specific immunoassays. General principles of hapten design are summarized by Szurdoki *et al.* (1995). A hapten strategy for benzimidazoles has been elaborated by Brandon *et al.* (1995). Several monoclonal antibodies were generated using different haptens that allowed for both types of immunoassays. In the case of compounds that do not possess functional or easily accessible groups, these have to be introduced and then sometimes the whole compound has to be reconstructed requiring advanced organic-chemical methods.

## Polyclonal vs. Monoclonal antibodies

In principle, any warm-blooded animal with an immunoglobulin-comprising immune system may be used for the generation of antibodies. In practice, commonly rodents such as rabbits, rats and mice are the animals of choice for small scale production; sheep, goat, monkey, horse, pig, etc. for larger scale production. A slightly different antibody, IgY, is produced by chickens. The advantage of using chickens for the generation of antibodies is that the antibody is present in egg yolk and can readily be purified from the eggs. All such antibodies are Y-shaped proteins constituted of 4 peptide chains as discussed above. Antibodies raised in experimental animals and isolated from immune serum are populations of several species of antibodies having different characteristics as affinity, selectivity and specificity for the target compound. In addition, polyclonal antibodies inherently are limited in amount and therefore may pose the risk that, once consumed, can never be exactly reproduced. To overcome this problem, one can resort to the technique of monoclonal and/or recombinant antibody production and genetic engineering. Production of monoclonal antibodies starts in the same way as for polyclonals, except that mainly mice are used for immunisation. After an appropriate period, antibody-producing splenocytes or B-lymphocytes are isolated and fused with immortalizing myeloma cells to yield hybridomas. These can be cultured infinitely and the aimed antibody can be isolated from the culture medium. Procedures for the production of monoclonal antibodies, being beyond the scope of this article, can be found in Sambrook *et al.* (1989) and Harlow *et al.* (1988). Recombinant antibodies and antibody fragments require genetic engineering of antibody genes into vectors and introduction in, e.g., bacterial or insect cells (Ausubel *et al.*, 1995; Lackuow, *et al.*, 1991; Miller, 1988; Summers *et al.*, 1987; Choudary *et al.*, 1995). Phage antibodies represent another particular type of antibody, wherein the gene for the aimed antibody or fragment thereof is manipulated into a phage chromosome such that it is expressed at the tip of the pili. In this form the phages can be used in an assay, but as an alternative the phages may be manipulated in a way that the antibody fragments are released into the culture medium for use in an immunoassay (Lee *et al.,* 1995).

In addition to the conventional polyclonal and monoclonal antibodies, an alternative has been developed by Ablynx (Ghent, Belgium), the co-called nanobodies. Nanobodies only contain the heavy chains and are derived from dromedaries and llamas. They are much smaller than the common immunoglobulins and much more stable with regard to pH and temperature. A depiction of nanobodies in comparison to normal IgG is given in Fig. 1. These nanobodies are intended for clinical use in the battle against diseases such as cancer, but different application such as in environmental analysis can be envisioned.

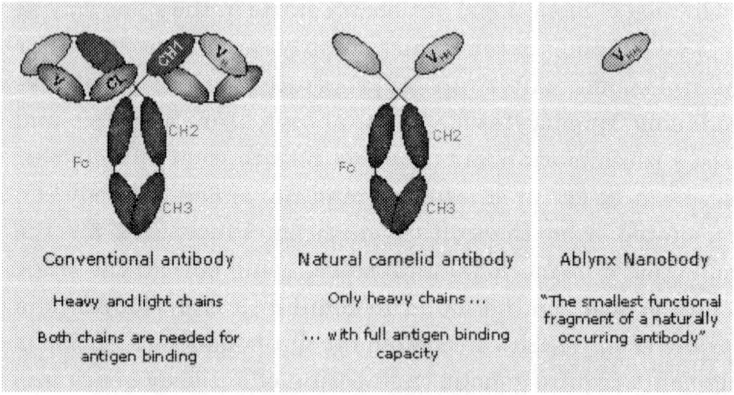


**Fig. 1 :** Illustration of IgG and nanobody

(Source : www.ablynx.be)

## Immunisation

Immunisation generally starts with the injection of the immunogen in adjuvans, for example, Freunds complete adjuvant. Booster injections are given about each three weeks and small blood samples are taken to check for antibody titer. Therefore, the co-called capture antigen/hapten is used. Capture antigen/hapten is similar to the immunogen, except that in the case of haptens a different carrier protein is used to avoid the capture of antibodies against the protein used for synthesizing the immunogen. Capture antibody is coated onto microtiter plates, the immune serum is added in several dilutions and binding is detected using a labeled second antibody, e.g., anti-rabbit IgG coupled to an enzyme such as HRP (horse radish peroxidase). The antibody titer rises in the course of time and reaches a plateau after some months, with sometimes a small decrease later on. An example is given in Fig. 1.

## Development of IA

Once an antibody has been obtained, one has to make a choice with regard to intended use, the format of the IA to be used as well as the method for detection. Further, the type of sample to analyse such a drinking water, surface water, ground water, wastewater, effluent, soil, sediment, snow, air, etc. should be taken into consideration with respect to sample matrix effects. Principles, assay design and fundamentals have been reviewed (Hefle, 1995; Chenesky and Mahony, 1996).

## Format/labels

Immunoassay can be designed in several formats. The first classification is in homogeneous and heterogeneous methods. Heterogeneous assays require separation of bound and unbound fractions, whereas homogeneous assays provide a signal as result of the binding of antibody-antigen. Homogeneous methods are divided in homologous and heterologous assays. Heterogeneous methods can be divided in competitive and non-competitive methods, direct and indirect assays. Examples include the most commonly used ELISA (enzyme-linked immunosorbent assay), IMEA (immunometric enzyme assay), RIA (radioimmunoassay), IRMA (immune radiometric assay), fluorescent/time resolved fluorescent/polarization fluorescent or (bio/chemi)luminescent immunoassays, particle-based assays (based on polymeric or paramagnetic beads), flow-injection immunoassay (FIIA), lateral flow systems, dip sticks. Depending on the choice of format, the label and the corresponding detection system has to be designed. As mentioned, the ELISA is the most commonly used immunoassay system, either in direct or in indirect format. Direct ELISA involves the coating of microtiter plates with antibody, washing, optionally blocking of remaining active sites and washing, addition of enzyme tracer (usually HRP-conjugated antigen/hapten) and sample, washing, and finally addition of coloring reagent such as TMB plus hydrogen peroxide. The resulting absorbances are read using a microtiter plate reader. From the sigmoid standard curve, wherein the zero binding gives the highest value and the high-level standard the lowest value, the concentrations in the samples are calculated. Indirect ELISA comprises coating of antigen or hapten conjugated to carrier protein such as OVA onto microtiter plates, blocking, washing, addition of antibody and sample, washing, addition of enzyme-conjugated second antibody, washing, addition of coloring reagent, followed by reading of absorption values and calculation as above.

## Parameters and Validation

Initially, an immunoassay is designed by optimizing the combination of antibody and detection means. For example, in direct ELISA the concentrations of antibody for coating and of labelled antigen (tracer) are chosen such that the corresponding absorption is between 1.0 and 2.0. Therefore, a so-called checkerboard analysis is set up, meaning that antibody and tracer are each added to a microtiter plate in various dilutions and the best combination is taken for futher investigation, taken into account the background found which should not exceed about 0.2 absorption units. Thereafter the assay has to be validated based on the usual parameters such as standard curve, working range, detection limit, precision (intra- and interassay variation), specificity/cross-reactivity, linearity, accuracy, recovery and matrix effects.

The standard curve is established using the target compound in a series of dilutions in assay buffer or pure water and the concentrations chosen should range from zero to the background point of the curve, wherein IC50 is often used for comparison purposes. From this curve the working range is determined and optimally should cover concentrations to be detected in real samples. The detection limit of the assay may be determined at the 90 % binding point, but the concentration at 3 S.D. from the zero binding point is statistically more correct (Geiß and Einax, 2001; Brady, 1995). To determine the specificity of the assay several related and unrelated compounds are tested for cross-reactivity, which is expressed in the percentage binding of the test compound in relation to the target compound at the IC50 point using the formula: [concentration test compound at IC50 / concentration target compound at IC50] * 100 %. The linearity of an assay is determined by serially diluting a high-level sample followed by measurement. A correlation between dilution factor or concentration found and concentration expected near 1.0 (linear regression analysis) indicates high linearity, which means that real samples can be diluted to be within the working range without interference. In the case the value for linearity deviates considerably, the cause has to be found and may be in matrix effects. Accuracy is generally assessed by comparing results of an immunoassay with a conventional reference method. Recovery means that any concentration of target compound is reproducibly measured in the assay. In general, this parameter is determined by adding various concentrations of compound to a sample and analysing blanc and added samples in one run. Ideally, a correlation factor of 1.0 is found, although a small deviation does not have to affect the assay as long as it is reproducible. As with any analytical method for a diversity of sample types, matrix effects may markedly influence results. These effects may be caused by various interfering substances such as heavy metals, ionic strength, humic acids, cell debris, particulate matter, etc. Although, immunoassays typically are rather insensitive for matrix effects, in case these occur, a solution may sometimes be found in constructing the standard curve in blanc sample matrix, for example, particular surface water or soil extract without target compound. To illustrate the validation parameters, our assay for ibuprofen will be discussed below.

## Immuno Affinity Chromatography (IAC)

Immunoaffinity chromatography is the technique wherein an antibody is covalently coupled onto a solid support and the produced column is used for the capture of target compound from a complex aqueous sample. Any onbound material is passed into the flow-through and the bound target compound can be eluted using appropriate solvents. Such columns may be used to isolate, purify and optionally concentrate any compound(s) for which an antibody has been generated. The advantage is that in particular highly polar compounds can be easily extracted in contrast to conventional extraction techniques, that the antibody provides high specificity and that much lower amounts of organic solvents are required. The size of the column is readily adjustable to a particular application and, for example, several hundreds of mls of can be passed through the column and elution can be performed in a volume of about one ml, allowing a high concentration factor. The eluate will then be further analysed with any methods as desired. Optionally, the IAC column may be inserted in an on-line system connected to, e.g., HPLC or LC-MS.

The principle and technique, types of solid supports, coupling chemistry and applicability of IAC has been described. For example, overviews of silica-based and agarose-based solid supports have been described by van Mohan and Lyddiatt (1992) and Sommeren *et al.* (1993), respectively. General principles of on-ine IAC-LC were discussed by de Frutos (1992), de Frutos and Regnier (1995), Lucas *et al.* (1995); IAC/GC-MS was reviewed by Tsikas (2001); and IAC-CE by Heegaard and Kennedy (2002). Generally, polyclonal and monoclonal antibodies are used for coupling to solid supports, but antibody fragments such as Fv and scFv may also be employed resulting in very stable immunoadsorbents (Berry and Pierce, 1993). Application of IAC for the detection of various classes of compounds is extensively mentioned in literature. Examples of pesticides and metabolites include imidazolinone compouds in soil and plant extracts (Wong *et al.*, 1995), terbutryne in drinking water (Dietrich and Krämer 1995), 2,4-D and atrazine in water (Kim *et al.*, 1993), carbofuran in water and crude potato extract (Rule *et al.* 1994), atrazine in water (Thomas *et al.* 1994), trisulfuron in soil extract (Ghildyal and Kariofillis 1995), phenylurea herbicides in plant material (Lawrence *et al.*, 1996), atrazine and degradation products in river and groundwater (Rollag *et al.*, 1996). The analysis of antibiotics using IAC coupled with several different antibodies was performed by Märtlbauer *et al.* (1996); various aflatoxines were determined in airborne dust using IAC-LC by Kussak *et al.* (1995); mycotoxines such as ochratoxin A and zearalenone were detected by using IAC-HPLC in foods (Eskola *et al.*, 2002). IAC columns for PCDDs/PCDFs were developed by Shelver *et al.* (2002); and for PAHs using sol-gel glass immunosorbent by Schedl *et al.* (2001). EDCs often occur in very low concentrations in the environment, while they show potent activities; a method based on IAC extraction coupled with LC/ESI-MS for the analysis of wastewater was reported by Ferguson *et al.* (2001). In addition to single compounds or groups of related compounds, also micro-organisms may be isolated, purified and concentrated from complex samples, followed by any detection method, such as RT-PCR for waterborne enteric viruses in drinking water supplies (Schwab *et al.*, 1996).

## Immunosensors

Sensors constitute a rather new development for real-time detection of contaminants in the environment and among these, immunosensors have found to be very promising due to sensitivity and specificity. Although, the principle of the sensor has long been known in the form of the pH electrode, detection of specific target compounds has in fact only begun in the 1990s. Sensors exist in various formats and the main parts comprise the sensing part, the interface and the processing part. The combination of an electrochemical electrode with a biological system such as an enzyme has led to a large variety of enzyme sensors. Important improvements have been made by the introduction of fiber optics wherein phenomena of adsorption, fluorescence, bio/chemiluminscence or phosphorescence are employed for signal detection. Alternative detection techniques comprise semiconductor (ISFET), piezoelectric, impedance, and SPR transducers. In addition to enzymes, various other biological systems can be used for the construction of a biosensor, such as micro-organisms, tissues, organelles, receptors and antibodies or fragments thereof. The latter form, the immunosensor, will be discussed here. For the different biosensor types reference is made to a list of review. General principles and designs have been described by Turner (1991, 1992), Tran Minh Canh (1993), Skladal (1997), Marazuela and Moreno-Bondi (2002), Patet (2002) and Wolfbeis (2004). Surveys of commercial biosensors were reported by Myszka (1998); Rich and Myszka (2000), Baird and Myszka (2001), Rich and Myszka (2002). Affinity-based biosensors including immunosensors as well as applications therefore are discussed by Sadik and van Emon (1996), Hock (1997), Marty *et al.* (1998), Rekha *et al.* (2000), Rogers (2000), Luppa *et al.* (2001), Marazuele-Bondi (2002), Suri *et al.* (2002) and Harris *et al.* (2004). An antibody/antigen sensor array based on chemiluminescence and CCD detection for multi-analyte analysis of pesticides was designed by Weller *et al.* (1999). With regard to target compounds, in these reviews some lists are given, for example, pesticides, antibiotics, micro-organisms, toxines detected using enzyme sensors (Patet, 2002) or immunosensors (Suri *et al.*, 2002); PCBs using disposable immunosensors (Rich and Myszka, 2002); metals, bacteria, DNA using fiber optic biosensors (Wolfbeis, 2004). Several compound-specific immunosensors for environmental analysis have been reported. For example, for Clostridium botilinum toxin A (fiber optic, Ogert *et al.*, 1992; Kuma *et al.*, 1994), parathion (fiber optic, Anis *et al.*, 1992), 2,4-D and or 2,4,5-T (amperometric/fiber optic, Bauer *et al.*, 1996; Dzantiev & Zherdev, *1996*; Piras *et al.*, 1996; Wittmann *et al.*, 1996; Wilmer *et al.*, 1997), cholera toxin (fiber optical, Hale *et al.*, 1996), Newcastle disease virus (evanescent wave guide, Lee & Thompson, 1996), atrazine (fiber optic, Mouvet *et al.*, 1996; amperometric, Lopez *et al.*, 1998), toxic Chattonella marina (red tide) (piezoelectric, Nakanishi *et al.*, 1996), fumonisin B (fiber optic, Thompson and Maragos, 1996), carbaryl (flow-through, Gonzalez-Martinez *et al.*, 1997), TNT/RDX (fiber optic, Shrivar-Lake *et al.*, 1997; van Bergen *et al.*, 2000; Kusterbeck *et al.*, 2000), anthrax spores (flow through, Scholl *et al.*, 2000), EDCs (receptor, SPR, Sesay and Cullen, 2001; Hock *et al.*, 2002). However, most of the developed biosensors remain academic. One exception is the River Analyser developed in a EU project RIANA, which is a multi-analyte immunosensor that has been validated for on-line use in the river Rhine (Mallat *et al.*, 2001; Barzen *et al.*, 2002; Tschmelak *et al.*, 2004). Herein fluorescent signals are recorded at several spots where different antibodies against pesticides and industrial chemicals are coupled. Most of the recent developments in immunosensor are made on the Biacore$^{TM}$, an SPR-based apparatus manufactured by Biacore AB, Uppsala, Sweden, of which the Spreeta$^{TM}$ is a simplified and much cheaper version. Our own work included the design of immunosensor assay for bisphenol A on both types of SPR-sensors (Marchesini *et al.,* 2005). An antibody for bisphenol A (BPA) raised against 4,4-bis(4-hydroxyfenyl) valeric acid (BVA) was used in the Biacore biosensor in a competitive assay, wherein BPA, BVA and some structurally related stilbenes were tested. The results are depicted in Fig. 2. The detection limit was found to be approx. 7 ng $ml^{-1}$ for BVA, 10 ng/ml for BPA [70% cross-reactivity (CR)], 5000 ng $ml^{-1}$ for dienestrol (0.1 % CR) and >5000 ng/ml for DES and hexestrol (<0.1% CR). The results on the Spreeta were similar (data not shown).

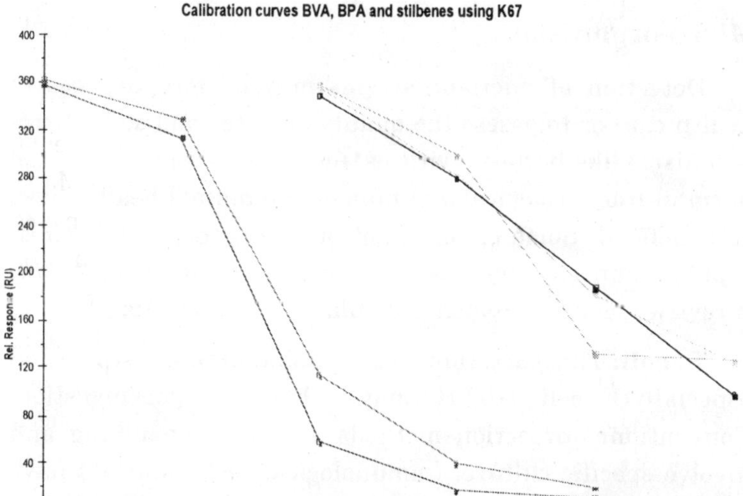


**Fig. 2 :** Cross-reactivity in Biacore sensorassay for bisphenol A

## Target substances/compounds

Substances that may exhibit adverse effects on populations or organisms include single compounds, bacteria and viruses. The first class comprises pesticides, industrial and household products and wastes, toxins, pharmaceuticals, and many other organic compounds. The conventional analytical chemical techniques as described above are suitable for overall detection and quantification. In addition, some immunochemical techniques have been approved for monitoring and early warning control (US EPA, IUPAC). Detection of micro-organisms requires different detection methods, such as bioassays, toxicity assays and specific culturing, optionally in combination with colorimetric, enzymatic, immunochemical or other typing and/or visualizing techniques. The various classes of polluting target compounds include the following:

## Micro-organisms

Detection of micro-organisms may be for purposes of health care or to assess the quality of water and soil. Micro-organisms like bacteria, viruses, fungi, phages may either be harmful from ecological and human and animal health view, or beneficial. Some examples of micro-organisms for which rapid immunochemical tests were developed are given below. A review has been published by Black and Finch (1993).

**E. coli:** This bacterium is an inhabitant of intestines and especially E. coli O157:H7 may be harmful upon ingestion. Conventional detection methods are time-consuming and involve specific culture. Immunological tests and kits have been developed using Fab antibody fragments coated onto paramagnetic beads for separation and fluorescein isothiocyanate conjugated anti-O157 antibody for detection. Numbers of bacteria and duration of the test are superior to known methods. (Pathak, 2001).

**Bacillus anthracis:** Although, known for its toxin anthrax that is used for terroristic attacks, Bacillus anthracis is also a target organism in environmental analysis. An overview of the state of the art in detection methods has been given by Beyer *et al.* (2003). In general, B. anthracis is detected by culturing and PCR analysis.

**Campylobacter:** Environmental waters are considered as a significant source of Campylobacter causing outbreaks of human infections. New detection methods involve a combination of PCR and ELISA after enrichment culture. This assay is able to detect even damaged of viable nonoculturable forms of Campylobacter. [Sails *et al.* 2002].

**Aflatoxin-producing moulds:** Detection of moulds producing aflatoxins was described by Yong and Cousin (2001). Although, this immunoassay was developed for Aspergillus parasiticus, A. flavus, A. sojae and A. oryzae in food, it may optionally be applied to soil samples.

**Rotaviruses:** Gastroenteritis caused by the consumption of shellfish and drinking water contaminated with rotaviruses may be lethal, in particular for infants. Conventional methods using cell culture assays lack sensitivity and are time-consuming. An immunological assay was developed including cell culture from oyster meat and immunofluorescence monoclonal antibodies against the capsid glycoprotein of VP7. Recoveries obtained were close to 100%. (Santos *et al.,* 2002).

**Nitrospira-like bacteria:** Oxidation of nitrite to nitrate is the energy source of chemolithoautotrophic nitrite oxiders. They are ubiquitous in terrestrial and aquatic environments. Most nitrite oxidizers belong to the genus Nitrobacter. In the study of Bartosch *et al.* (2001) an immunoblotting technique using monoclonal antibody and TEM for confirmation was used for detection and identification without culturing.

**Diatoms:** Ground water is often used as drinking water from domestic wells. Such groundwater may be contaminated by surface water through leakage from, e.g., lakes. The presence of diatoms is a measure for surface water influence and ground water quality. Therefore, a direct immunoassay (ELISA) was developed by C.E. Walker *et al.* (2005) using monoclonal antibodies.

**Cryptosporidium:** Cryptosporidiosis is a worldwide disease in human caused by the transmission of oocysts from contaminated drinking water, food and recreational water (Fayer *et al.,* 2000). Infection can be life-threatening and effective therapy is not available. Moreover, oocysts are resistant to disinfectants. Detection and typing of Cryptosporidium species is difficult and time-consuming in a conventional way. Oocysts measure 4-6 μm and contain antigens to be used for the generation of antibodies. According to the article above, there have been developed several immunological-based detection methods, although the specificity of these methods often is low. Furthermore, the concentration of oocysts in a sample is often very low. A solution of this problem has been offered by Pezzana *et al.* (2000). They optimized the Gelman "Envirochek capsule" for concentration of oocysts from drinking water in combination with paramagnetic beads coated with anti-Cryptosporidium antibodies for separation and FITC-labeled monoclonal antibody for examination using an epifluorescent microscope.

**Pasteuria penetrans:** This is an obligate parasitic, gram-positief bacterium of several plant parasitic nematodes and daphnia. Detection and quantification of Pasteuria spores has been integrated in pest management programs. Fould *et al.* (2001) describe the immunological assessment of Pasteuria penetrans in soil samples using polyclonal antibodies in an ELISA.

**Phytium sulcatum:** The presence of Phytium sulcatum in soil is the cause of plant diseases like root browning and may adversely affect crops. For the detection of this fungal organism in infested fields a monoclonal antibody as well as an immunoassay was developed by Kageyama *et al.* (2002).

**Nematodes:** Rapid identification and quantification of plant-parasitic nematodes, being economically important pathogens, are required as part of pest-management strategies. Chen *et al.* (2001) describe the development of methods to capture specifically pathogenic nematodes from soil and water. They lectin-coated beads, immunofluorescent assays as well as immuno-magnetic capture for the recovery and quantification of nematodes.

**Basidiomycetes:** Soil quality depends on the function of fungi in nutrient cycling through decomposition, among others. Responsible agents are, e.g., soil-aggregating basidiomycetes that produce lignin decomposing enzymes. In order to be able to assess the presence of these beneficial micro-organisms, broad-spectrum polyclonal antibodies and ELISA have been designed by Caesar-TonThat *et al.* (12001).

Many more references to immunochemical detection methods for micro-organisms can be found in literature. To determine which ones should be included in monitoring programs for water quality control, the occurrence in drinking water and surface water should be known. A survey was conducted in 2004 by the RIWA (Rhine Water Works) in surface water used for the production of drinking water for the presence of water borne viruses [de Roda Husman *et al.*, 2004]. Several viruses have been found, such as infectious enteroviruses, F-specific phages, somatic phages, reoviruses, noroviruses and rotaviruses. This study was performed by using RT-PCR of virus RNA. In such cases, it would be desirable to develop specific immunoassays for monitoring control of water quality of surface water as well as drinking water.

## Toxins

In general, toxins are produced by organisms as defence means against predators.With respect to human health, those that may be present in food and water pose some particular problems. In the scope of the present discussion, in particular, attention will be given to marine and seafood toxins, bacterial enterotoxins, mycotoxins and microcystines. Marine and seafood toxins are exemplified by brevetoxins, okadaic acid, ciguatoxin (Hokama *et al.* 1992; Hokama and Yoshikawa-Ebesu, 2001; Baden *et al.,* 1995). Bacterial enterotoxins are often the cause of severe diseases and epidemics. Several of these toxins enter the environment by wastewater and faeces. Some examples are Staphylococcus enterotoxin B, Clostridium toxin, Botulinum toxin, difteria, tetanus, etc. Mycotoxins are produced by moulds that may be grown on cereals and these include aflatoxins, zearalenone, zeranol, ochratoxin, deoxynivalenol, fuminisins, T-2 and HT-2 toxins (Visconti *et al.,* 2005; Paepens *et al.,* 2004; Tuomola *et al.,* 2002; Usleber *et al.,* 1993). Microcystines consist of a group of complex, highly stable compounds that are intracellularly produced by blue-green algae or cyanobacteria in high concentrations and are released in surrounding surface water posing a serious global public health issue (Figueiredo *et al.,* 2004). The occurrence of toxic cyanobacteria in the Netherlands has been assessed during a survey (Hoogenboezem *et al.,* 2004). Microcystines are toxic for animals and humans (recreative watersports) causing skin and lung irritation and eventually liver cancer. Blooms of these micro-organisms arise during warm period with low wind. In such periods, the intracellular concentration of microcystines may rise up to more than 5000 $\mu gL^{-1}$ and the extracellular concentration to more than a few hundreds of $\mu g$ $ml^{-1}$. An immunoassay for microcystines has been reported by

McDermott *et al.* (1995), Weller *et al.* (2001). For most of the above toxins there are commercial kits available.

## Pesticides

Pesticide is the generic name for substances used to combat various pests. The can be classified in herbicides, insecticides, fungicides, acaricides, nematicides, bactericides, rodenticides, algicides, disinfectants, and many other biocides. The first immunoassays for environmental analysis were directed to pesticides. Since that time, the number of publications about all types of immunoassays and kits for various types of pesticides has accumulated enormously, including several reviews (Meulenberg *et al.,* 1995; Meulenberg 1997, 1998; Watts and Hegarty 1995; Krotzky & Zeeh 1995; Sherry 1995; Tsung-Che 1995; Szurdoki 1996 Several classes of pesticides have been targeted for immunoassay development, such as organochlorine, organophosphorus, carbamate, (di)thiocarbamate, chlorophenoxycarboxylic acid, triazine, halogenated nitro aromatic, pyrimidine, anilide, urea, carboximide, benzimidazole, dipyridinium, morpholino and triazole pesticide compounds. The majority of environmental immunoassays consists of enzyme immunoassays. At this moment fewer new immunoassays are described and more emphasis is laid on those compounds that pose problems in conventional assays, such as highly polar compounds with regard to extraction difficulties. Furthermore, there also is interest in assays for metabolites, group-specific in stead of compound-specific assays, and multi-analyte immunoassays. The latter form should allow the detection and quantification of more than one pesticide in one run, because major disadvantage of standard immunoassay is the fact that each assay or kit is designed for the analysis of several samples for one target compound.

## Industrial substances

Among the thousands of substances of anthropogenic origin, several classes of industrial contaminants have gained interest due to their persistence, toxicity, high levels, etc. These include PCBs, PAH, dioxins, dioxine-like compounds, phenolic compounds, benzofurans, brominated flame retardants, plasticisers, detergents, metabolites of all these, and many others (Andresen *et al.*, 2004). Industrial contaminants have been listed in the several priority lists as mentioned above, e.g., in EC Directives, IUPAC, US EPA, and given in Eljarrat and Barcelo (2003). Reviews about immunochemical assays can be found in Puig & Barcelo (phenols; 1995) and Watts & Hegarty (pesticides and organics; 1995). For example, PCBs ELISA have been developed by Johnson *et al.* (2001) for oily soil samples, and Franek *et al.* (2001). Dioxins can be measured with immunoassays developed by Matveeva *et al.* (2001) (phosphorescent), Shimomura *et al.* (2001) (ELISA), Shan *et al.* (2001) (soil). Chlorophenols encompass numerous compounds with various numbers of chlorosubstituents. An indirect competitive immunoassay for 2,4,6-trichlorophenol, used as insecticide, bactericide, antiseptic and a byproduct of chlorinating procedures, in the combustion processes and in wastewater of paper and textile industry, has been designed by Galve *et al.* (2002). Dehydroabietic acid, a toxic substance in pulp effluents may be detected using the ELISA of Li *et al.* (1994). Occupational exposure leads to detectable levels in urine and for this purpose an ELISA procedure has been described by Galve *et al.* (2002) for halogenated and brominated compounds. It will be appreciated that such assay can also be employed for environmental analysis.

## Pharmaceuticals/Antibiotics

In the 1990s there was mention of the presence of pharmaceuticals in the environment, especially surface water, wastewaters and effluents of WWTPs at levels comparable to those of pesticides (Buser *et al.*, 1998a). In view of the bioactivity of pharmaceuticals, including antibiotics on humans and animals, together with the lack of knowledge about effects on other organisms, this item has attracted attention of water quality control agencies. In particular, the long term exposure to a combination of various pharmaceuticals at subtoxic level may affect humans (via drinking water) and animals. The occurrence and fate of pharmaceuticals in surface water was already reported by Richardson (1985) and by Halling-Sorensen *et al.* (1998). In the 1990s several surveys were conducted in Germany and Switzerland, where various pharmaceuticals were detected including lipid regulators, antiphlogistics, betablockers, antidepressants, anticancer agents, contrast agents [Stan *et al.*, 1994; Stumpf *et al.*, 1996; Buser *et al.*, 1998a,b; Buser *et al.*, 1999; Ternes, 1998]. Some examples of compounds found at many sites in detectable levels are clofibric acid, ibuprofen, diclofenac. Rönnefart *et al.* (2002) published a list of pharmaceuticals produced and used in Germany in 2001 and also the measures taken and regulations established in recent years. Mons (2004) reviews a conference held in 1993 in the USA about the presence of pharmaceuticals and the effect of purification methods. A RIZA Report (Schrap *et al.*, 2003) describes the results of an extensive survey in the Netherlands. Among the 12,000 human and 2,500 veterinary drugs approved, 100 active compounds were monitored in wastewater, surface water and drinking water at 12 different sites. Some of these compounds were found at quite high levels, such as ibuprofen up to 17 $\mu gl^{-1}$ and naproxen up to 29 $\mu gl^{-1}$ in household waste water. Although, the removal efficiency of these antiphologistics compounds in purification may be up to 95 %, ibuprofen has even been found in drinking water. Analytical methods used in the above investigations included GC, LC and MS. Immunochemical assays for environmental monitoring purposes are scarce. Only ELISAs for ibuprofen and naproxen have been developed and validated (Meulenberg *et al.,* 2005) and an ELISA for fibrates is currently in the validation stage. The one for ibuprofen will be discussed in more detail below. Further, compounds posing problems due to their occurrence in surface water are antibiotics, that may lead to resistent micro-organisms. Antibiotics are used in human and veterinary medicine. They comprise several classes of compounds: penicillines, ß-agonists, sulfonamides, tetracyclins, chloramphenicol, streptomycin, macrolides, etc. These classes are composed of several related compounds, which are structurally related. Antibiotics belonging to the class of sulfonamides may be detected as a group by employing a generic assay as described by Spinks *et al.* (2002) and Korpimäki *et al.* (2004) at the lower ng $ml^{-1}$ level. A review of the production of polyclonal and monoclonal antibodies and the corresponding tracers was published by Märtlbauer (1994). Similarly, and ELISA for isoxazolyl penicillines was developed by Usleber *et al.* (1994).

## Hormone disruptors

Although, concern about hormonal effects of contaminating substances has been expressed already by Colborn (1993, 1996), it was not until the second half of the last decade of the twentieth century that the public was alerted about possible effects of non-hormonal compounds on the endocrine system, in particular the reproductive system by estrogen-mimicking substances. Since that time the number of publications about so-called endocrine disrupting compounds (EDCs) has been exponentially growing, congresses and workshop have addressed the issue (Damstra *et al.,* 2002; Barcelo, 1997) and surveys been conducted. Effects of endogenous and pharmaceutical hormonal compounds may for the greater part be found in the clinical and pharmaceutical literature, but for unknown EDCs new bioassays had to be developed and validated. With regard to pesticides there already existed archives made for approval of the individual compounds, including effects on reproduction of animals and extrapolated to humans. However, such tests often take several generations, especially with mammals such as rats and mice, in order to come to any conclusion and, thus, are not practical for environmental analysis. Therefore, in addition to population statistics, in vitro assays have been designed using cell lines or engineered organisms and analytical-chemical methods have been developed to be able to measure both endogenous and exogenous EDCs in the environment at the low levels they often occur. One of the investigations performed on organismal level is the histological examination of water organisms such as fish, molluscs, alligators etc. on sex changes. Further, the production of the female protein vitellogenin in male liver is an indication of sex changes in fish. Upon a search in various databases, an inventory was made of the Dutch situation with regard to the production, use, and risks of compounds exhibiting xeno-estrogenic action and the presence in drinking water sources and drinking water (Denneman *et al.,* 1998). Several classes were mentioned: natural and synthetic hormones, pesticides, alkylphenols and alkylphenolethoxylates, phthalates, dioxines, phytoestrogens, solvents and drugs. Drinking water appeared to contain in detectable concentrations of more than 1.0 $\mu gl^{-1}$ e.g. atrazine, bis(2-ethyl-hexyl)phthalate, 4-nonylphenol, styrene. Subsequently, a large survey was conducted wherein various types of samples were collected including wastewater, STP effluents, suspended matter, STP sludge, manure, rainwater, surface water and suspended matter, sediment as well as biota. Using HPLC several classes of compounds were analysed: hormones, bisphenol A, alkylphenols and alkylphenolethoxylates, phthalates, polybrominated diphenylethers and polybrominated biphenyls. The results of this LOES project have been published [Verhaak *et al.*, 2002].

Rapid assays for EDCs comprise bioassays as mentioned above and immunoassays. The latter can be used to detect and quantitate assessed compounds showing hormone disrupting activity. Examples of the former are the Two-Hybrid system (Lee *et al.*, 2002) wherein pesticides, alkylphenols and several industrial chemicals were tested and found active as EDCs. EDC detection using a yeast recombinant assay with expression of the human progesterone receptor was employed in a monitoring study in Spain (Garcia-Reyero *et al.*, 2001). Herein positive samples were confirmed by chemical analysis and comprised estrogens and polar surfactants. Receptor assays are described by Takeyoshi *et al.* (2002), Granek and Rishpon (2002), Seifert *et al.* (1999). A vitellogenin ELISA was developed by Ohkubo *et al.* (2003). Estrogen analysis in the form of a multi-analyte assay wherein cross-reactivity of the antibody used was taken into a profit for the detection of several estrogens, was reported by Dieterly *et al.* (2003). A RIA for phytoestrogens was developed by Lapcik *et al.* (2003) and both a fluorescent immunoassay and a heterogeneous assay using total internal reflection fluorescence for estrogens in complex samples by Coille *et al.* (2002).

Natural, synthetic and xeno-estrogens in the environment have gained worldwide attention due to their possible adverse effect on human reproduction and as a potential cause of sex-hormone related cancers, which has led to the development of bioassays and analytical tests as referred to above, as well as several surveys and monitoring programs. However, pollutants may also mimick other types of hormones such as thyroids and corticosteroids. The main endogeneous thyroidal compounds are represented by T4 and T3, and any distrubance of the hormonal equilibrium in human blood may affect metabolism and well-being. The same applies for corticosteroidal hormones, of which the stress-hormone cortisol is the main representative. In order to address the possible effects of pollutants showing thyroidal activity, an investigation was performed to develop a biosensor assays for the assessment of such activity in the scope of a EU grant (EVK1-CT-2001-55002, Marie Curie Host Fellowship). Therefore, the main transport proteins of T4/T3 in human blood, TTR and TBG, were used as binding proteins in a Biacore sensorassay. Various compounds were tested and the results have been published [Marchesini *et al.*, 2005]. By way of illustration, the affinity of a range of industrial compounds in these assays is given in Table 1.

**Table 1 :** Cross-reactivities in TTR/TBG Biacore sensorassay

*Experimental and literature values of the Relative Potency (RP) of the Thyroid Disrupting Chemicals evaluated using the rTTR and TBG-basezd Biosensor Inhibition Assays*

| | **RP** | | **RP value from literature** | |
|---|---|---|---|---|
| | **RTTR** | **TBG** | **rTTR** | **TBG** |
| **L-Thyroxine (T4)** | 1 | 1 | 1 | 1 |
| Triiodothyronine (T3) | 0.03 ± 0.005*[d] | 0.02± 0.004 * | - | - |
| Pentachlorophenol | 0.53 ± 0.1* | < 0.001 | 1.74 ± [15] | 0.001 [15] |
| Pentabromophenol | 0.64 ± 0.1* | < 0.001 | 7.14 ± 1.11[13] | - |

*Contd.*

| | | | | |
|---|---|---|---|---|
| Bisphenol A (BPA) | < 0.001* | < 0.001 | < 0.001 | - |
| TetrabromoBPA | 1.5 ± 0.2[d] | < 0.001 | 10.6 ± 1.29[14] | - |
| TetrachloroBPA | 0.75 ± 0.2*[d] | < 0.001 | 0.76 ± .07[14] | - |
| 4-OH PCB 14 | 4.36 ± 0.5* | < 0.001 | 3.9 ±[9] | < 0.001 [9] |
| PCB 14 | < 0.001 | < 0.001 | 0.59 | |

Results shown are means ± SD of triplicate measurements performed in different days. Values that differ significantly (Student's t test $P < 0.05$)): From T4 are indicated * , from the following compound with higher RP [d]

## Ibuprofen ELISA

As an example of a validation study, the results for our ibuprofen antibody are shown (Meulenberg et al., 2005). The antibody was raised in rabbits and isolated by extraction caprylic acid. The usual parameters were determined and summarized as follows. Using an antibody designated M51, a standard curve (Fig. 3) was set up with a working range of 10 – 10,000 nM and a detection limit of 5 nM. The linearity of the assay showed a regression line with a linear relation of $y = 0.7948 x + 745$; $R^2 = 0.9628$, which is a highly significant correlation. Using spiked WWTP effluent and river water (Meuse) the matrix effects were determined in comparison to ibuprofen in demi-water. Matrix effects in these types of water appeared negligible and the deduced recovery was approx. 100 %. The precision of the ELISA expressed as intra- and inter-assay variation was determined by using a control sample containing about 3100 nM of ibuprofen and analysing in 8-fold on three different occasion. The intra-assay variation varied from 11 % to 18 % and the inter-assay variation was 18 %. Cross-reactivities in the ibuprofen assay are shown in Table 2.

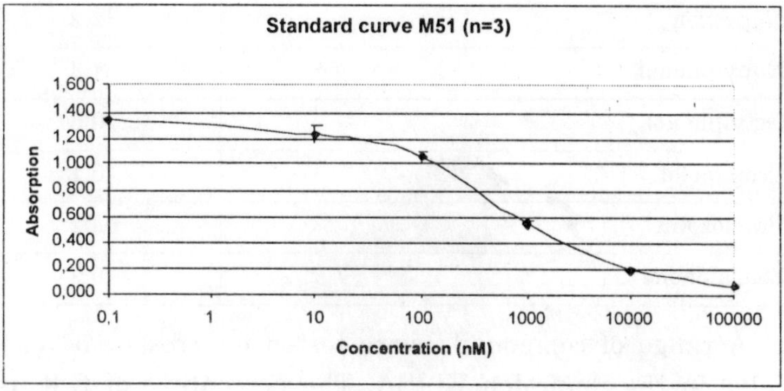


**Fig. 3 :** Standard curve of ibuprofen ELISA

Serial dilutions of a ibuprofen stock solution were added in the ELISA; results of the assay (n = 3) are expressed in absorption values.

**Table 2 :** Cross-reactivities in ibuprofen ELISA

| Substance | % C.R. |
|---|---|
| Bezafibrate | 0.4 |
| Bisphenol A | 0.6 |
| Carazolol | 0.04 |
| Chlorpyrifos | 0.3 |
| Clofibric acid | 0.3 |
| Diclofenac | 0.02 |
| Erythromycine | 0.1 |
| Fenitrothion | 0.5 |
| Fenofibrate | 0.5 |
| Gemfibrozil | 0.2 |
| Ibuprofen | 100 |
| Metoprolol | 0.1 |

*Contd.*

| | |
|---|---|
| Naproxen | 2.2 |
| Nonylphenol | 1.3 |
| Octylphenol | 0.6 |
| Propanolol | 0.1 |
| Vinclozolin | 0.02 |
| Zearalenone | 0.2 |

A range of compounds were tested for cross-reactivity (C.R.) in the ibuprofen ELISA. The percentage of C.R. is calculated at the 50 % binding point (IC50). The binding of the target compound is set at 100 %. The antibody (M51) is found to be highly specific for ibuprofen.

## Conclusions

In addition to the well-known conventional analytic methods for the detection of pollutants in the environment, rapid assays comprising biotests and immunochemical techniques may be used. Biotests include various types of toxicity tests and assays for hormone disrupting activities. Immunochemical techniques include immunoassays for direct detection and quantification of compounds and organisms; immunoaffinity chromatography (IAC) as a pretreatment tool for isolation, purification and concentration of target compounds; and immunosensors for real-type detection. Pollutants have been described in terms of the several classes of compounds and organisms. For numerous target substances, immunoassays and IAC columns have been developed. Moreover, immunosensors are broadly in development. From the above, it will be clear that for the monitoring of pollutants in the environment in order to trace sources and decrease or eliminate contaminating substance, the biotests and immunochemical techniques can be used as rapid cost-effective tools.

## References

Andresen, J.A., Grundmann, A. and Bester, K. (2004) Organophosphorus flame retardants and plasticisers in surface waters. Sci. Total Environ., 332 : 155-166.

Anis, A.N, Wright, J. Roger, K.R., Thompson, R.G., Valdes, J.J. and Eldefrawi, M.E. (1992) A fiber-optic immunosensor for detecting parathion. Anal. Lett., 25 (4): 627-635.

Ausubel, F.M., Brent, R., Kingston, R.E., Moore, D.D., Seidman, J.G., Smith, J.A. and Struhl, K. (1995) *Current Protocols in Molecular Biology*, Vol. 1 and 2, Wiley Interscience, New York.

Baden, D.G., Melinek, R., Sechet, V., Trainer, V.L., Schultz, V.L, Schultz, D.R., Rein, K.S, Tomas, C.R., Delgado, J. and Hale, L. (1995) Modified immunoassays for polyether toxins: Implications of biological matrixes, metabolic states, and epitope recognition. J. AOAC Int., 78 (2): 499-508.

Baird, C.L. and Myszka, D.G. (2001) Current and emerging commercial optical biosensors. J. Mol. Recogn., 14: 261-268.

Ballschmiter, K., Hackenberg, R., Jarman, W.M. and Looser, R. (2002) Man-made chemicals found in remote areas of the world: The experimental definition for POPs. Environ. Sci. & Pollut. Res., 9 (4): 274-288.

Barcelo, D. (ed.) (1997) *Endocrine disrupting compounds: Environmental analysis and effects.* TRAC, 16 (10): 544-619.

Bartosch, S, Hartwig, C., Spieck, E. and Bock, E. (2001) Immunological detection of *Nitrospira*-like bacteria in various soils. Microb. Ecol., 43: 26-33.

Barzen, C., Brecht, A. and Gauglitz, G. (2002) Optical multiple-analyte immunosensor for water pollution control. Biosensors & Bioelectronics, 17: 289-295.

Bauer, C.G., Eremenko, A.V., Ehrentreich-Förster, E., Bier, F.F., Makower, A., Halsall, H.B., Heineman, W.R. and Scheller, F.W. (1996) Zeptomoe-detecting biosensor for alkaline phosphatase in an electrochemical immunoassay for 2,4-dichlorophenoxyacetic acid. Anal. Chem., 68 (15): 2453-2458.

Behmisch, P.A., Hosoe, K. and Sakai, S. (2001) Bioanalytical screening methods for dioxins and dioxin-like compounds –

a review of bioassay/biomarker technology. Environment Int., 27: 413-439.

Berry, M.J. and Pierce, J.J. (1993) Stability of immunoadsorbents comprising antibody fragments: Comparison of Fv fragments and single-chain Fv fragments. J. Chromat., 629: 161-168.

Beyer, W., Bartling, C. and Neubauer, H. (2003) Zum Stand der Nachweisverfahren für *Bacillus anthracis* in klinischen und Umweltproben. Tierärztl. Umschau, 58: 653-662.

Black, E.K. and Finch, G.R. (1993) Detection and occurrence of waterborne bacterial and viral pathogens. Water Environ. Res., 65 (4): 295-300.

Blaise, C., Gagné, F. and Bombardier, M. (2000) Recent developments in microbiotesting and early millenium prospects. Water, Air, and Soil Pollution, 123: 11-23.

Brady, J.F. (1995) *Interpretation of immunoassay data.* Chapter 19 *In : Immunoanalysis of Agrochemicals.* (Eds. J.O. Nelson, A.E. Karu and R.B. Wong) ACS, Washington, pp. 266287.

Brandon, D.L., Binder, R.G., Bates, A.H. and Montague, W.C. Jr. (1995) Hapten strategy for benzimidazole pesticides, drugs, and metabolites. Chapter 6 *In : New Frontiers in Agrochemical Immunoassay.* (Eds. D.A. Kurtz, J.H. Skerritt, and L. Stanker) AOAC Int., Arlington, pp. 77-89.

Bruzzonoti, M.C., Sarzanini, C. and Mentasti, E. (2000) Preconcentration of contaminants in water analysis. J. Chromat. A, 902: 289-309.

Buser, H-R., Müller, M.D. and Theobald, N. (1998a) Occurrence of the pharmaceutical drug clofibric acid and the herbicide mecoprop in various Swiss lakes and in the North Sea. Environ. Sci. Technol., 32 (1): 188-192.

Buser, H-R., Poiger, T. and Müller, M.D. (1998b) Occurrence and fate of the pharmaceutical drug diclofenac in surface waters: Rapid photodegradation in a lake. Environ. Sci. Technol., 32 (22): 3449-3456.

Buser, H-R., Poiger, T. and Müller, M.D. (1999) Occurrence and environmental behavior of the chiral pharmaceutical drug ibuprofen in surface waters and in wastewater. Environ. Sci. Technol., 33: 2529-2535.

Caesar-TonThat, T.C., Shelver, W.L., Thorn, R.G. and Cochran, V.L. (2001) Generation of antibodies for soil aggregating basidiomycete detection as an early indicator of trends in soil quality. Appl. Soil Ecol., 18: 99-116.

Cahn, T.M. (ed.) (1993) *Biosensors*. Chapman & Hall and Masson, Paris.

Chen, Q., Robertson, L., Jones, J.T., Blok, V.C., Phillips, M.S. and Brown, D.J.F. (2001) Capture of nematodes using antiserum and lectin-coated magnetised beads. Nematology, 3 (6): 593-601.

Chernesky, M.A. and Mahony, J.B. (1996) Immunoassays: principles and assay design. Virology Methods Manual, Academic Press Ltd.

Choudary, P.V., Lee, H.A., Hammock, B.D. and Morgan, M.R.A. (1995) *Recombinant antibodies: New Tools for Immunoassays*. Chapter 13 In : New Frontiers in Agrochemical Immunoassays. (Eds. D.A. Kurtz, J.H. Skerritt and L. Stanker) AOAC Int., Arlington, pp., 171-185.

Coille, I., Reder, S., Bucher, S. and Gauglitz, G. (2002) Comparison of two fluorescence immunoassay methods for the detection of endocrine disrupting chemicals in water. Biomol. Eng., 18 : 273-280.

Colborn, T., Dumanoski, D. and Myers, J.P. (eds.) (1996) *Our Stolen Future*. Abacus, London.

Colborn, T., Von Saal, F. and Soto, A. (1993) Developmental effects of endocrine-disrupting chemicals in wildlife and humans. Environ. Health Persp., 101: 378-384.

Dabek-Zlotorzynska, E., Chen, H. and Ding, L. (2003) Recent advances in capillary electrophoresis and capillary electrochromatography of pollutants. Electrophoresis, 24: 4128-4149.

Damstra, T., Barlow, S., Berman, A., Kavlock, R. and Van der Kraak G. (eds.) (2002) *Global Assessment of the State-of-the-Science of Endocrine Disruptors*, WHO/PCS/EDC.

De Frutos, M. (1995) Chromatography-immunology coupling, a powerful tool for environmental analysis. TRAC, 14 (3): 133-140.

De Frutos, M. and Regnier, F.E. (1992) Tandem chromatographic-immunological analyses. ACS Report.

De Roda Husman, A.M., Lodder, W.J., Penders, E.J.M., Krom, A.P., Bakker, G.L. and Hoogenboezem, W. (2004) Viruses in the Rhine and source waters for drinking water production. RIWA, Amsterdam.

Denneman, W.D., Heeg, N., Palsma, A.J. and Janssen, H.M.J. (1998) Xeno-estrogens and drinking water sources. RIWA, Amsterdam.

Dieterle, F., Reder, S. and Gauglitz, G. (2003) Crossreactivity – a disadvantage turns into an advantage for the field biosensor. Technisches Messen. 70 (12): 569-573.

Dietrich, M. and Krämer, P. (1995) Continuous immunochemical determination of pesticides via flow injection immunoanalysis using monoclonal antibodies against terbutryne immobilized to solid support. Food Agric. Immunol., 7: 203-220.

Doherty, F.G. (2001) A review of the Microtox® toxicity test system for assessing the toxicity of sediments and soils. Water Qual. Res. J. Canada, 36 (3): 475-518.

Dzantiev, B.B., Zherdev, A.V., Yalaev, Sitdikov, R.A., Dmitrieva, N.M. and Moreva, I.Yu. (1996) Electrochemical immunosensors for determination of the pesticides 2,4-dichlorophenoxyacetic acid and 2,4,5-trichlorophenoxyacetic acid. Biosensors & Bioelectronics, 11 (1/2): 179-185.

Eeltink, S., Rozing, g.P. and Kok, W.Th. (2003) Recent applications in capillary electrochromatography. Electrophoresis, 24: 3935-3961.

Eljarrat, E. and Barcelo, D. (2003) Priority lists for persistent organic pollutants and emerging contaminants based on their relative toxic potency in environmental samples. TRAC, 22 (10): 655-665.

Eskola, M., Kokkonen, M. and Rizzo, A. (2002) Applicatin of manual and automated systems for purification of ochratoxin A and zearalenone in cereals with immunoaffinity columns. J. Agric. Food Chem., 50: 41-47.

Fayer, R., Morgan, U. and Upton, S.J. (2000) Epidemiology of *Cryptosporidium*: transmission, detection and identification. Int. J. Parasitol., 30 : 1305-1322.

Ferguson, P.L., Iden, C.R., McElroy, A.E. and Brownawell, B.J. (2001) Determination of steroid estrogens in wastewater by immunoaffinity extraction coupled with HPLC-Electrospray-MS. Anal. Chem., 73 (16): 3890-3895.

Figueiredo, D.R., Azeiteiro, U.M., Esteves, S.M., Goncalves, F.J.M. and Pereira, M.J. (2004) Microcystin-producing blooms – a serious global public health issue. Ecotoxicol. Environ. Safety, 59: 151-163.

Finet, JP. (ed.) (1998) *Ligand coupling reactions with heteroatomic compounds.* Tetrahedron Organic Chemistry Series, Vol. 18, Elsevier Science Ltd.

Flurer, C.L. (2003) Analysis of antibiotics by capillary electrophoresis. Electrophoresis, 24: 4116-4127.

Fochtman, P., Raszka, A. and Nierzedska, E. (2000) The use of conventional bioassays, microbiotests, and some "rapid"methods in the selection of an optimal test battery for the assessment of pesticides toxicity. Environ. Toxicol., 15 (5): 376.384.

Fould, S., Dieng, A.L., Davies, K.G., Normand, P. and Mateille, T. (2001) Immunological quantification of the nematode parasitic bacterium *Pasteuria penetrans* in soil. FEMS Microbiol. Ecol., 37: 187-195.

Franek, M. Deng, A., Kolar, V. and Socha, J. (2001) Direct competitive immunoassay for the coplanar polychlorinated biphenyls. Anal. Chim. Acta, 444: 131-142.

Galve, R, Sanchez-Baeza, F., Camps, F. and Marco, M.P. (2002a) Indirect competitive immunoassay for trichlorophenol determination. Rational evaluation of the competitor heterology effect. Anal. Chim. Acta, 452: 191-206.

Galve, R., Nichkova, M., Camps, F., Sanchez-Baeza, F. and Marco, M.P. (2000b) Development and evaluation of an immunoassay for biological monitoring chlorophenols in urine as potential indicators of occupational exposure. Anal. Chem., 74: 468-478.

Garcia-Reyero, N., Grau, E. Castillo, M., Lopez de Alda, M.J., Barcelo, D. and Pina, B. (2001) Monitoring of endocrine disruptors in surface waters by the yeast recombinant assay. Environ. Toxicol. Chem., 20 (6): 1152-1158.

Geiß, S. and Einax, J.W. (2001) Comparison of detection limits in environmental analysis – is it possible ? An approach on quality assurance in the lower working range by verification. Fres. J. Anal. Chem., 370 : 673-678.

Ghildyal, R. and Kariofillis, M. (1995) Determination of triasulfuron in soil: affinity chrmoatography as a soil extract cleanup procedure. J. Biochem. Biophys. Meth., 30: 207-215.

Gizzi, G., Hoogenboom, L.A.P., Von Holst, C., Rose, M. and Anklam, E. (2005) Determination of dioxins (PCDDs/PCDFs) and PCBs in food and feed using the DR CALUX® bioassay: Results of an international validation study. Food Additives Contaminants, 22 (5): 472-481.

Gonzalez-Martinez, M.A., Morais, S., Puchades, R., Maquiera, A., Abad, A. and Montoya, A. (1997) Monoclonal antibody-based flow-through immunosensor for analysis of carbaryl. Anal. Chem., 69: 2812-2818.

Gosling, J.P. (1996) *Enzyme Immunoassay*. Chapter 13, *In : Immunoassay*, pp., 287-308. Academic Press.

Granek, V. and Rishpon, J. (2002) Detecting endocrine-disrupting compounds by fast impedance measurements. Environ. Sci. Technol., 36: 1574-1578.

Hale, Z.M., Payne, F.P., Marks, R.S., Lowe, C.R. and Levine, M.M. (1996) The single mode tapered optical fibre loop immunosensor. Biosensors and Bioelectronics, 11 (1/2): 137-148.

Halling-Sorensen, B., Nors Nielsen, S., Lanzky, P.F., Ingerslev, F., Holten Lützhoft, H.C. and S.E. Jorgensen (1998) Occurence, fate and effects of pharmaceutical substances in the environment – A review. Chemosphere, 36 (20) : 357-393.

Harlow, E. (ed) (1988) *Antibodies: A Laboratory Manual*. Cold Spring Harbor Laboratory Press, Cold Spring Harbor, N.Y.

Harris, R.D., Luff, B.J., Wilkinson, J.S., Wilson, R., Schiffrin, D.J., Piehler, J., Brecht, A., Abuknesha, R.A. and Mouvet, C.

(2004) Integrated optical surface plasmon resonance biosensor for pesticide analysis. Research Journal 1995/6, University of Southampton.

Heegaard, N.H.H. and Kennedy, R.T. (2002) Antigen-antibody interactions in capillary electrophoresis. J. Chromat. B, 768: 93-103.

Hefle, S.L. (1995) Immunoassay fundamentals. Food Technol., Febr., pp. 102-107.

Hock, B. (1997) Antibodies for immunosensors—A review. Anal. Chim. Acta, 347: 177-186.

Hock, B., Seifert, M. and Kramer, K. (2002) Engineering receptors and antibodies for biosensors. Biosensors & Bioelectronics, 17: 239-249.

Hokama, Y. and Yoshikawa-Ebesu, J.S.M. (2001) Ciguatera fish poisoning: a foodborne disease. J. Toxicol. – Toxin Reviews, 20 (2): 85-139.

Hokama, Y., Hong, T.W.P., Isobe, M., Ishikawa, Y. and Yasumoto, T. (1992) Cross-reactivity of highly purified okadaic acid (OA), synthetic spiroketal east sphere of OA and ciguatoxin. J. Clin. Lab. Anal., 6: 54-58.

Hoogenboezem, W., Wagenvoort, A.J. and Blaauboer, K. (2004) The occurence of toxic cyanobacteria. RIWA, Amsterdam

Hoogendoorn, E. and van Zoonen, P. (2000) Recent and future developments of liquid chromatography in pesticide trace analysis. J. Chromat. A, 892: 435-453.

Imbenotte, M., Azaroual, N., Cartigny, B., Vermeersch, G. and Lhermitte, M. (2003) Detection and quantitation of xenobiotics in biological fluids by 1H NMR spectroscopy. J. Toxicol. Clin. Toxicol., 41 (7): 955-962.

Jeannot, R. and Sauvard, E. (2000) Determination of pesticides and some of their degradation products in ground and surface water by LC/MS. Int. J. Food Sci., 2 (12): 219-231.

Johnson, J.C., van Emon, J.M., Clarke, A.N. and Wamsley, B.N. (2001) Quantitative ELISA of polychlorinated biphenyls in an oily soil matrix using supercritical fluid extraction. Anal. Chim. Acta, 428: 191-199.

Kageyama, K., Kobayashi, M., Tomita, M., Kubota, N., Suga, H. and Hyakumachi, M. (2002) Production and evaluation of monoclonal antibodies for the detection of *Phytium sulcatum* in soil. J. Phytopathol., 150: 97-104.

Kim, B.B. and Vlasov, E.V. (1993) Immunoaffinity chromatographic method for the detection of pesticides. Anal. Chim. Acta, 280: 191-196.

Köhler, S., Belkin, S. and Schmid, R.D. (2000) Reporter gene bioassays in environmental analysis. Fres. J. Anal. Chem., 366 : 769-779.

Koppen, G., Covaci, A., Van Cleuvenbergen, R., Schepens, P., Winneke, G., Nelen, V. and Schoeters, G. (2001) Comparison of CALUX-TEQ values with PCB and PCDD/F measurements in human serum of the Flanders environmental and health study (FLEHS). Toxicol. Lett., 123: 59-67.

Korpimäki, T. Brockmann, E-C., Kuronen, O, Saraste, M., Lamminmäki, U and Tuomola, M. (2004) Engineering of a broad specificity antibody for simultaneous detection of 13 sulfonamides at the maximum residue level. J. Agric. Food Chem., 52: 40-47.

Krotzky, A.J. and Zeeh, B. (1995) Immunoassays for residue analysis of agrochemicals: proposed guidelines for precision, standardization and quality control. Pure & Appl. Chem., 67 (12): 2065-2088.

Kuma, P., Colston, J.T. and Chambers J.P. (1994) Detection of botulinum toxin using an evanescent wave immunosensor. Biosensors & Bioelectronics, 9: 57-63.

Kussak, A., Andersson, B. and Andersson, K. (1995) Determination of aflatoxins in airborne dust from feed factories by automated immunoaffinity column clean-up and liquid chromatography. J. Chromat. A, 708: 55-60.

Kusterbeck, A.W., Gauger, P.R. and Charles, P.T. (2000) Environmental applications of the NRL flow immunosensor. *In : Rapid Methods for Analysis of Biological Materials in the Environment,* pp., 79-85. (Eds. P.J. Stopa and Bartoszcze) Kluwer Academic Publishers.

Lackuow, V.A. *et al.* (1991) Cloning and expression of heterologous genes in inesct cells with baculovirus vectors. *Recombinant*

*DNA Technology and Applications.* (Eds. C. HO, A. Prokop and R. Bajpai)McGraw-Hill, NY.

Lapcik, O., Stursa, J., Kleinova, T., Vitkova, M., Dvorakova, H., Klejdus, B. and Moravcova, J. (2003) Synthesis of hapten and conjugates of coumestrol and development of immunoassay. Steroids, 68: 1147-1155.

Larsson, P.O., Glad, M., Hansson, L., Mansson, M-O., Ohlson, S. and Mosbach, K. (1983) *High-performance liquid affinity chromatography. In : Advances in Chromatography, Vol.* 21, pp., 41-85. (Eds. J.C. Giddings, E. Grushka, J. Cazes, and P.R. Brown) Marcel Dekker Inc.

Lawrence, J.F., Ménard, C., Hennion, M-C., Pichon, V., Le Goffic, F. and Durand, N. (1996) Use of immunochromatograpy as a simplified cleanup technique for the liquid chromatographic determination of phenylurea herbicides in plant material. J. Chromat. A, 732: 277-281.

Lec, H.A., Alcocer, M.J.C., Lacarra, T.G., Jeenes, D.J. and Morgan, M.R.A. (1995) Recombinant antibodies: Expression in Escherichia coli using plasmid and phagemid vectors and application to food analytes. Chapter 14 *In : New Frontiers in Agrochemical Immunoassay.* (D.A. Kurtz, J.H. Skerritt, and L. Stanker) AOAC Int., Arlington pp., 187-196.

Lee, H.S., Miyauchi, K., Nagata, Y., Fukuda, R., Sasagawa, S., Endoh, H., Kato, S., Horiuchi, H., Tagaki, M. and Ohta, A. (2002) Employment of the human estrogen receptor ß ligand-binding domain and co-activator SRC1 nuclear receptor-binding domain for the construction of a yeast two-hybrid detection system for endocrine disruptors. J. Biochem., 131: 399-405.

Lee, W.E. and Thompson, H.G. (1996) Detection of Newcastle disease virus using an evanescent wave immuno-based biosensor. Can. J. Chem., 74: 707-712.

Lemieux, G.A. and Bertozzi, C.R. (1998) Chemoselective ligation reactions with proteins, oligosaccharides and cells. TIBTECH, 16: 506-513.

Li, K., Chester, M., Kutney, J.P., Saddler, J.N. and Breuil, C. (1994) Production of polyclonal antibodies for the detection of dehydroabietic acid in pulp mill effluents. Anal. Lett., 27 (9): 1671-1688.

Lopez, M.A., Ortega, F., Dominguez and Katakis, I. (1998) Electrochemical immunosensor for the detection of atrazine. J. Mol. Recogn., 11: 178-181.

Lucas, A.D., Gee, S.J., Hammock, B.D. and Seiber, J.N. (1995) Integration of immunochemical methods with other analytical techniques for pesticide residue determination. J. AOAC Int., 78: 585-591.

Luppa, P.B., Sokoll, L.J. and Chan, D.W. (2001) Clin. Chim. Acta, 314: 1-26.

Mallat, E., Barzen, C., Abuknesha, R., Gauglitz, G. and Barcelo, D. (2001) Fast determination of paraquat residues in water by an optical immunosensor and validation using capillary electrophoresis-ultraviolet detection. Anal. Chim. Acta, 427: 165-171.

Marazuela, M.D. and Moreno-Bondi, M.C. (2002) Fiber-optic biosensors – an overview. Anal. Bioanal. Chem., 372: 664-682.

Marchesini, G.R., Meulenberg, E., Haasnoot, W. and Irth, H. (2004) Biosensor immunoassays for the detection of bisphenol A. Anal. Chim. Acta, 528 (1): 37-45.

Marchesini, G.R., Meulenberg, E., Haasnoot, W., Mitzuguchi, M. and Irth, H. (2005) Biosensor recognition of thyroid disrupting chemicals using transport proteins. Anal. Chem., submitted.

Märtlbauer, E., Usleber, E., Schneider, E. and Dietrich, R. (1994) Immunichemical detection of antibiotics and sulfonamides. Analyst, 119: 2543-2548.

Märtlebauer, E., Dietrich, R. and Usleber, E. (1996) Immunoaffinity chromatrography as a tool for the analysis of antibiotics and sulfonamides. Chapter 13 *In : Veterinary Drug Residues.* pp. 121-131. ACS Series.

Marty, J.-L., Leca, B. and Noguer, T. (1998) Biosensors for the detection of pesticides. Analusis Magazine, 26 (6): M144-M149.

Matveeva, E.G., Gribkova, E.V., Sanborn, J.R., Gee, S.J., Hammock, B.D. and Savitsky, A.P. (2001) Development of a homogeneous phosphorescent immunoassay for the detection of polychlorinated dibenzo-p-dioxins. Anal. Lett., 34 (13): 2311-2320.

McDermott, C.M., Feola, R. and Plude, J. (1995) Detection of cyanobacterial toxins (microcystins) in waters of Northeastern Wisconsin by a new immunoassay technique. Toxicon, 33 (11): 1433-1442.

Meulenberg, E.P. (1997) Immunochemical detection of environmental and food contaminants: Development, validation and application. Food Technol. Biotechnol., 35 (3): 153-163.

Meulenberg, E.P. (1998) Pesticides, immunoassays. *In : Encyclopedia of Environmental Analysis and Remediation.* (Ed. R.A. Meyers) John Wiley & Sons, Inc.

Meulenberg, E.P., Peelen, G.O.H, Lukkien, E. and Koopal, K. (2005) Immunochemical detection methods for bioactive pollutants. Intern. J. Environ. Anal. Chem., 85 (12-13): 861-870.

Meulenberg, E.P., W-H. Mulder and P.G. Stoks (1995) Immunoassays for pesticides. Environ. Sci. Technol., 29 (3): 553-561.

Miller, L.K. (1988) *Vectors : A Survey of Molecular Cloning Vectors and Their Uses.* (Eds. R.L. Rodriguez and D.T. Denhardt) Buttersworth, Boston.

Mohan, S.B. and Lyddiatt, A. (1992) Silica-based solid phases for affinity chromatography: Effect of pore size and ligand location upon biochemical activity. Biotechnol. Bioengg., 40: 549-563.

Mons, M. (2004) International investigation into pharmaceuticals in water. H2O, 25/26: 14.

Motohashi, N., Nagashima, H. and Parkanyi, C. (2000) Supercritical fluid extraction for the analysis of pesticide residues in miscellaneous samples. J. Biochem. Biophys. Meth., 43: 313-328.

Mouvet, C., Amalric, L., Broussard, S., Lang, G., Brecht, A. and Gauglitz, G. (1996) Reflectrometric interference spectroscopy for the determination of atrazine in natural water samples. Environ. Sci. Technol., 30 (6): 1846-1851.

Myszka, D.G. (1999) Survey of the 1998 optical biosensor literature. J. Mol. Recogn., 12: 390-408.

Nakanishi, K., Karube, I., Hiroshi, S., Uchida, A. and Ishida, Y. (1996) Detection of the red tide-causing plankton

*Chattonella marina* using a piezoelectric immunosensor. Anal. Chim. Acta, 325: 73-80.

Ogert, R.A., Brown, J.E., Singh, B.R., Shriver, L.C. and Ligler, F.S. (1992) Detection of *Clostridium botulinum* Toxin A using a fiber optic-based biosensor. Anal. Biochem., 205: 306-312.

Ohkubo, N., Mochida, K., Adachi, S., Hara, A., Hotta, K., Nakamura, Y. and Matusbara, T. (2003) Development of enzyme-linked immunosorbent assays for two forms of vitellogenin in Japanese common goby (*Acanthogobius flavimanus*). Gen. Compar. Endocrin., 131: 353-364.

Paepens, C., De Saeger, S., Sibanda, L., Barna-Vetro, I, Léglise, I., Van Hove, F. and Van Peteghem, C. (2004) A flow-through enzyme immunoassay for the screening of fumonisins in maize. Anal. Chim. Acta, 523: 229-235.

Palmer, G., McFadzean, R., Killham, K., Sinclair, A. and Paton, G.I. (1998) Use of *LUX*-based biosensors for rapid diagnosis of pollutants in arable soils. Chemosphere, 36 (12): 2683-2697.

Patel, P.D. (2002) (Bio)sensors for measurement of analytes implicated in food safety: a review. TRAC, 21 (2): 96-115.

Pathak, S.P. and Gopal, K. (2001) Rapid detection of *Escherichia coli* as an indicator of faecal pollution in water. Ind. J. Microbiol., 41: 139-151.

Pezzana, A., Vilaginès, Ph., Bordet, F., Coquard, D., Sarrette, B. and R. Villaginès, R. (2000) Optimization of the Envirochek capsule method and immunomagnetic separation procedure for the detection of low levels of *Cryptosporidium* in large drinking water samples. Water Sci. Technol., 41 (7): 111-117.

Piras, L., Adami, M., Fenu, S., Dovis, M. and Nicolini, C. (1996) Immunoenzymatic application of a redox potential biosensor. Anal. Chim. Acta, 335: 127-135.

Poinsot, V., Bayle, C. and Couderc, F. (2003) Recent advances in amino acid analysis by capillary electrophoresis. Electrophoresis, 24: 4047-4062.

Ponsati, B., Giralt, E. and Andreu, D. (1989) A synthetic strategy for simultaneous purification-conjugation of antigenic peptides. Anal. Biochem., 181 (2): 389-395.

Puig, D. and Barcelo, D. (1995) Determination of phenolic compounds in water and waste water. TRAC, 15 (8): 362-375.

Rekha, K., Thakur, M.S. and Karanth, N.G. (2000) Biosensors for the detection of organophosphorous pesticides. Crit. Rev. Biotechnol., 20 (3): 213-235.

Rich, R.L. and Myszka, D.G. (2000) Survey of the 1999 surface plasmon resonance biosensor literature. J. Mol. Recogn., 13: 388-407.

Rich, R.L. and Myszka, D.G. (2001) Survey of the 2000 commercial optical biosensor literature. J. Mol. Recogn., 14: 273-294.

Rich, R.L. and Myszka, D.G. (2002) Survey of the year 2001 commercial optical biosensor literature. J. Mol. Recogn., 15: 352-376.

Richardson, M.L. and Bowron, J.M. (1985) The fate of pharmaceuticals in the aquatic environment. J. Pharm. Pharmacol., 37 (1): 1-12.

Richardson, S.D. (2001) Mass spectrometry in environmental sciences. Chem. Rev., 101 (2): 211-254.

Richardson, S.D. (2004) Environmental mass spectrometry: Emerging contaminants and current issues. Anal. Chem., 76 (12): 3337-3364.

Rogers, K.R. (2000) Principles of affinity-based biosensors. Mol. Biotechnol., 14: 109-129.

Rollag, J.G., Beck-Westermeyer, M. and Hage, D.S. (1996) Analysis of pesticide degradation products by tandem high-performance immunoaffinity chromatography and reversed-phase liquid chromatography. Anal. Chem., 68 (20): 3631-3637.

Rönnefart, I., Koschorreck, J. and Kolossa-Gehring, M. (2002) *Arzneimittel in der Umwelt. Mitteilungsblatt der Fachgruppe Umweltchemie und Oekotoxikologie,* 8, No. 4.

Rule, G.S., Mordehai, A.V. and Henion, J. (1994) Determination of carbofuran by on-line immunoaffinity chromatography with coupled-column liquid chromatography/mass spectrometry. Anal. Chem., 66 (2): 230-235.

Sadik, O.A. and Van Emon, J. (1996) Applications of electrochemical immunosensors to environmental monitoring. Biosensors & Bioelectronics, 11 (8): i-xi.

Sails, A.D., Bolton, F.J., Fox, A.J., Wareing, D.R.A. and Greenway, D.L.A. (2002) Detection of *Campylobacter jejuni* and *Campylobacter coli* in environmental waters by PCR enzyme-linked immunosorbent assay. Appl. Environ. Microbiol., 68 (3): 1319-1324.

Sambrook, J, Fritsch, E.F., Maniatis, T. and Nolan, C. (eds.) (1989) *Molecular Cloning: A Laboratory Manual.* Cold Spring Harbor Laboratory Press, Cold Spring Harbor, N.Y.

Santos, C.S., Rigotto, C., Simöes, C.M.O. and Barardi, C.R.M. (2002) Detection of viable Rotaviruses in shellfish by means of cell culture and immunofluorescence assay. J. Food Sci., 67 (5): 1868-1871.

Sasano, R., Hamada, T., Kurano, M. and Furuno, M. (2000) On-line coupling of solid-phase extraction to gas chromatography with fast solvent vaporazion and concentration in an open injector liner. Analysis of pesticides in aqueous samples. J. Chromat. A, 896: 41-49.

Schedl, M., Wilharm, G., Achatz, S., Kettrup, A., Niessner, R. and Knopp, D. (2001) Monitoring polycyclic aromatic hydrocarbon metabolites in human urine: Extraction and purification with a sol-gel glass immunosorbent. Anal. Chem., 73: 5669-5676.

Schmitt-Kopplin, P. and Frommberger, M. (2004) Capillary electrophoresis – mass spectrometry: 15 years of developments and applications. Electrophoresis, 24: 3837-3867.

Scholl, P.F., Bargeron, C.B., Phillips, T.E., Wong, T., Abukaker, S., Groopman, J.D., Strickland, P.T. and Benson, R.C. (2000) Immunoaffinity based phosphorescent sensor platform for the detection of bacterial spores. *In : In-vitro Diagnostic Instrumentation,* (Ed. G.E. Cohn) Proceedings of SPIE, vol. 3913, Washington.

Schrap, M., Pijnenburg, J. and Geerdink, R. (2004) Prefluorinated compounds in Dutch surface water. RIZA Report 2004.25/2004.037, Rijkswaterstaat.

Schwab, K.J., De Leon, R. and Sobsey, M.D. (1996) Immunoaffinity concentration and purification of waterborne enteric viruses for detection by reverse transcriptase PCR. Appl. Environ. Microbiol., 62 (6): 2086-2094.

Seifert, M., Haindl, S. and Hock, B. (1999) Development of an enzyme linker receptor assay (ELRA) for estrogens and exoestrogens. Anal. Chim. Acta, 386: 191-199.

Sesay, A.M. and Cullen, D.C. (2001) Detection of hormone mimics in water using a miniturased SPR sensor. Environ. Monitoring Assessment, 70: 83-92.

Shan, G., Leeman, W.R., Gee, S.J., Sanborn, J.R., Jones, A.D., Chang, D.P.Y. and Hammock, B.D. Highly sensitive dioxin immunoassay and its application to soil and biota samples. Anal. Chim. Acta., 444: 169-178.

Shelver, W.L., Shan, G., Lee, S.J., Stanker, L.H. and Hammock, B.D. (2002) Comparison of immunoaffinity column recovery patterns of polychlorinated dibenzo-p-dioxins/polychlorinated dibenzofurans on columns generated with different monoclonal antibody clones and polyclonal antibodes. Anal. Chim. Acta, 457: 199-209.

Sherry, J.P. (1995) Immunodetection of ecosystem contaminants. Research, application and acceptance in Canda. Chapter 24 *In : Immunoanalysis of Agrochemicals.* pp.335-353. ACS, Washington.

Shimomura, M., Nomura, Y., Lee, K-H., Ikebukuro, K. and Karube, I. (2001) Dioxin detection based on immunoassay using a polyclonal antibody against octa-chlorinated dibenzo-p-dioxin (OCDD). Analyst, 126: 1207-1209.

Shrivar-Lake, L.C., Donner, B.L. and Ligler, F.S. (1997) On-site detection of TNT with a portable fiber optic biosensor. Environ. Sci. Technol., 31 (3): 837-841.

Skladal, P. (1997) Advances in elctrochemical immunosensors. Electroanalysis, 9 (10): 737-745.

Spinks, C.A., Wyatt, G.M., Everest, S., Jackman, R. and Morgan, M.R.A. (2002) Atypical antibody specificity: advancing the development of a generic assay for sulphonamides using heterologous ELISA. J. Sci. Food Agric., 82: 428-434.

Stan, H-J., Heberer, T. and Linkerhägner, M. (1994) Occurrence of clofibric acid in the aquatic system – Is the use in human medical care the source of the contamination of surface, ground and drinking water? Vom Wasser, 83: 57-68.

Stumpf, M., Ternes, T.A., Haberer, K. Seel, P. and Baumann, W. (1996) Determination of pharmaceuticals in sewage plants and river water. Vom Wasser, 86: 291-303.

Summers, M.D. *et al.* (1987) A manual of methods for baculovirus vectors and insect cell culture procedures. Texas Agricultural Experimental Station Bulletin, No. 1555.

Suri, C.R., Raje, M. and Varshey, G.C. (2002) Immunosensors for pesticide analysis : Antibody production and sensor development. Crit. Rev. Biotechnol., 22 (1): 15-32.

Suzuki, G., Takigami, H., Kushi, Y. and Sakai, S. (2004) Evaluation of mixture effects in a crude extract of compost using the CALUX bioassay and HPLC fractionation. Environ. Int., 30: 1055-1066.

Szurdoki, F., Bekheit, H.K.M., Marco, M-P., Goodrow, M.H. and Hammock, B.D. (1995) *Important factors in hapten design and enzyme-linked immunosorbent assay development.* Chapter 4 *In : New Frontiers in Agrochemical Immunoassay.* (Eds. D.A. Kurtz, J.H. Skerritt, and L. Stanker) AOAC Int., Arlington, pp. 39-63.

Szurdoki, F., Jaeger, L., Harris, A., Kido, H., Wengatz, I., Goodrow, M.H., Szekacs, A., Wortberg, M., Zheng, J., Stoutamire, D.W., Sanborn, J.R., Gilman, S.D., Jones, A.D., Gee, S.J. Choudary, P.V. and Hammock, B.D. (1996) Rapid assays for environmental and biological monitoring. J. Environ. Sci. Health, B31 (3): 451-458.

Takeyoshi, M., Yamasaki, K., Sawaki, M., Nakai, M., Noda, S. and Takatsuki, M. (2002) The efficacy of endocrine disruptor screening tests in detecting anti-estrogenic effects downstream of receptor-ligand interactions. Toxicol. Lett., 126: 91-98.

Ternes, T.A. (1998) Occurrence of drugs in German sewage treatment plants and rivers. Water Res., 32 (11): 3245-3260.

Thomas, D.H., Beck-Westermeyer, M. and Hage, D.S. (1994) Determination of atrazine in water using tandem high-performance immunoaffinity chromatography and reversed-phase liquid chromatography. Anal. Chem., 66 (21): 3823-3829.

Thompson, V.S. and Maragos, C.M. (1996) Fiber-optic immunosensor for the detection of fumonisin B1. J. Agric. Food. Chem., 44 (4): 1041-1046.

Tschmelak, J., Proll, G. and Gauglitz, G. (2004) Verification of performance with the automated direct optical TIRF immunosensor (River Analyser) in single and multi-analyte assays with real water samples. Biosensors & Bioelectronics, 20 (4): 743-752.

Tsikas, D. (2001) Affinity chromatography as a method for sample preparation in gas chromatography / mass spectrometry. J. Biochem. Biophys. Meth., 49: 705-731.

Tsunch-Che, T. (1995) Immunochemical methods for detection of toxins and pesticides. Chapter 31 *In : Molecular Methods in Plant Pathology*. (Eds. R.P. Singh and U.S. Singh) CRC Lewis Publishers, pp., 445-460.

Tuomola, M., Cooper, K.M., Lahdenperä, S., Baxter, G.A., Elliott, C.T., Kennedy, D.G. and Lövgren, T. (2002) A specificity-enhanced time-resolved fluoroimmunoassay for zeranol employing the dry reagent all-in-one-well principle. Analyst, 127: 83-86.

Turner, A.P.F. (2001) *Advances in Biosensors, Vol. 1*, JAI Press Ltd., London.

Turner, A.P.F. (2002) *Advances in Biosensors, Vol. 2*, JAI Press Ltd., London.

Usleber, E., Lorber, M., Straka, M., Terplan, G. and Märtlbauer, E. (1994) Enzyme immunoassay for the detection of isoxazolyl penicillin antibiotics in milk. Analyst, 119: 2765-2768.

Van Bergen, S.K., Bakaltcheva, I.B., Lundgren, J.S. and Shriver-Lake, L.C. (2000) On-site detection of explosives in groundwater with a fiber optic biosensor. Environ. Sci. Technol., 34: 704-708.

Van der Lelie, D., Verschaeve, L., Regniers, L. and Corbisier, P. (2000) *Use of bacterial tests (the VITOTOX® genotoxicity test and the BIOMET heavy metal test) to analyze chemicals and environmental samples*. New Microbiotests for Routine Toxicity Screening and Biomonitoring. (Eds. G. Persoone, C. Janssen, and De W. Coen) Kluwer Academic/Plenum Publishers.

Van Sommeren, A.P.G., Machielsen, P.A.G.M. and Gribnau, T.C.J. (1993) Comparison of three activated agaroses for use in affinity chromatography: effects on coupling performance and ligand leakage. J. Chromat., 639: 23-31.

Vethaak, A.D., Rijs, G.B.J., Schrap, S.M., Ruiter, H., Gerritsen, A. and Lahr, J. (2002) Estrogens and xeno-estrogens in the aquatic environment of the Netherlands. RIZA/RIKZ Report 2002-001, Lelystad.

Visconti, A., Lattanzio, V.N.T., Pascale, M. and Haidukowsky, M. (2005) Analysis of T-2 and HT-2 toxins in cereal grains by immunoaffinity clean-up and liquid chromatography with fluorescence detection. J. Chromat. A, 1075: 151-158.

Volpi Ghiradini, A., Ghetti, P.F., Di Leo, V. and Pantani, C. (1998) Microtox® solid-phase bioassay in sediment toxicity assessment. Proceedings of the International Association for Theoretical and Applied Limnology, Congress in Sao Paulo, 1995. Published in Verh. Internat. Verein. Limnol., 26: 2393-2397.

Walker, C.E., Schrock, R.M., Reilly, T.J. and Baehr, A.L. (2005) A direct immunoassay for detecting diatoms in groundwater as an indicator of the direct influence of surface water. J. Appl. Phycol., 17: 81-90.

Waterval, J.C.M., Lingeman, H., Bult, A. and Underberg, W.J.M. (2001) Derivatization trends in capillary electrophoris. Electrophoresis, 21: 4029-4045.

Watts, C.D. and Hegarty, B. (1995) Use of immunoassays for the analysis of pesticides and some other organics in water samples. Pure & Appl. Chem., 67 (8/9): 1533-1548.

Weller, M.G., Schuetz, A.J., Winklmaier, M. and Niessner, R. (1999) Highly parallel affinity sensor for the detection of environmental contaminants in water. Anal. Chim. Acta, 393: 29-41.

Weller, M.G., Zeck, A., Eikenberg, A., Nagata, N., Ueno, Y. and Niessner, R. (2001) Anal. Sci., 17: 1445-1448.

Wilmer, M., Trau, D., Renneberg, R. and Spener, F. (1997) Amperometric immunosensor for the detection of 2,4-dichlorophenoxyacetic acid (2,4-D). Anal. Lett., 30 (3): 515-525.

Wittmann, C., Bier, F.F., Eremin, S.A. and Schmid, R.D. (1996) Quantitative analysis of 2,4-dichlorophenoxyacetic acid in water samples by two immunosensing methods. J. Agric. Food. Chem., 44: 343-350.

Wolfbeis, O.S. (2004) Fiber-optic chemical sensors and biosensors. Anal. Chem., 76: 3269-3284.

Wong, R.B., Pont, J.L., Johnson, D.H., Zulalian, J., Chin, T. and Karu, A.E. (1995) Immunoaffinity chromatography applications in pesticide metabolism and residue analysis. Chapter 5 *In : Immunoanalysis of Agrochemicals.* pp. 235-247, ACS, Washington.

Yong, R.K. and Cousin, M.A. (2001) Detection of moulds producing aflatoxins in maize and peanuts by an immunoassay. Int. J. Food Microbiol., 65: 27-38.

CHAPTER 9

# CYTOCHROME P450: A TOOL TO ASSESS ORGANIC XENOBIOTIC EXPOSURE IN ORGANISMS

**V. Gayathri and P.A. Azeez**

EIA Division, Sálim Ali Centre for Ornithology and Natural History
Anaikatty, Coimbatore – 641 108, India

## ABSTRACT

Several studies show that Cytochrome P450 and associated enzymes are good as biomarkers for a variety of pollutants. Among the CYP1A-associated monooxygenases, particular interest was seen among researchers on EROD induction. Extensive studies have suggested that monooxygenase can serve as a biochemical marker for exposure to PAH- and PCB-types of pollutants. EROD induction appears to be a reliable surrogate measure of exposure of organics analysis in invertebrates, fish, birds and mammals. A number of techniques are available for measuring CYP1A induction such as Western blotting, enzyme linked immunosorbent assay, Polymerase chain reaction (PCR) techniques, radioimmuno assay and detection of mRNA using cDNA probes. The present topic attempts a brief review of cytochromes and associated enzymes as biomarker for micro-organic contaminants in the environment.

**Keywords**: Cytochrome P450, CYP1A-associated monooxygenase, Biomarkers EROD induction, micro-organic contamination, PAH, PCB, dioxins

## Introduction

Polycyclic aromatic hydrocarbons (PAHs) and polychlorinated biphenyls (PCBs) are two classes of organic compounds widely distributed in the environment. PCBs are known to be lipophilic in nature and resistant to biotransformation and accumulate in organism along the food chain. They bring forth several toxic effects on reproductive, nervous, dermal, immune and endocrine systems in organisms. Several PCBs are carcinogenic and there are indications that they may perhaps bind covalently *in vitro*, via metabolic activation, to cellular macromolecules such as DNA. PAHs, while being less persistent than PCBs in environment, are environmentally of importance since many individual PAHs after metabolic activation are genotoxic (Ostby and Krokje, 2002; Mohanraj and Azeez, 2003).

Genotoxic compounds possess a major challenge because they can alter reproduction, enhance aging process and induce tumors or cancers in exposed individuals. The damage can also be transmitted to the offspring. Development of methods, which might predict genotoxic impact of environmental contaminants before serious effects on the ecosystems occur, is therefore very important (Ostby and Krokje, 2002). One approach, which may help to decrease the degree of uncertainty in estimating such risks, is incorporation of appropriate biomarkers that can provide information on exposure at the population levels, and biological responses and response-modifying factors at the individual level studies (Kyrtopoulos *et al.*, 2001).

Biomarkers are indicators of current or historical contact of an organism with an environmental agent. These are xenobiotically induced variations in cellular or biochemical components or processes, structures, or functions measurable in a biological system or sample. Biomarkers provide a functional measure of exposure that integrates the rate of exposure and bioavailability of the toxicant of interest. The biomarkers may be only an indicator of exposures or may be directly related to an adverse outcome. Even with exposures or stress, if the organism is not forced out of its normal homeostatic range or is not required to use energy that would normally go into growth or reproduction adverse outcome is unlikely to be observed (Blankenship and Giesy, 2002).

Long-term exposure to PAHs and PCBs may cause different effects. The cytochrome P450 system is involved in the activities that commence with exposure to both the groups of compounds. Families of cytochromes, the heme-containing enzymes have evolved in response to the necessity to metabolize toxic compounds and are a major component of organism's defense against toxic chemicals in their environment. Cytochrome P450 (the number referring to the wavelength at which the cytochrome could be detected) is an enzyme involved in oxidation, reduction, and hydroxylation reactions, also called mixed functional oxidases (MFOs). The cytochrome P450 monooxygenase system (CYP) consists of many structurally related iso-enzymes involved in the metabolism of both endogenous and exogenous compounds. The enzymes associated with Cytochrome P450 catalyze oxidative conversion of lipophlic xenobiotics into entities that are more water-soluble and, thus, can be readily excreted and / or detoxified (Gravato and Santos, 2002a, b). Cytochrome P450 dependent enzymes include Ethoxy Resorufin-O-Deethyalse (EROD), Benzo [a] Pyrene Hydrolase (B [a] PH), and Aryl Hydrocarbon Hydroxylase (AHH) (Peakall, 1992). Planar compounds such as Benzo [a] pyrene (B [a] P) and 3,3′, 4,4′- Tetra Chloro Biphenyls (TCB) are known to interact with the CYP1A subfamily. CYP1B plays important roles in the metabolism of these compounds. CYP1 inducers such as (B [a] P) and TCBs, operate through the aryl hydrocarbon receptor (AhR), a ligand-activated transcription factor that regulates their expression (Stegman and Hahn 1994; Hahn 2001, 2002).

Induction of CYP1A and associated enzymes has been extensively discussed worldwide as a biomarker of exposure to organic pollution in the liver and other tissues (Aas *et al.*, 2000; Ayroton *et al.*, 1990; Bucheli and Fent 1995; Custer *et al* 2001a, 2002; Palace *et al.*, 2001; Peakall 1992; Scholz and Segner, 1999). The present review focuses on induction of CYP1A family by pollutants like PAHs, PCBs and dioxin-like compounds and application of CYP1A associated enzymes as biomarkers of organic pollutants. This review is not intended to give a complete overview of the available literature, but rather to brief on the topic.

## Mechanism of action

The mechanism of action of PCBs, Polychlorinated Dibenzo Furans (PCDFs) and Polychlorinated Dibenzo-p-Dioxins (PCDDs) proceed via initial binding to a high-affinity, low-capacity cytosolic receptor protein. Early experiments examining the induction of Aryl Hydrocarbon Hydroxylase (AHH) activity revealed a relationship between Halogenated Aromatic Hydrocarbons (HAH) structure and the ability to induce AHH. These results, in combination with those obtained using various inbred strains of mice, suggested the presence of specific receptors that recognized these compounds. Subsequently, a cytosolic protein was identified that bound 2,3,7,8-Tetrachloro Dibenzo-p-Dioxin (TCDD) saturably with high affinity, and exhibited the properties of a receptor. This "TCDD receptor" has been identified and characterized in a wide range of species and tissues and has been designated as the Aryl Hydrocarbon Receptor (AhR) (Denison *et al.*, 1998). Poland and Kuntson (1982) found good correlation between ability of PCDDs to induce AHH activity and their toxic potency. They concluded that the cytosol binding protein, by a variety of criteria, had the *in vitro* properties expected of the receptor for the induction of CYP1A. Several lines of investigation strongly suggested that the Ah locus was the structural gene for the cytosol receptor in mice.

The AhR regulates the P450 gene. The overall mechanism of induction of CYP1A1 gene expression is presented in Fig. 1. As the contaminants such as the HAHs and PAHs diffuse, probably by passive diffusion, through the plasma membrane they bind with high affinity to the cytoplasmic AhR complex. Subsequent to the ligand binding, the ligand: AhR complex undergoes transformation, during which at least two molecules of hsp90 and other bound proteins dissociate from the complex. The liganded AhR moves to the nucleus and accumulates within it. In the nucleus, it is converted into its high affinity DNA binding form following its association with AhR Nuclear Translocator (ARNT) and possibly other proteins. The binding of these transformed heterometic TCDD: AhR complexes to dioxin responsive elements (DREs) upstream of the CYP1A1 gene leads to DNA bending, chromatin and nucleosome disruption, increased promoter accessibility, increased rates of transcription, initiation of the CYP1A1 gene, the subsequent accumulation of CYP1A1-specific mRNA and increased synthesis of microsomal cytochrome P4501A1 (Whitlock *et al.*, 1996).

All of the high-affinity AhR ligands identified to date are planar, hydrophobic molecules and include several classes of HAHs (PCB, PCDF, PCDDs, etc.), PAHs (such as B [a] P, 3-methylchoantherene, flavones, rutacarpine alkaloids), aromatic amines and other chemicals. The affinity of binding of TCDD and other HAHs is in nanomolar to micromolar range while PAHs bind with affinity in picomolar to nanomolar range. This difference was positively correlated with observed differences in the toxic and biological potency of these classes of chemicals, with HAHs being significantly more active. Available evidence suggests that the differences in potency between HAHs and PAHs are likely due to a combination of the higher AhR binding affinity and increased resistance of HAHs to metabolic degradation, which results in

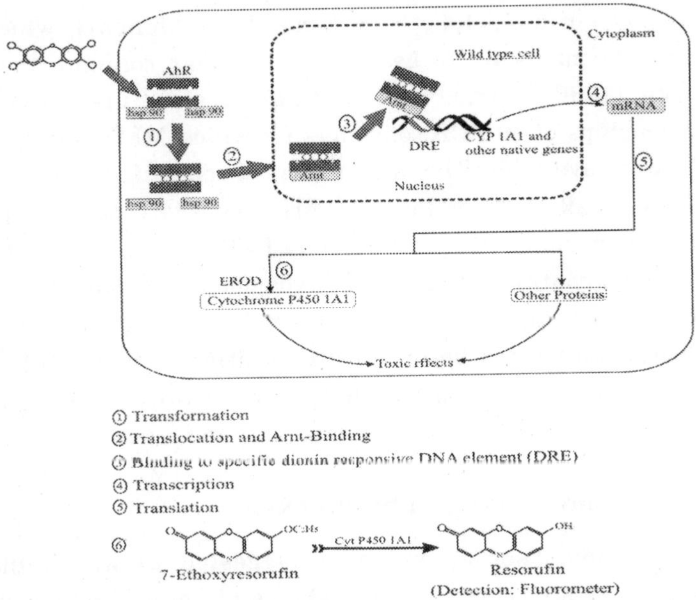


**Fig. 1 :** Mechanism of AhR action: Ah receptor-mediated mechanism of induction of gene expression by exogenous and endogenous chemicals

sustained AhR occupancy and persistent activation of gene expression. While it can be generalized that ligand-binding specificity and ranking potency of HAH and PAH ligands are similar for AhRs among species and tissues, they are not identical and significant differences do exist among them (Denison *et al.,* 1998). Safe (1986) addressed the receptor response specificity and concluded that response specificity to Ah receptor ligands was a complex process that depends not only on the receptor levels but also on various other factors.

The ability of specific PCBs, PCDFs and PCDDs to induce the P450I system is greatly influenced by the degree of chlorination and the chlorine substitution pattern. The most toxic PCBs are those that are unsubstitued in the ortho positions i.e. 3,3′, 4,4′, 5, 5′-hexa chloro-biphenyl, which allows the molecule to assume a co-planar configuration. Clarke (1986) carried out a study of structure-activity relationships of 50 PCB congeners for which MFO induction data were available. The author divided compounds into five groups: weak P450 or inactive, primary P448, mixed type inducers, primary P450 and entirely P450. It was the second group that contains the most toxic congeners, including those listed above, and was characterized by having both para position substituted and the ortho positions unsubstituted. Mason *et al.* (1987) suggests that the most toxic PCDFs and PCDD are those substituted in the 2, 3, 7 and 8 position.

## Cytochrome P450 as a biomarker

The biomarker approach is suggested as a suitable strategy for studying sublethal effects of pollutants and in providing an early signal of possible adverse effects in organisms (Bergman and Mayer, 1992; Cormier and Racine 1992; Dyers *et al.,* 1992; Gesamp 1995; Jenkins and Sanders 1992; Payne *et al.,* 1987; Sanders 1992; Sunahara *et al.,* 2002; Varanasi *et al.,* 1986; Varanasi *et al.,* 1992). In examining effect of pollutants on communities and in epidemiological studies also biomarkers are expected to be very valuable (Goldstein, 1981). As markers of early biological effect, mainly cytogenic end-points were used for monitoring toxic exposure. CYP1A has been the most extensively studied cytogenic endpoint in association with pollutants exposure (Monosson and Stegeman, 1992; Schoket *et al.*, 1998, 2001; Woodin *et al.*, 1887). The CYP1A subfamily is highly inducible by PAHs and PAH-like compounds. Therefore, CYP1A induction, estimated for instance by EROD activity, has been widely used as a biomarker for planar organic contaminants like PAHs (Bucheli and Fent, 1995). Various studies have showed that PCB isomers and congeners had similar potencies to induce AHH, EROD and BaPH (Peakall, 1992).

Several commercial PCB mixtures as inducers of AHH and EROD activity in *in vitro* tests have been presented in several studies (Bosveld *et al.,* 1995, 2000; Giesy and Kannan, 1998; Safe 1994, 1997/1998, Sanderson and van den Berg 1999, Vanden Berg *et al.*, 1998). Sawyer *et al.,* (1984) determined several Arochlor and Kanechlor mixtures *in vivo* (EROD induction in male Wistar rat) and *invitro* studies (AHH and EROD induction in H4IIE cells). Correlation between *invivo* and *invitro* induction potencies of these mixtures were also reported. The studies revealed the close relationship between the induction of the various CYP1 enzyme systems and xenobiotics.

Among the CYP1A-associated monooxygenases, EROD induction is of particular interest (Gravato and Santos, 2002a,b). EROD induction is a reliable surrogate measure of exposure of planar organochlorine residue analysis in fish, birds and mammals (Palace *et al.*, 2001). PAH compounds of petrogenic origin have shown as potent inducers of CYP1A in several fish species, in both laboratory experiments as well as in field studies (Aas *et al.,* 2000). It was also shown that the AHH and EROD activity of mixtures of PCBs- Arochlors, Kanechlor and other environmentally important mixtures were essentially a summation of the individual PCBs and PCDFs.

## Techniques to measure CYP1A induction

A number of techniques for measuring CYP1A induction are available. Among them the common ones are assays of catalytic function, such as EROD or AHH, and immunochemical measurements of CYP1A protein, such as Western blotting, enzyme linked immunosorbent assay, Polymerase chain reaction (PCR) techniques, radioimmuno assay and detection of mRNA using cDNA probes.

Certain studies have measured induction of immuno-detectable CYP1A proteins on exposure to inducers at concentrations as low as 0.0001 μM (Hahn *et al.,* 1996; Kennedy *et al.*, 1996). Ostby and Krokje (2002) showed marked induction of CYP1A proteins detected by Western blotting on treatment with low concentration of TCB and B [a] P. The study suggests that the technique is a very sensitive to CYP1A induction, capable of satisfactorily detecting induction by environmentally relevant concentrations of inducers. Earlier, Bradlaw and Casterline (1979) and Bradlaw *et al.,* (1980) used AHH-bioassay to examine several dioxin and dioxin-like compounds, Arochlors, food extracts and fish samples. The AHH activity was measured by conversion of B [a] P to 3-hydroxy-B [a] P in microsomal fractions of liver cells. They detected picogram ranges of TCDD-equivalents in the samples.

Fluorescence-based catalytic assays for P450 induction study have been employed widely for several reasons. Fluorometric assays such as those based on alkylated homologues of resorufin and coumarin involve a relatively minimal amount of sample manipulation. Fluorescence of the metabolized substrate in these assays can be read directly in the vessels in which the reaction takes place. This is particularly useful in the assays of cultured cells where the assay can be performed in the wells of multi-well culture plates (Kennedy *et al.,* 1993, 1995). Trust *et al.,* (2000) measured EROD, the catalytic function of Hydrocarbon –inducible CYP1A, using a kinetic modification of the plate-based bioassay of Kennedy *et al.,* (1993).

Currently, the EROD is commonly used measuring the binding of the dioxin-like compounds to the AhR and the subsequent induction of CYP1A related de-ethylation of 7-ethoxyresorufin to resorufin (e.g. Behnisch *et al.*, 2001a, b; Till *et al.,* 1997). Micro titer plate adaptation of the EROD assay was employed by Fisher *et al.,* (2003) to measure the CYP1A activity in *Chironomus riparius* larvae. They documented that modification of EROD assay permit detection of CYP1A activity in individual larvae. For EROD bioassay several cell lines were used such as the rat H4II cell line (Behnisch *et al.*, 2001a,b; Giesy *et al.*, 1994; Till *et al.,* 1997), the Chicken Embryo Hepatocytes (CEH) (Kennedy *et al.,* 1993, 1995), cultured chicken embryo liver (Engwall and Hjelm, 2000), Hepa 1 (mouse), Human Hepatoma HepG2 and Hep3 (Ohta *et al.,* 1998) and fish cell lines like RTL-W1 (Clemon *et al.,* 1994). Micro–EROD bioassay with H4IIE cells were also used for similar studies. The detection limits for EROD induction by TCDD were found varying noticeably with the kinds of cell lines used for the study (Sanderson *et al.,* 1996; Tillitt *et al.,* 1991; Kennedy *et al.,* 1996; Brunstrom *et al.,* 1995).

## CYP1A induction in different taxa

### *Invertebrates*

Fisher *et al.* (2003) measured CYP1A activity in individual *Chrinomus riparius* using a micro titer plate adaptation of the EROD assay. Sensitivity of this biomarker was tested by exposing larvae to Phenobarbital (0.5 and 1.0 mM) and Permethrin (1 and 10$\mu g^{-1}$ g). Both the chemicals induced EROD activity in *C. riparius* larvae up to 1.58 fold with Phenobarbital and 2.47 fold with Permethrin. EROD induction was pronounced largely after 48 hours. Feeding levels prior to exposure also had a significant effect on EROD activity. It was highest when larvae were fed double the normal ration.

Ismert *et al.*, (2002) investigated snail *Helix aspera* about the effect of exposure to naphthalene (NAP), a PAH. They examined certain xenobiotic-metabolizing enzymes, which were dependent on CYP1A and associated with glutathione, such as EROD, Ethoxy Cumarin-O-Deethylase (ECOD) and Pentoxy Resorufin-O-Dealkylase (PROD). The study found organ-specific responses as the animals were treated with NAP, highlighting the necessity of considering such complexities when organisms are proposed as indictors of pollution exposure. Induction of metabolizing activities could be an excellent tool to predict a specific toxicity and could be used as potential biomarkers of NAP exposure.

### *CYP1A Induction in fish*

In fish, many environmental pollutants including PAHs and PCBs are known to induce CYP1A-dependent monooxygenases. Some studies, that elaborate such results are listed in Table 1. It is reported, that fish monooxygenases, heat shock proteins (Hsp), and superoxide dismutase among several similar others can serve as biochemical markers of exposure to a variety of pollutants like PAH and PCB types, and metals (Ueng *et al.*, 1996; Eeva *et al.*, 2000; Li *et al.*, 2002). Luxon *et al.*, (1987) measured AHH activity in lake trout from several sites around the Great Lakes and used samples from an interior provincial park as a control. The AHH activity in lake trout collected from the western end of Lake Ontario averaged ten times higher than control from Lake Superior while that from Lake Huron was substantially lower. Casterline *et al.*, (1983) examined fish to test the hypothesis that AHH induction could be used as biological screen to select samples for chemical analysis of PCBs, PCDDs and PCDFs. The TCDD equivalency was calculated for each sample; while seven samples fell on a curve relating AHH activity to TCDD equivalents, one had notably higher AHH activity than expected. Although, the sample size of this particular experiment is small for the results to be deemed conclusive, it suggests that such biological screening could be of use to decide on samples for other expensive chemical analysis.

**Table 1 :** Biomarkers for exposure and effects from micro-organics – Select studies

| Name of Species | Endpoint | Authors |
|---|---|---|
| | **PCBs** | |
| **Mammals** | | |
| Sprague-Dawley rats | EROD activity from exposure to soil | Fouchecourt *et al.* (1998) |
| Mink | EROD activity | Shipp *et al.* (1998) |
| Polar Bear | CYP1A induction | Letcher *et al.* (1996) |
| **Birds** | | |
| Japanese quail | MFO induction and blood levels of PCBs | Marsili *et al.* (1996) |
| Common tern eggs | CYP1A induction by TCB | Hoffman *et al.* (1993) |
| **Fish** | | |
| Fish (general) | P450 induction | Stegeman and Lech (1991) |
| **Amphibians** | | |
| Leopard frogs | P450 induction | Huang *et al.* (1998) |
| | **PAHs** | |
| **Mammals** | | |
| Human lymphocytes | AHH initiating the conversion of B [a] P to genotoxic form | Mane *et al.* (1990) |

*Contd.*

| | | |
|---|---|---|
| Human lymphoblast | AHH induction and gene mutation | Crespi *et al.* (1985) |
| Hamster | Liver fraction containing P488 induction | Phillipson and Ioannide (1989) |
| **Birds** | | |
| Herring gulls | Hepatic EROD induction | Lee *et al.* (1985) |
| **Fish** | | |
| Atlantic cod | CYP1A induction with skin ulcer | Aas *et al.* (2000) |
| Sea bass | Liver P450 content and induction of liver EROD activity | Gravato and Santos (2002a) |
| **Invertebrates** | | |
| Snail | CYP-specific activities higher inn kidney | Ismert *et al.* (2002) |

Induction of EROD and AHH in the deep-sea fish *Corphaenoides armatus* and PCBs on a congener-specific basis was examined by Stegeman *et al.* (1986). Induced forms of CYP1A were confirmed by the immunoblot technique. Stegeman *et al.* (1987), who used the same technique to study in winter flounder in coastal Massachusetts, also found strong correlation between EROD and AHH activity and between the activities of both the enzymes and CYP1A equivalents calculated from the immunoblot technique. Earlier, Foureman et *al.*, (1983) after examining over 400 fish during a three-year period found reasonable correlation between EROD and AHH in the same fish species. The large sample size is important to establish frequency distributions, as there were large variations (over 500 fold in the case of EROD) in activity. In addition, Palace *et al.* (2001) found a strong correlation between liver 3,3′, 4, 4′-tetra chlorobiphenyls (TCB) concentration and EROD activity in fish. Fish liver EROD data from *in vivo* studies were reported to be related to that from *in vitro* investigations (Schramm and Rehmann, 2000; Schramm *et al.,* 2001).

In order to perform environmental risk assessment with regard to oil contamination in the sea, Aas *et al.* (2000) selected EROD activity as biomarker in Atlantic cod. EROD activity was found generally increasing throughout the exposure period indicating increased biotransformation efficiency. The lowest nominal concentration of dispersed oil in water (0.06ppm) corresponded to 0.3ppb measured total PAH concentration in the water. Atlantic cod exposed to this concentration showed higher induction of CYP1A than the control. The authors conclude that these dose-response data may serve as useful contributions while assessing environmental risk from marine oil pollution. Among fish captured from even minimally contaminated areas Collier *et al.,* (1989) found a substantial proportion having high activities of AHH enzymes. The results agree with other studies (Foureman *et al.,* 1983; Stegeman *et al.,* 1987) reporting apparent induction of these types of hepatic enzymes in winter flounder captured from relatively uncontaminated sites. It seems that hepatic AHH activity is a sensitive tool for use in environmental monitoring programs, although further analyses are very essential to conclusively establish it.

Estimated EROD levels in liver of cod by Aas *et al.* (2000) were relatively lower than earlier reported levels in the same species (Beyer *et al.,* 1996; Goksoyr *et al.,* 1994). Several liver samples of fish from Hogervarde exhibited low or undetectable levels of EROD in spite of a high PAH metabolite content in bile. Tributyl tin (TBT), from antifouling paint of ships, could be a possible inhibitor of CYP1A metabolism in that area (Fent and Stegeman, 1993). Stegeman and Lech (1991) suggested that a low EROD activity in fish might be an adaptation to a chronic exposure to high levels of PAH. Hence, Aas *et al.* (2000) caution that when monitoring pollution effects in fish exposed to high levels of PAH over a long period, CYP1A induction assays must be used with care and always together with other parameters.

Time-related response in liver EROD activity, with falling liver EROD activity after exposures longer than 8 hours, whereas liver P450 remaining high was reported by Gravato and Santos, (2002b). Earlier, Andersson *et al.* (1985) and Lemarie *et al.* (1996) had found supporting results, in their experiments on rainbow trout. Pacheco and Santos (1998) also found comparable result after 4 days exposure in eel treated with a single injection of BNF. According to Tate (1988), channel catfish injected with BNF (50 mg $kg^{-1}$) demonstrated a significant liver EROD induction after 2 days treatment. While the EROD activity decreased with longer exposures (12 days), the liver P450 content remained significantly higher than control. The result showed that the liver EROD activity to be an adequate biomarker for short exposures of Juvenile sea bass to BNF, since it decreased in a time dependent manner.

## *CYP1A Induction in birds*

In avian embryos brain asymmetry and hepatic microsomal EROD activity are potential bioindicators of PCB and TCDD contamination. Brain asymmetry in birds has been associated with TCDD and related compounds and holds promise as a biomarker of contaminant exposure and its effects (Henshel *et al.,* 1997). EROD induction in livers of double-crested cormorant embryos in relation to PCB concentrations and toxic equivalent (TEQ) has been reported earlier. Sanderson *et al.* (1994) reported a relationship between TCDD exposure and EROD induction in cormorant embryos. Davis *et al.* (1997) documented differences in EROD activities in embryos of cormorants among locations in

California and Oregon and suggested that these differences were because of exposure to dioxin-like compounds. In one study, Custer *et al.* (2001b) revealed that the EROD activity in the liver of cormorant embryos was significantly higher in the Wisconsin colonies and correlated with PCBs and TEQs of aryl hydrocarbon-active PCB congeners relative to TCDD.

Tillitt *et al.* (1988, 1989, 1991) reported EROD-induction in the rat hepatoma cell line, using egg samples from fish-eating birds collected from 41 colonies in Michigan and Ontario. They found significant differences in the ability of egg composites from various regions around the Great Lakes to cause induction. The relative ranking of colonies correlated well with known areas of contamination, with materials from Great Bay and Saginaw Bay giving the highest and those on Lake Superior the lowest values.

Elliott *et al.* (1991) reported EROD induction with residue levels of 182 ppm for PCB 105, 119 ppm for PCB 153 and 3.3 ppm for PCB 126 in American kestrel in adipose tissue. In another study, Elliott *et al.*, (1996) calculated bald eagle toxicity reference values (TRVs), based on hepatic CYP1A enzyme induction of 100 and 210ng. No significant concentration-related effects for morphological, physiological or histological parameters, such as chick growth, edema or density of thymic lymphocytes, were observed at these concentrations. It appears that hepatic CYP1A induction is more sensitive than some of the developmental endpoints.

The PCB congeners injected into the yolk sac of chicken eggs at an early stage of development (4 days of incubation) revealed a significant correlation between, EROD inducing potencies and embryo lethality (Brunstrom, 1989). On the basis of relative AHH induction, Kubiak *et al.* (1989) estimated the potencies of individual PCB congeners as TCDD-TEQs in state-endangered Forster's terns. The authors compared the reproductive success of a Green Bay colony of Forster's terns with that of a successful inland colony. Hepatic MFO activity (AHH) was 3 fold higher in Green bay hatchlings indicating the high degree of PCBs that possibly decreases reproductive success.

### *CYP1A Induction in mammals*

It is important to note, as pointed out by Phillipson and Ioannides (1989), that the level of P450 isoenzyme proteins in unexposed animals was relatively low. Support for this statement was provided by the data demonstrating uninduced hamster liver fractions that contain high-cytochrome P488 levels, converted both B [a] P and benzo [a] anthracene to mutagens. It was felt that repeated exposures were required to induce the requisite enzyme systems to metabolize these pro-mutagens to ultimate mutagenic/carcinogenic forms. Ostby and Krokje (2002) evaluated CYP1A induction in rat hepatoma cell line Fao, as biomarkers of exposure to organic compounds such as PAHs and PCBs, in environmentally relevant concentrations. In their study CYP1A proteins were induced at B [a] P concentration of 0.0001 μM and increased with increasing concentrations up to 10 μM. Marked induction of immunodetectable CYP1A protein was also seen after treating Fao cells with increasing concentrations of TCB up to 1 μM.

Tillitt *et al.* (1991) followed cell bioassays to detect dioxin-like activity in extracts of environmental compartments such as soil, water and biota. The H4IIE rat hepatoma cell bioassay has been widely used for such purposes. In this assay, EROD-inducing potencies of single compounds and environmental samples were determined from complex dose response curves and compared to that of the TCDD in order to express the biological potency of the tested samples in TCDD-equivalents (TCDD-EQs).

## CYP1A Induction as a biomarker for Carcinogenicity

Several PAHs are known as carcinogens. A prerequisite for conversion of PAHs into the active bay region diol epoxides is the presence of cytochrome P450 (*CYP1A*) and associated enzymes. These enzymes responsible for the conversion can be found primarily in the liver, but are also present in lung, intestinal mucosa and other tissues. Thus, factors such as distribution in the target tissue(s), solubility and intracellular localization proximate to these enzymes figure prominently in the expression of PAHs carcinogenicity. In order to assess any correlation between carcinogenic potency and the ability to induce P450 isoenzymes, several indices of P450 isoenzymes activity [such as O-demethylation of ethoxyresourfin, metabolic activation of 2 amino-6-methyldipyride (1,2, -α 3′, 2′ d) imdazol (Glu-p-I) to mutagens and immunological detection of polyclonal antibodies against purified rat P450I] were measured in microsomal preparations incubated with benzo (a) pyrene and benzo (e) pyrene (B [e] P) (Ayroton *et al.*, 1990). While both PAHs amplified several parameters of P450I activity, B [a] P was found markedly more potent than B [e] P. The carcinogenic potency of the PAHs tested could be predicted by the degree to which they induced these enzymes.

## Cytochrome P450 in comparative studies

Induction of Cytochrome P450 dependent EROD activity can be used extensively to compare toxicity of micro-organics in different organisms or to compare among micro-organics with respect to their toxicity. Comparative study of TEQs of organic mixture would be useful to monitor their degree of toxicity. This could be solidly revealed by EROD bioassay. Dubois *et al.* (1996) reported much higher Arochlor 1254 induced EROD activity *in vitro* in fetal rat hepatocytes than in human or quail cells. Schmitz *et al.* (1996) made a comparison of TEQs of the PCB mixtures- Arochlor 1254 and Clophen A 50 by EROD bioassay (H4IIE). In Arochlor 1254 and Clophen A50, PCB-126 contributed for 95/90% of the EROD and 64/40% of the TEQ. Similarly, a comparison of relative potency (REP) of B [a] P and a complex mixture of PAHs as inducers of hepatic microsomal EROD activity were done by Chaloupka *et al.* (1993) in the B6C3F1 mouse. EROD induction potencies of B [a] P and the MGP-PAH mixture showed that the mixture was approximately 700 times more potent than expected based on the B [a] P contents of the mixture. The Table 2 briefs some of the advantages of such biomarkers in pollutant related studies.

**Table 2:** Advantages of CYP1A as biomarker

| Advantages | Authors |
|---|---|
| • CYP1A induction, estimated by EROD activity widely used as a biomarker for organic contaminants | Bucheli and Fent 1995, Peakall 1992 |
| • Biotransformation efficiency due to oil contamination can be assessed by CYP1A induction | Aas *et al.*, 2000 |
| • PHAH exerting their toxicity through the cytosol receptor can be analyzed by induction of CYP1A | Poland and Kuntson, 1982 |
| • Correlation between *in vivo* and *in vitro* induction potencies of organic mixtures to induce CYP1A | Sawyer *et al.*, (1984) |
| • Induction of CYP1A even at low concentration of environmental inducers | Østby and Krøkje (2002) |
| • Period of micro-organics exposure can be determined by using CYP1A as there was a time-related response | Gravato and Santos (2002b), Andersson *et al.*, (1985), Lemaire *et al.*, (1996), Pacheco and Santos (1998), Tate (1988) |

*Contd.*

| | |
|---|---|
| • Decreases reproductive success of the birds due to micro organics detected even at the early stage of embryonic development by induction of CYP1A | Brunstrom (1989), Sanderson *et al.* (1994), Davis *et al.* (1997) |
| • Induction of CYP1A used to compare the TEQs of micro organics which would be useful to monitor their degree of toxicity | Schmitz *et al.*, 1996, Chaloupka *et al.*, 1993 |
| • The immunosuppressive effects of micro organics studied by CYP1A induction | Lubet *et al.*, 1984 |
| • Availability of appropriate fast analytical techniques | |

Leece *et al.* (1986) showed that 2,3,4,5- tetra chloro-p-terphenyl was more active than either 2,3,4,5-terta chloro-o or m-terpentyl as an inducer of EROD activity. Toftgard *et al.* (1986) also supported such observations. They reported that a polychlorinated terphenyl (PCT) mixture with a low degree of chlorination, Arochlor 5432, was a potent inducer of liver micrososomal CYP, AHH and EROD activity, where as Arochlor 5460 and the unchlorinatedc o-, m- and p-terphenyls were weak inducers.

Several studies have shown that the EROD activity of a PAH fraction has a similar or higher activity than the dioxin fraction in complex mixtures such as fly ashes or sediments (Till *et al.*, 1997; Gale *et al.*, 2000). The dose-response AhR-binding activities (in rat hepatic cytosols) and the AHH/EROD induction potencies (in rat H4IIE cells) were determined for 29 PAHs (Piskorska- Pliszczynska *et al.*, 1986). It was apparent that the magnitude of these *in vitro* responses was strongly structure dependent. Dibenzo [a, h] anthracene, 7-methylbenzo [a] anthracene and 3-methyl cholanthrene exhibited high affinities for receptor protein than TCDD. All of these compounds that were active in the receptor binding and monooxygenase enzyme induction assays possessed one common structural feature, namely the presence of a phenanthrene structure fused with at least one benzo ring.

Clemons *et al.* (1994) compared the EROD activity for several dioxin-like compounds with a rainbow trout cell line (RTL-W1) and a rat hepatoma cell line (H4IIE). With the exception of 1,2,3,6,7,8-HCDD and 1,2,3,7,8-PCDF, all of the fish RTL-W1 derived relative potencies were significantly higher (2 to 8 fold) than that determined using H4IIE. In one study, Li *et al.* (2002) compared TEQ values analyzed by Micro-EROD, enzyme immuno assay and chemical analysis in several samples. They concluded that for all environmental samples, the EROD-TEQ was higher than the values from chemical analysis. Induction of CYP1A1 (P4501A1) and P4501A1 specific EROD activity by TCDD was investigated in human spleenic lymphocytes cultures by Jeong and Yang (1996). EROD activity was induced by TCDD in mitogen-stimulated blast cells. The expression of P4501A1 mRNA was increased by TCDD in mitogen-stimulated cells as detected by northern blot analysis. These findings support that TCDD induced the expression of P4501A1 gene, resulting in an increased EROD induction, can be used appreciably as a biomarker.

Lubet *et al.* (1984) studied the immunosuppressive effects of dibenzo [a, h] anthracene in AHH-inducible mice (C57BL/6) and AHH-non-inducible mice (DBA/2N) by intraperitoneal and oral administration. The results suggested that AHH inducibility was effective in finding the immunosuppressive activity of PAHs. Gravato and Santos (2002a) performed a comparative toxicity study of β-naphthoflavone (BNF), B [a] P and Naphthalene (NAPH), in terms of liver P450 content and induction of liver EROD activity in sea bass. Significant increase in P450 content and liver activity induction in the order of BNF > B [a] P > NAPH was found, indicating BNF as the most potent toxic compound among the three. The authors reported that NAPH failed to induce EROD activity. This result were partially agreed with Bols and coworkers (1999), who failed to obtain EROD activity induction by NAPH in a trout cell line.

## Limitations of CYP1A as biomarker

To assess exposure to PCBs and other AhR-active chemicals induction of enzymes, such as EROD and AHH, is one of the commonly used biomarker technique. However, there are some limitations to this approach, and need to be kept in mind while designing studies and interpreting the results. Some of the noted drawbacks are listed in the Table 3. Blankenship and Giesy (2002) indicate that dose-response curves can be problematic to interpret due to inhibition of EROD inducer. For example, if only a single concentration of an extract is tested in a cell bioassay system, it may be possible that no EROD induction is observed despite the presence of PCBs in high concentrations. To overcome this problem, researchers have measured actual protein levels (rather than activity). In addition, the use of other enzyme systems or cell lines (such as H4IIE-luc) in conjointly was found useful.

**Table 3 :** Selected limitations of CYP1A as Biomarker

| Limitations | Authors |
|---|---|
| • Dose-response curves can be problematic. | Blankenship and Giesy (2002) |
| • When using catalytic activity (e.g., EROD, AHH) inhibition or inactivation of the catalyst. | Hahn *et al.* (1993), |
| • Lack of EROD induction due to mutant protein in the AhR mechanism of action. | Celander *et al.* (1996) |
| • AHH activity might be too sensitive to moderate to high levels of contamination. | Collier *et al.* (1989) |

An important consideration while using catalytic activity (such as EROD and AHH) to measure CYP1A induction is the possibility that inhibition or inactivation of the catalyst may accompany induction at high concentrations of some inducers. Studies of CYP1A induction in cultured cells often report concentration-effect relationships characterized by an increase in catalytic activity at low concentrations of inducer (Hahn *et al.*, 1993). In the study by Hahn *et al.*, (1993), the maximum induction of EROD activity was seen at 0.1 μM TCB in PLHC-1 cells; the EROD activity at higher concentrations (1 and 10 μM) was lower. In contrast, in the same study immunoreactive CYP1A proteins increased with increasing concentration up to 10 μM TCB. There are studies reporting TCB inhibiting EROD activity in PLHC-1 cells, but no inhibition of CYP1A proteins at the same TCB concentrations. It seems that CYP1A catalytic rates do not always reflect the amount of catalyst. These phenomena could lead to an underestimation of the degree of induction, or to the conclusion that there is no induction at all, based only on catalytic activity. Immunochemical determination of CYP1A protein, or measurement of CYP1A mRNA, provides important, complementary information in such cases. For proper evaluation of field data, it is strongly recommended to measure induction of CYP1A at both protein and enzyme activity levels (Bucheli and Fent, 1995).

Gravato and Santos (2002b) showed a decrease in EROD activity in sea bass cells exposed to high BNF concentration and stated that it was an indicator of cytotoxicity. This was because, sea bass liver somatic index has been used as a general liver health indicator that is sensitive to environmental contaminants (Adams *et al.*, 1990). Gravato and Santos (2002b) also signified that this can be confirmed by determining Alanine amino transferase (ALT) assay, which could assess liver damage after xenobiotic exposure. The authors also add that the liver EROD activity may be due to cell damage, since ALT measurements confirm this hypothesis.

A problem encountered with the use of EROD as biomarker is a lack of EROD induction that was reported in fish at a PCB-contaminated site in New Bedford Harbor due to a mutant protein involved in the AhR mechanism of action (Celander *et al.*, 1996). A study conducted by Collier *et al.*, (1989) states that AHH activity might be too sensitive to be used in discriminating between areas of moderate to high levels of contamination. Collier *et al.* (1989) also observed that fish captured from low contaminated area showed high induction of AHH activity. Similar findings emphasized the importance of using several indicators, such as levels of fluorescent aromatic compounds (FACs) in bile and measurement of DNA damage in environmental monitoring programs, to study contaminant exposure effects. Several studies as discussed above have reported Cytochrome associated enzymes activity induction as biomarkers for xenobiotic exposures. Joined with other appropriate indicators these biomarkers may be very helpful as early warning systems of contamination. However, there are significant limitations to their use to predict effects. Differences of species, sex, season, reproductive status, nutrition and co-contamination also may add on to its complexity. Such limitations and complexities need to be addressed by further research.

## Conclusions

Cytochrome P450, as a tool has high potential to advance knowledge about the degree of xenobiotic exposure in living organisms. The advanced technologies, their applications and publications have shown the popularity and importance of this biomarker. It is felt that CYP450 may help understanding different classes of xenobiotics, their mechanisms of toxicity and their biopotency in the environment. It may also help identify low-level exposure to function as an early warning system so that necessary management measures can be adopted. However, some challenges must be confronted successfully by further studies for this tool to be widely used. Further details of the mechanisms by which CYP1A1 and associated enzymes / proteins interact with specific xenobiotics or its groups need to be described. Standard testing procedures and co-indicators need to be identified to make their utility scientifically robust. Other indicators such as ALT can be used together with CYP1A1 to meet accepted performance criteria.

## References

Aas, E., Baussant, T., Balk, L., Liewenborg, B. and Anderson, O. K. (2000) PAH metabolites in bile, cytochrome P4501A and DNA adducts as environmental risk parameters for chronic oil exposure: a laboratory experiment with Atlantic cod. Aquat. Toxicol., 51: 241-258.

Adams, S..M., Shurgart, L. R., Southworth, G. R. and Hinton, D. E. (1990) *In: Biomarker of Environmental Contamination* (Eds. J.F. McCarthy and L.R Shugart). CRC Press. Boca Raton.FL, 333-353.

Andersson, T., Pesonen, M. and Johanson, C. (1985) Differential induction of cytochrome P450-dependent monooxygenase, epioxide hydrolase, glitathione transferase and UDP glucuronosyl transferase activites in the liver of the rainbow trout by β-Naphthoflavone or clophen A50. Biochem. Pharmocol., 34: 3309-3314.

Ayroton, A. D., McFarlane, M. and Walker, R. (1990) Induction of the P450 I family of proteins by polycyclicaromatic hydrocarbons: Possible relationship to their carcinogenicity. Toxicol, 60 (1-2): 173-186.

Behnisch, P. A., Hosoe, K. and Sakai, S. (2001a) Bioanalytical screening methods for dioxins and dioxin-like compounds-a review of bioassay/biomarker technology. Envionment International, 27: 413-439.

Behnisch, P. A., Hosoe, K. and Sakai, S. (2001b) Combinatorial bio/chemical analysis of dioxin and dioxin-like compounds in waste recycling, feed/food, humans/wildlife and the environment. Envionment International, 27: 495-519.

Bergman, H. L. and Mayer, F. L. (1992) Development of bioindicators for environmental protection programmes in estuarine ecosystems: philosophy and strategy, *In : Ecological Indicators*, (Eds. D. H. McKenzie, D. E. Hyatt and V. J. McDonald) Vol II. Elsevier Appl. Sci., pp., 1517-1518.

Beyer, J., Sandvik, M., Hylland, K., Fjeld, E., Egaas, E., Aas, E., Skare, J. U. and Goksoyr, A. (1996) Contaminant accumulation and biomarker responses in flounder (*Platichthy flesus* L) and Atlantic cod (*Gadus morhua* L.) exposed by caging to polluted sediments in Sorifjirden, Norway. Aquat. Toxicol, 36 (1): 75-98.

Blankenship, A. L. and Giesy, J. P. (2002) Use of biomarkers of exposure and vertebrate tissue residue in the hazard characterization of PCBs at contaminated sites – application to birds and mammals. *In : Environmental Analysis of Contaminated Site*, (Eds. G. I. Sunhara, A. Y. Renoux, C. Thellen, C. L. Guadet and A. Pilon) John Wiley and Sons, pp. 153-190.

Bols, N. C., Schirmer, K., Joyce, E. M., Dixon, D. G., Greenberg, B. M. and Whyte, J. J. (1999) Ability of polycyclic aromatic hydrocarbons to induce 7-ethoxyresorufin -O-deethylase activity in a trout liver cell line. Ecotoxicol. Environ. Safety, 44: 118-128.

Bosveld, A. T. C., Nieboer, R., de Bont, J., Murk, Aj., Feyk, L. A., Giesy, J. P. and van den Berg, M. (1995) Biochemical and developmental effects of dietary exposure to Polychlorinated biphenyls 126 and 153 in common tern chicks (*Sterna hirundo*). Environ. Toxicol. Chem., 19: 719-730.

Bosveld, A. T. C., Verhallen, E., Seinen, W. and van den Berg, M. (1995) Mixture interactions in the in vitro CYP1A1 induction bioassay using chicken embryo hepatocytes. Organohalogen Compounds, 25: 309-312.

Bradlaw, J. A. and Casterline, J. J. (1979) Induction of enzyme activity in cell culture: a rapid screen for detection of planar polychlorinated organic compounds. J. Assoc. Anal. Chem., 62: 904-916.

Bradlaw, J. A., Garthoff, L. H., Hurley, N. E. and Firestone, D. (1980) Comparitve induction of aryl hydrocarbon hydroxlase activity in vitro by analogues of dibenzo-p-dioxin. Food. Cosmet. Toxicol., 18: 627-635.

Brunstrom, B. (1989) Toxicity of coplanar polychlorinated biphenyls in avian embryos. Chemosphere., 19: 765-768.

Brunstrom, B., Engwall, M. and Hjelm, K. (1995) EROD induction in cultured chick embryo liver: A sensitive bioassay for dioxin-like compounds in environmental pollutants. Environ. Toxicol. Chem., 14 (5): 837-842.

Bucheli, T. D. and Fent, K. (1995) Induction of cytochrome P450 as a biomarker for enviornmental contamination in aquatic ecosystems. Crit. Rev. Environ. Sci. Technol., 25 (3): 201-268.

Casterline, J., Bradlaw, J., Puma, B. and Ku, Y. (1983) Screening of fresh water fish extracts for enzyme-inducing substances by an aryl hydrocarbon hydroxylase induction bioassay technique. J. Assoc. Anal. Chem., 66: 1136-1139.

Celander, M., Steggeman, J. J. and Forlin, L. (1996) CyP1-, CYP2B- and CYP3A-like proteins in rainbow trout (Oncorbyncbus mykiss) liver: CYP1A2-specific down-regulation after prolonged exposure to PCB. Mar. Enviorn. Res., 42: 283-286.

Chaloupka, K., Harper, N., Krishnan, V., Santosefano, M., Rodriguez, L. V. and Safe, S. (1993) Synergistic activity of PAH mixtures as Ah receptor agonists. Chem. Biol. Interact., 89: 141-58.

Clarke, J. U. (1986) Structure-activity relationships in PCBs: Use of principal components analysis to predict inducers of mixed-function oxidase activity. Chemosphere, 15: 275-287.

Clemons, J.H., Van den Heuvel, M.R., Stegman, J.J., Dixon, D.G. and Bols, N.C. (1994) Comparison of toxic equivalent factors for selected dioxin and feeran congeners derived using fish and mammalian liver cell lines. Can. J. Fish. Aquat. Sci., 51 : 1577-1584.

Collier, T. K., Eberhart, B. L., Stein, J. E. and Varanasi, U. (1989) Aryl hydrocarbon hydroxylase-A 'New' monitoring tool in the status and trends program. Oceans., 2: 18-21.

Cormier, S. M. and Racine, R. N. (1992) Biomarkers of environmental exposure and multivariate approaches for assessment and monitoring. *In : Ecological indicators*, (Eds. D.H. Mckenzie, D.E. Hyatt and V.J. McDonald) Vol II. Elsevier Appl. Sci., pp., 229-242.

Crespi, C. L., Liber, H. L. and Behymer, T. D. (1985) A human cell line sensitive to mutation by particle-borne chemicals. Mutat. Res., 157: 71-75.

Custer, T. W., Custer, C. M. and Hines, R. K. (2002) Dioxins and congener-specific polychlorinated biphenyls in three avian species from the Wisconsin River, Wisconsin. Environ. Pollut., 119: 323-332.

Custer, T. W., Custer, C. M., Dickerson, K., Allen, K., Melancon, M. J. and Schmidt L. J. (2001a) Polycyclic aromatic hydrocarbons, Aliphatic hydrocarbons, trace elements and monooxygenase activity in birds nesting on the North Platte river, Casper, Wyoming, USA Environ. Toxicol. Chem., 20: 624-631.

Custer, T. W., Custer, C. M., Hines, R. K., Stromborg, K. L., Allen, P. D., Melancon, M. J. and Henshel, D. S. (2001b) Organochlorine contaminants and biomarker response in double-crested cormorants nesting in Green Bay and Lake Michigan, Wisconsin, USA. Archives. Environ. Contam. Toxicol., 40: 89-100.

Custer, T. W., Hines, R. K., Melancon, M. J., Hoffman, D. J., Wickliffe, J. K., Bickham, J. W., Martin, J. W. and Henshel D. S. (1997) Contaminant concentrations and biomarker response in great blue heron eggs from 10 colonies on the upper Mississippi river, USA. Environ. Toxicol. Chem., 16: 260-271.

Davis, J. A., Fry, D. M. and Wilson, B. W. (1997) Hepatic ethoxyresorufin-O-deethylase activity and inducibility in wild populations of double-crested cormorants (*Phalacrocorax auritus*). Environ. Toxicol. Chem., 16: 1441-1449.

Denison, M. S., Phelan, D. and Elferink, C. J. (1998) The Ah Receptor signal transduction pathway. *In : Toxicant-Receptor Interactions*, (Eds. M. S. Denison and W. G. Helferich) Taylor and Francis, pp. 3-32.

Dubois, M., de Waziers, I., Thome, J. P. and Kremers, P. (1996) P450 induction by Archolor 1254 and PCB-77 in cultured hepatocytes from rat, quail and man :interspecies comparison. Comp. Biochem. Physiol., 113C (1): 51-9.

Dyers, S. D., Dickson, K. L. and Zimmerman, E. G. (1992) Use of stress proteins in fish as indicators of environmental effects and exposure. *In : Ecological indicators*, (Eds. D. H. McKenzie, D. E. Hyatt and V. J. McDonald) Vol II. Elsevier Appl. Sci., pp., 1529-1530.

Eeva, T., Tanhuanpaa, S., Tabergh, C., Airaksinen, S., Nikinmaa, M. and Lehikoinen, M. (2000) Biomarkers and fluctuating asymmetry as indicators of pollution- induced stress in two hole-nesting passerines. Functional Ecology, 14: 235-243.

Elliott, J. E. S., Kennedy, W., Jeffrey, D. and Shutt, L. (1991) Polychlorinated biphenyls (PCB) effects on the hepatic mixed function oxidase and porphyria on birds II. American kestrel. Comp Biochem Physiol. C Comp. Pharmacol. Toxicol., 99: 141-145.

Elliott, J.E., Norstrom, R. J., Lorrenzen, A., Hart, L. E., Phillibert, H., Kennedy, S. W., Stegeman, J. J., Bellward, G. and Cheng, K. M. (1996) Biological effects of polychlorinated dibenzo-p-dioxins, dibenzofurans and bophenyls in bald eagle (Haliaeetus teucocepbalus) chicks. Environ. Toxicol. Chem., 15: 782-793.

Engwall, M. and Hielm, K. (2000) Uptake of dioxin-like compounds from sewage sludge into various plant species-assessment of levels using sensitive bioassay. Chemosphere, 40 : 1189-1195.

Fent, K. and Stegeman, J.J. (1993) Effects of tributylin in vivo on hepatic cytochrome P 450 forms in marine fish. Aquat. Toxicol., 24(3) : 219-240.

Fisher, T., Crane, M. and Callaghan A. (2003) Induction of cytochrome P450 activity in individual *Chironomus riparius*

Meigen larvae exposed to xenobiotics. Ecotoxicol. Environ. Safety., 54: 1-6.

Fouchecourt, M. O., Berny, P. and Riviere, J. L. (1998) Bioavailability of PCBs to male laboratory rats maintained on litters of contaminated soils: PCB burden and induction of alkoxyresorufin-O-dealkylase activities in liver and lung. Arch. Environ. Contam. Toxicol., 35: 680-687.

Foureman, G. L., White, N. B. Jr and Bend, J. R. (1983) Biochemical evidence that Winter Flounder (*Pseudopleuronects americanus*) have induced hepatic cytochrome P450-dependent monooxygenase activities. Can. J. Fish. Aquat. Sci., 40: 854-865.

Gale, R. W., Long, E. R., Schwartz, T. R. and Tillitt, D. E. (2000) Evalution of planar halogenated and polycyclic aromatic hydrocarbons in estuarine sediments using ethooxyresorufin-O-deethylase induction of H4IIE cells. Environ. Toxicol. Chem., 19: 1348-1359.

Gesamp (IMO/FAO/UNESCO/WMO/WHO/IAEA/UN/UNEP Joint group on the Scientific Aspects of Marine environmental Protection) (1995) Biological indicators and their use in the measurement of the condition of the marine environment. Rep. Stud. GESAMP.

Giesy, J. P. and Kannan, K. (1998) Dioxin- like and non-dioxin-like toxic effects of PCBs: implications for risk assessment. Crit. Rev. Toxicol., 28: 511-569.

Giesy, J. P., Ludwig, J. P. and Tillit, D. E. (1994) Dioxin, Dibenzofurans, PCBs and colonial fish eating water birds. *In : Dioxines and Health*, (Ed. A. Schecter) Plenum press, pp., 249-307.

Goksoyr, A., Beyer, J., Husøy, A. M., Larsen, H. E., Westrheim, K., Wilhelmsen, S. and Kulngsøyr, J. (1994) Accumulation and effect of aromatic and Chlorinated hydrocarbons in juvenile Atlantic cod (*Gadus morhua* L.) caged in polluted fjord (Sørifjirden, Norway). Aquat. Toxicol., 29 (1): 21-35.

Goldstein, I. F. (1981) The use of biological markers in studies of health effects of pollutants. Environ. Res. 25: 236-240.

Gravato, C. and Santos, M. A. (2002a) Juvenile Sea Bass liver P450, EROD induction, and Erythrocytic genotoxic responses to

PAH and PAH-like compounds. Ecotoxicol. Environ. Safety, 51: 115-127.

Gravato, C. and Santos, M. A. (2002b) β-Naphthoflavone liver EROD and Erythrocytic Nuclear Abnormality Induction in juvenile *Dicentrarchus labrax* L. Ecotoxicol. Environ. Safety, 52: 69-74.

Hahn, M. E. (2001) Dioxin Toxicology and the aryl hydrocarbon receptor: Insight from fish and other non-traditional models. Mar. Biotechnol. 3: S224-S238.

Hahn, M. E. (2002) Aryl hydrocarbon receptors:diversity and evolution. Chemico-Biological Interations, 141: 131-160.

Hahn, M. E., Lamb, T. M., Schultz, M. E., Smolowitz, M. and Stegeman, J. J. (1993) Aquat. Toxicol. 26: 185-208.

Hahn, M. E., Woodward, B. L., Stegeman, J. J. and Kennedy, S. W. (1996) Rapid assessment of induced cytochrome P450 1A protein and catalytic activity in fish hepatoma cells grown in multiwell plates: response to TCDD, TCDF and two planar PCBs. Environ. Toxicol. Chem., 15: 582-591.

Henshel, D. S., Martin, J. W., Norstrom, R., Elliott, J., Cheng, K. M. and DeWitt, J. C. (1997) Morphometric abnormalities in double-crested cormorant chicks exposed to polychlorinated dibenzo-p-dioxins, dibenzofurans and biphenyls. J. Great Lakes Res., 23: 11-26.

Hoffman, D. J., Smith, G. J. and Rattner, B. A. (1993) Biomarkers of contaminant exposure in common terns and black -crowned night herons in the Great Lakes. Environ. Toxicol. Chem., 12: 1095-1103.

Huang, Y. W., Melancon, M. J., Jung, R. E. and Karasov, W. H. (1998) Induction of cytochrome P450 associated monooxygenase in Northern Leopard frogs *Rana pipiens* by 3,3',4,4',5-pentachloro biphenyl. Environ. Toxicol. Chem., 17: 1564-1569.

Ismert, M., Oster, T. and Bagrel, D. (2002) Effcets of atmosphereic exposure to Naphthelene on xenobiotic-metabolising enzymes in the snail Helix aspera. Chemosphere, 46: 273-280.

Jenkins, K. D. and Sanders, B. M. (1992) Monitoring with biomarkers: a multi-tiered framework for evaluating the ecological impacts of contaminants. *In : Ecological indicators,* (Eds. D. H. Mckenzie, D. E. Hyatt and V. J. McDonald) Vol II. Elsevier Appl. Sci. pp. 1279-1293.

Jeong, H. G. and Yang, K. H. (1996) Expression of 2,3,7,8-tetrachlorodibenzo-p-dioxin -inducible cytochrome P450 1A1 in human splenic lymphocyte cultures. Cancer Lett., 98 (2): 193-198.

Kennedy, S. W., Jones, S. P. and Bastien, L. J. (1995) Efficient analysis of cytochrome P450 IA catalytic activity, prophyrins and total protein in chicken embryo hepatocyte cultures with a fluorescent plate reader. Anal Biochem., 226: 362-370.

Kennedy, S. W., Lorenzen, A. and Norstrom, R. (1996) Chicken embryo hepatocyte bioassay for measuring cytochrome P4501A-based 2,3,7,8-tetrachloro dibenzo-p-dioxin equivalent concentrations in environmental samples. Environ. Sci. Technol., 30: 706-715.

Kennedy, S. W., Lorenzen, A., James, C. A. and Collins, B. T. (1993) Ethoxyresorufin-O-deethylase and prophyrin analysis in chicken embryo hepatocyte cultures with a fluorescent plate reader. Anal. Biochem., 211: 102-112.

Kubiak, T. J., Harris, H. J., Smith, L. M., Schwartz, T. R., Stalling, P. L., Trick, L., Sielo, D. E., Docherty, P. D. and Erdman, T. C. (1989) Micro contaminants and reproductive impairment of the Forster's Tern in Green Bay, Lake Michigan 1983. Arch. Environ. Contam. Toxicol., 18: 706-727.

Kyrtopoulos, S. A., Georgiadi, P., Autrup, H., Demopoulous, N., Farmer, P., Haugen, A., Katsouyanni, K., Lambert, B., Ovrebo, S., Sram, R., Stefanou, G. and Topinka, J. (2001) Biomarkers of genotoxicity of urban air pollution -Overview and descriptive data from a molecular epidemiology study on populations exposed to moderate-to-low levels of polycyclic aromatic hydrocarbons:the AULIS project. Genetic Toxicol. Environ. Mutagenesis., 496: 207-228.

Lee, Y. Z., Leighton, F. A., Peakall, D. B., Norstrom, R. J., O'Brien Payne.J.F. and Rahimtula, A. D. (1985) Effects of ingestion of Hibernia and Prudhoe Bay oils on hepatic and renal mixed function oxidase in nestling herring gulls (Larus argenatus). Environ. Res., 36: 248-255.

Leece, B. D., Denomme, M. A., Li, S. M., Towner, R. A., Gyorkos, J. W., Chittim, B. G. and Safe, S. (1986) Effects of individual terphenyls and polychlorinated terphenyls on rat hepatic microsomal cytochrome P4500 dependent monoxygenase: structure-activity relationships. Arch. Toxicol., 59 (3) 186-189.

Lemaire, P., Forlin, L. and Livingstone, D. R. (1996) Response of hepatic biotransformation and antioxidant enzymes to CYP1A-inducers (3-methylcholanthrene, b-Nahthoflavone) in sea bass (*Dicentrachus labrax*), dab (*Limanda limanda*) and rainbow trout (*Oncorhynchus mykiss*). Aquat. Toxicol., 36: 141-160.

Letcher, R. .J., Norstrom, R. J., Lin, S., Ramsay, M. A. and Bandiera, S. M. (1996) Immnoquantification and microsomal monooxygenase activities of hepatic cytochromes P4501A and P4502B and chlorinated hydrocarbon contaminant levels in polar bear (*Ursus maritimus*). Toxicol. Appl. Pharmacol., 137: 127.

Li, W., Wu, W. Z., Xu, Y., Li, L., Schramm K. W. and Kettrup, K. (2002) Measuring TCDD equivalents in environmental samples with Micro-EROD assay: Comparison with HRGC/HRMS data. Bull. Environ. Contam. Toxicol., 68: 111-117.

Li, W., Yin, D., Zhang, A. and Wang, L. (2002) Toxicity of chloroanilines and effects on superoxide dismutase activities in serum of crucian carp (*Carassius auratus*). Bull. Environ. Contam. Toxicol., 69: 630-636.

Lubet, R. A., Brunda, M. J. and Lemaire, B. (1984) Polycyclic hydrocarbon: induced immunotoxicity in mice: Role of the Ah locus. *In : Mechanisms, methods and metabolism: Polynuclear aromatic hydrocarbons*, (Eds. M. Cooke, A. J. Dennis) 8th International Symposium. Columbus, OH: *Battelle Press*, pp. 843-855.

Luxon, P. L., Hodson, P. V. and Borgmann, U. (1987) Hepatic aryl hydrocarbon hydroxylase activity of Lake Trout (*Salvelinus namaycush*) as an indicator of organic pollution. Environ. Toxicol. Chem., 6: 549-657.

Mane, S. S., Purnell, D. M. and Hsu, I. C. (1990) Genotoxic effects of five polycyclic aromatic hydrocarbons in human and rat mammary epithelial cells. Environ. Mol. Mutagen., 15 (2): 78-82.

Marsili, L., Fossi, M. C., Casini, S. and Focardi, S. (1996) PCB levels in bird blood and relationship to MFO responses. Chemosphere, 33: 699-710.

Mason, G., Zacharewski, T., Denomme, M. A., Safe, L. and Safe, S. (1987) Polybrominated dibenzo-p-dioxins and related compounds:Qualitative in vivo and in vitro structure-activity relationships. Toxicol., 44: 245-255.

Mohanraj, R. and Azeez, P. A. (2003) Polycyclic Aromatic Hydrocarbons in Air and their Toxic Potency. Resonance, 8 (9): 20-27.

Monosson, E, and Stegeman, J. J. (1992) Cytochrome p450 induction as a biomarker: Induction of "P450" (P450IAI) in winter flounder by 3,3', 4,4'-tetrachlorobiphenyl and by exposure to inducers in the field. *In : Ecological Indicators*, (Eds. D. H. McKenzie, D. E. Hyatt and V. J. McDonald) Vol II. Elsevier Appl. Sci. pp. 1552-1553.

Ohta, S., Tonorike, K., Kanatani, S., Nakao, T. Aozara, O. and Miyata, H. (1998) Development of risk assessment for dioxin amalogues and PAHs in the environmental samples by two kind of *in vitro* bioassay. Organohalogen compounds, 37 : 175-178.

Ostby, L. and Krokje, Å. (2002) Cytochrome P450 (CYP1A) induction and DNA adducts in a rat hepatoma cell line (Fao), exposed to environmentally relevant concentrations of organic compounds, singly and in combinations. Envrion. Toxicol. Pharmacol., 12: 15-26.

Pacheco, M. and Santos, M. A. (1998) Induction of liver EROD activity and genetoxic effects by polycylic aromatic hydrocarbons and resin acids on the juvenile eel. Ecotoxicol. Environ. Safety, 40: 71-76.

Palace, V. P., Allen-Gill, S. M., Brown, S. B., Evans, R. E., Metner, D. A., Landers, D. H., Curtis, L.R., Klaverkamp, J. F., Baron, C. L. and Lockhart, W. L. (2001) Vitamin and thyroid status in artic grayling (*Thymallus arcticus*) exposed to doses of 3,3',4,4'-tetrachlorobiphenyl that induce the phase I enzyme system. Chemosphere, 45: 185-193.

Payne, J. F., Fancey, L. L., Rahimuthullah A. D. and Porter, E. L. (1987) Review and perspective on the use of mixed-function oxygenases enzymes in biological monitoring. Comp. Biochem. Physiol., 86C: 233-245.

Peakall, D. (1992) Animal Biomarkers as Pollution Indicators, Chapman and Hall, London. pp. 291

Phillipson, C. E. and Ioannides, C. (1989) Metabolic activation of polycyclic aromatic hydrocarbons to mutagens in the Ames test by various animal species including man. Mutat. Res. Mar., 211 (1): 147-151.

Piskorska-Pliszczynska, J., Keys, B., Safe, S. and Newman, M. S. (1986) The cytosolic receptor binding affinities and AHH induction potencies of 29 polynuclear aromatic hydrocarbons. Toxicol. Lett., 34 (1): 67-74.

Poland, A. and Kuntson, J. C. (1982) 2,3,7,8 - Tetrachlorodibenzo-p-dioxin and related halogentaed aromatic hydrocarbons: Examination of the mechanism of toxicity. Annual Rev. Pharomacol. Toxicol., 22: 517-554.

Rattner, B. A., Melancon, M. J., Custer, T. W., Hothem, R. L., King, K. A., LeCaptain, L. J. and Spann, J. W. (1993) Biomonitoring environmental contamination with pipping black-crowned night-heron embryosL: induction of cytochrome P450. Environ. Toxicol. Chem., 12: 1719-1732.

Safe, S. (1986) Comparative toxicology and mechanism of action of polychlorinated dibenzo-p-dioxins and dibenzofurans. Annual. Rev. Pharomacol., 26: 371-399.

Safe, S. (1997/1998) Limitations of the TEF approach for risk assessment of TCDD and related compounds. Teratog. Carcinog. Mutagen., 17: 285-304.

Safe, S. H. (1994) Polychlorinated biphenyls (PCBs). Environmental impact, biochemical and toxic responses, and implications for risk assessement. Crit. Rev. Toxicol., 24 (2): 87-149.

Sanders, B. (1992) Stress proteins as molecular indicators for contaminant exposure and adverse biological effects. *In : Ecological Indicators*, (Eds. D. H. McKenzie, D. E. Hyatt and V. J. McDonald) Vol II. Elsevier Appl. Sci., pp. 1564-1565.

Sanderson, J. and van den Berg, M. (1999) Toxic Equivalency factors (TEFs) for halogenated aromatic hydrocarbons in wildlife. Organohalogen Compounds, 44: 433-436.

Sanderson, J. T., Aarts, J. M. M. J. G., Brouwer, A., Froese, K.L., Denson, M. S. and Giesy. J. P. (1996) Comparison of Ah receptor-mediated luciferase and ethoxyresorufin-O-deethylase induction in H4IIE cells: implications for their use as bioanalytical tools for the detection of Polyhalogenated aromatic hydrocarbons. Toxicol. Appl. Pharmacol., 137: 316-325.

Sanderson, J. T., Norstrom, R. J., Elliott, J, Hart LE, Cheng, K. M. and Bellward, G. D. (1994) Biological effects of polychlorinated dibenzo-p-dioxins, dibenzofurans and bophenyls in double-crested cormorant chicks (*Phalacrocorax auritus*). J. Toxicol. Environ. Hlth., 41: 147-265.

Sawyer, T. W., Vatcher, A. D. and Safe, S. (1984) Comparative aryl hydrocarbon hydroxlase activity induction activties of comercial PCBs in Wistar rats and hepatoma H4IIE cells in culture. Chemosphere, 13: 695-701.

Schmitz, H-J., Behnisch, P., Hagenmaier, A., Hagenmaier, H., Bock, K. W. and Schrenk, D. (1996) CYP1A1-inducing potency in H4IIE cells and chemical compostion of technical mixtures of polychlorinated biphenyls. Environ. Toxicol. Pharmocol., 1: 73-79.

Schoket, B., Papp, G., Levay, K., Mrackova, G., Kadlubar, F. F. and Vincze, I. (2001) Impact of metabolic genotypes on levels of biomarkers of genotoxic exposure. *In : Fundamental and Molecular Mechanisms of Mutagenesis,* 482: 57-69.

Scholz, S. and Segner, H. (1999) Inducion of CYP1A in primary cultures of rainbow trout (*Oncorhyncus mykiss*) liver cells: Concentration response relationships of four model substances. Ecotoxicol. Environ. Safety, 43: 252-260.

Schramm, K. W. and Rehmann, K. (2000) Biological in vitro investigation of PBT in industrial and environmental samples. Organohalogen Compounds, 45: 204-207.

Schramm, K. W., Klimm, C., Hofmaier, A. and Kettrup, A. (2001) Comparison of dioxin-like -response in vitro and chemical analysis of emissions and materials. Chemosphere. 42: 551-557.

Shipp, E. B., Restum, J. C., Giesy, J. P., Bursian, S. J., Aulerich R. J. and Helferich, W. C (1998) Multigene-rational study of the effects of consumption of PCB-contaminated carp from Saginaw Bay, Lake Huron on mink. 2. Liver PCB concentration and induction of hepatic cytochrome P-450 activity as potential biomarker for PCB exposure. J. Toxicol. Environ. Hlth., 54A: 377-401.

Stegeman, J. J., Kloepper-Sams, P. J. and Farrington, J. W. (1986) Monooxygenase induction and chlorobiphenyls in the deep-sea fish *Coryphanoides armatus.* Science. 231: 1287-1289.

Stegeman, J. J., Teng, F. Y. and Snowberger, E. A. (1987) Induced cytochrome P450 in winter flounder (*Pseudopleuronects americanus*) from costeal Massachusettus evaluated by catalytic assay and monoclonal antibody probes. Can. J. Fish. Aquat. Sci. 47: 1270-1277.

Stegma, J.J. and Hahn, M.E. (1994) Biochemistry and molecular biology of monoxygenases : Current Perspectives on forms, functions and regulation of cytochrome P 450 in aquatic species. *In : Aquatic Toxicology : Molecular, Biochemical and cellular Perspectives.* (Eds. D.C. Malins and G.K. Osteander). Lewis/CRC press, Boca Raton, FL., pp., 87-207.

Stegman, J.J. and Lech, J.J. (1991) Cytochrome P 450 monipooxygenase systems in aquatic species : Carcinogen metabolism and biomarkers for carcinogen and pollutant exposure. Environ. Hlth. Perspectives, 90 : 101-109.

Sunahara, G. I., Renoux, A. Y., Thellen, C., Gaudet, C. L. and Pilon, A. (2002) Use of biomarker of exposure and vertebrate tissue residues in the hazard characterization of PCBs at contaminated sites-application to birds and mammals. Envionmental Analysis of Conataminated Sites, 11, 153-180.

Tate, L. G. (1988) Characterization of phase I drug metabolism and the effect of b-Nahthoflavone in the liver and posterior kidney of the channel catfish, *Ictaurus punctatus*. Archives Environ. Contam. Toxicol., 17: 325-332.

Till, M., Behnisch, P., Hagenmaier, H., Bock, K. W. and Schrenk, D. (1997) Dioxin like components in incinerator fly ash:a comparison between chemical analysis data and results from a cell culture bioassay. Environ. Hlth. Perspectives., 105: 1326-1332.

Tillitt, D. E., Ankley, G. T. and Giesy, J. P. (1989) Planar chlorinated hydrocarbons (PCHs) in colonial fish-eating water birds eggs from the Great Lakes. Mar. Enviorn. Res., 28: 505-508.

Tillitt, D. E., Ankley, G. T. and Giesy, J. P. (1991) Characterization of the H4IIE rat hepatoma cell bioassays as a tool for assessing toxic potency of planar halogenated hydrocarbons in environmental samples. Environ. Sci. Technol., 25: 87-92.

Tillitt, D. E., Ankley, G. T., Giesy, J. P. and Keven, N. R. (1988) H4IIE hepatoma cell extract bioassays-derived 2, 3, 7, 8-tetrachlorodibenzo-p-dioxin equivalents (TCDD-EQ) from Michigan water bird colony eggs, 1986 and 1987 Report, pp., 63.

Toftgard, R., Nilsen, O. G., Carlstedt-Duke, J. and Glaumann, H. (1986) Polychlorinated biphenyls:alterations in liver morphology and induction of cytochrome P450. Toxicol., 41: 131-144.

Trust, K. A., Esler, D., Woodin, B. R. and Stegeman, J. J. (2000) Cytochrome P450 1A induction in sea ducks inhabiting nearshore areas of Prince William Sound, Alaska. Mar. Pollut. Bull., 40 (5): 397-403.

Ueng, Y. F., Liu, C., Lai, C. F., Meng, L. M., Hung, Y. Y. and Ueng, T. H. (1996) Effects of Cadmium and Envrionmental pollution on metalothionein and cytochrome P450 in tilapia. Envrion. Contam. Toxicol., 57: 125-131.

Van den Berg M., Birnbaum, L., Bosveld, A. T., Brunstrom, B., Cook, P., Feeley, M., Giesy, J. P., Hanberg, A., Hasegawa, R., Kennedy, S. W., Kubiak, T., Larsen, J. C., van Leeuwen, F. X., Liem, A. K., Nolt, C., Peterson, R. E., Poellinger, L., Safe, S. and Schrenk, D. (1998) Toxic Equivalency factors (TEFs) for PCBs, PCDDs for humans and wildlife. Environ. Hlth. Perspectives, 106: 775-779.

Varanasi, U., Collier, T. K., Williams, D. E. and Buhler, D. R. (1986) Hepatic cytochrome P450 isozymes and aryl hydrocarbon hydroxylase in English sole (*Parophrys vetulus*). Biochem. Pharmacol., 35: 2967-2971.

Varanasi, U., Stein, J. E., Johnson, L. L., Collier, T. K., Casillas, E. and Myers, M. S. (1992) Evaluation of bioindicators of contaminant exposure and effects in coastal ecosystems. *In : Ecological Indicators*, (Eds. D. H. McKenzie, D. E. Hyatt and V. J. McDonald) Vol. II. Elsevier Appl. Sci. pp., 461-498.

Whitlock, J. P. Jr., Okino, S., Dong, L., Ko, H., Clarke-Ketzenberg, R., Ma, Q. and Li, H. (1996) Induction of cytochrome P450 1A1: a model for analyzing mammalian gene transcription. FASEB J., 10: 809-818.

Woodin, B. R., Smolowitz, R. M. and Steggeman, J. J. (1997) Induction of Cytochrome P4501A in the intertidal fish (*Anoplarchus purpurescen*) by Prudhoe Bay crude oil and environmental induction in fish from Prince William Sound. Envrion. Sci. Technol., 31 (4): 1198-1205.

Zhang, J., Xu, Y., Li, W., Schramm, K. W. and Kettrup, A. (2002) Alterations in retinoids, tocopherol and microsomal enzyme activities in the liver of Silver Carp (*Hypophthalmichthys molitrix*) from Ya-ER Lake, China. Bull. Environ. Contam. Toxicol., 68: 660-667.